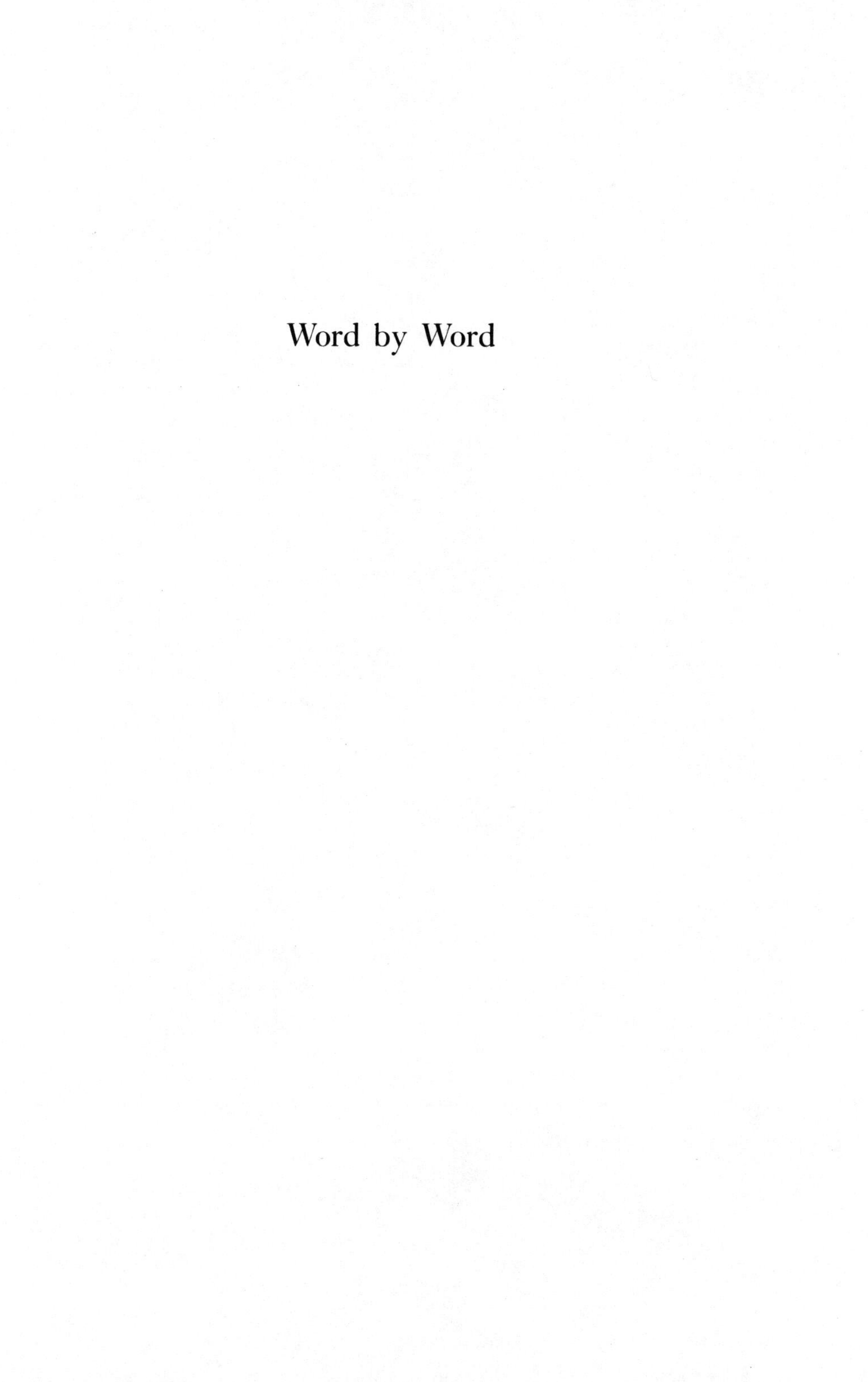

Word by Word

WORD *by* WORD

THE LANGUAGE OF MEMORY

Jonathan Morse

Cornell University Press

Ithaca and London

First published 1990 by Cornell University Press.

International Standard Book Number 0-8014-2383-x
Library of Congress Catalog Card Number 89-23931
Printed in the United States of America
Librarians: Library of Congress cataloging information appears on the last page of the book.

♾ The paper used in this publication meets the minimum requirements of the American National Standard for Permanence of Paper for Printed Library Materials Z39.48—1984.

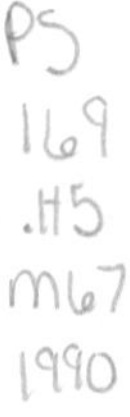

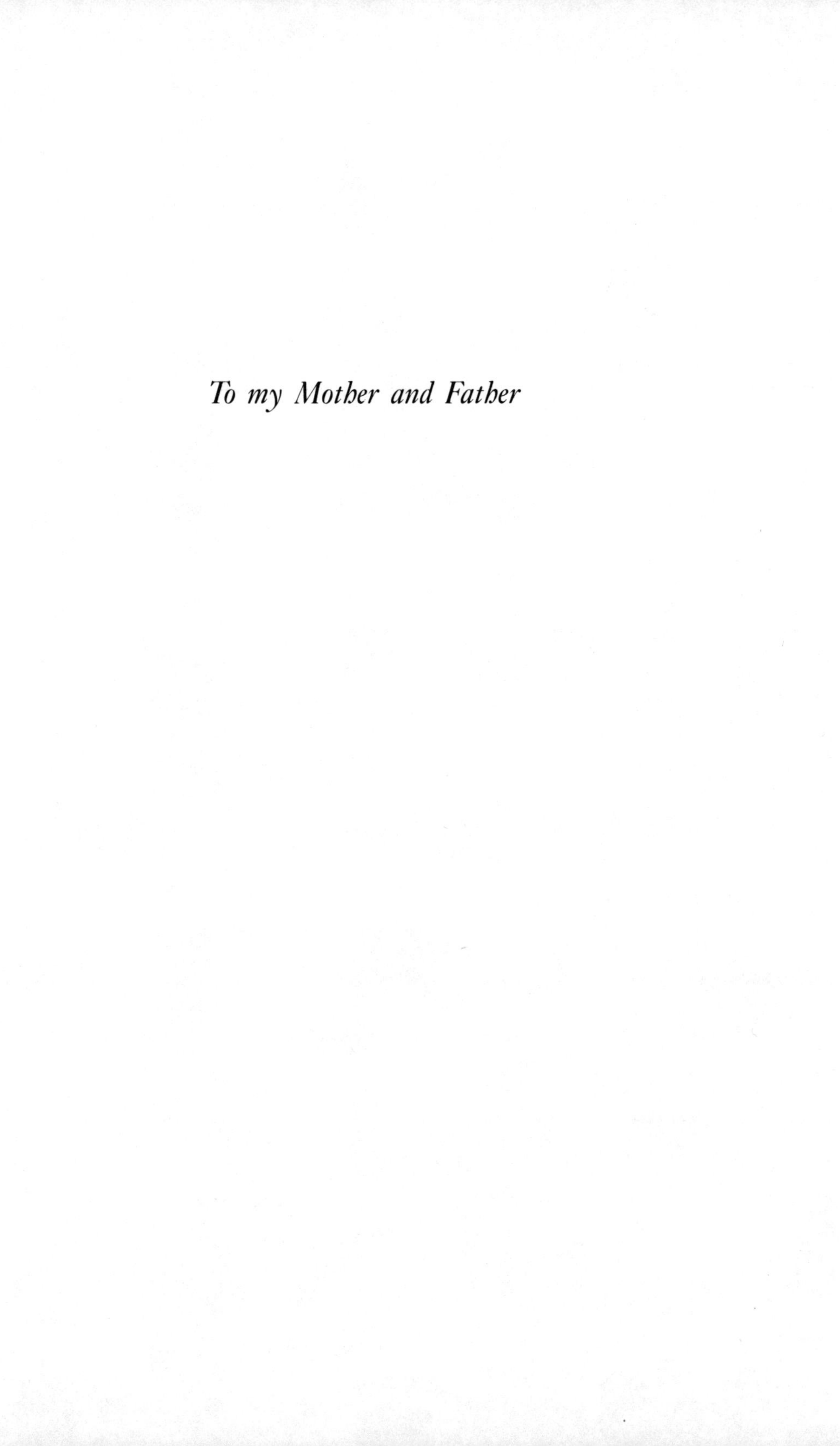

To my Mother and Father

Contents

Preface

This is a book about history in language. I don't claim universality for my thesis; the texts I deal with come from the last two hundred years, and the scope of my argument is meant to be limited roughly to the second half of the twentieth century.

Within those boundaries, however, I do want to make one broad claim at the beginning. Insofar as any culture has a unique history, it seems to me, that history will affect its literature not just in its paraphrasable content but at a more fundamental level. "History," in this sense, is more than an idea or a collection of data; it is a semantic construction that underlies every literary text: the lyric poems of Robert Frost as much as the novels of James A. Michener. History is only incidentally in the names and dates, but it is constitutively in the language. History is the shaping power that makes ephemeral sentences into remembered texts.

I offer this multiplication of terminology with some diffidence, and only because the redefinition brings with it a practical corollary. If we can characterize in linguistic terms the history underlying a literature, generically defined—American literature, say, or Jewish literature, or twentieth-century literature—we may be able to arrive at a useful understanding of the ways in which history and literature create each other. Literature is full of words that define and are defined by time, and it may be socially worth our while to learn to read them, each in its own culturally specific way. I think of this book as the down payment on such a reading.

We could note, by way of beginning to read, that some of the verbal constructions I discuss in this book are little worlds made of words: histories, *storie*, created under conditions in which the only historical reality that finally matters is the order imposed by the accepted meanings of words. Such texts—texts conceived under the conditions I will call virtual history—have at least this one thing in common: each destroys a way of perceiving preverbal reality and defines into existence, in its stead, a verbal parareality. To interpret one of these texts with respect to the nonverbal universe is therefore to try to read *through* the words to some source of coherence prior to definition. Such an interpretation is hard to carry out, but it seems to me historically necessary.

For some of the verbal and nonverbal documents of our century appear to tell us that we have been living through an era in which signification has placed itself in the service of death. Fredric Jameson has analyzed this process in the novels of Wyndham Lewis, and Robert Casillo has done the same for the poems of Ezra Pound. Lewis and Pound are literary figures, but perhaps the most terrible thing about language in the era of Lewis and Pound is that even at its most powerful, it has failed to help us imagine the reality for which it substitutes itself. There are *Endgame* and *Journey to the End of the Night* on the one hand, but on the other hand there are the photographs we have grown up with: the living skeletons of Buchenwald; the field full of Korean nationalists executed by the Japanese, by crucifixion. And the problem with those particular wordless documents is not that words have failed them but that readers have kept trying to bring words to bear. We have the statistic, as quoted by Alvin Rosenfeld: "More will be written about Adolf Hitler than about anyone else in history with the exception of Jesus Christ" (2).

If we sense that that prediction is troubling, it may be because we know too well how some of the words will be written. As I write this preface, for instance, a group of German historians is attempting to redefine the Hitler era in the palliative terms of a comparative world history of evil, and the educational authorities in Japan are sedulously replacing the textbooks of the MacArthur era with histories whose purpose is to render their readers unable to remember Nanking and Bataan. Meanwhile, a large proportion of Austria's electorate appears to have voted for President Waldheim because they believed he was a Nazi war criminal. The victories and defeats of 1945 seem to be ongoing and interchangeable, and it may be harder than we once thought to speak some of the words we once thought we had learned by heart. And of course such things have happened to language before, in other histories, under other circumstances.

Which implies this: culture bears a continually troubling, continually changing relation to the languages out of which we make our sense of a world present to us in time. One of the things I try to do in this book is to help us read some of those defining languages and recover the historical grammar that has made us mean what we mean for ourselves in our own time.

I hope that intention of mine springs from a moderately new idea. But in one academic respect, it makes my book retrograde. I am concerned in the first instance with rereading some primary texts, not with adding to the supply of general literary theory. I am concerned too with the ways in which verbal abstractions have come to be reified, not least as a part of literary theory. My own language will accordingly look impoverished. If the word "privilege" appears in this text, it is a noun, not a verb; if the words "thematic" or "combinatory" appear, they are adjectives, not nouns; if the word "resume" appears, it does not mean "summarize." As to the word "phallus," I don't think I even say it.

Nevertheless, this is an academic study, and my general debt to the theoreticians is large. For helping me read them, I am obliged to successive research committees and department chairs of the Department of English, University of Hawaii at Manoa, for granting me time away from the classroom; to James Woodress and J. Albert Robbins of *American Literary Scholarship* for assigning me three years' worth of homework in criticism; and, at the end, to Rudolf Schmerl, Director of Research Relations, University of Hawaii, for helping me meet the expenses of permission fees. But of course I owe most to the colleagues who have read chapters, sent me to the library, and lent me books and arguments. I single out Reinhard H. Friederich, Francine and Herbert Margulies,

Daniel Stempel, and Rob Wilson, but there are many others. For conversation and correspondence about Emily Dickinson, in particular, I thank Vivian R. Pollak.

In different form, portions of some of my chapters have benefited from their prior exposure to criticism in articles in *Georgia Review, Texas Studies in Literature and Language*, *Modern Fiction Studies*, and the *Yeats Eliot Review*, and in papers read at the T. S. Eliot centennial conference at the University of Arkansas at Little Rock; the twentieth-century literature conference, University of Louisville; and conferences of the International Association for Philosophy and Literature. To one book not cited in my bibliography my Dickinson chapters owe a pervasive general debt: Richard B. Sewall's *The Life of Emily Dickinson* (New York: Farrar, Straus, 1974). In 1986 I thought out loud about this book with a University of Hawaii graduate seminar whose members I now thank for asking and answering: Debra Dew, Tammy Nakamatsu, Patrick Uchigakiuchi, Joanna Yin, and Malynda Young. Three years later, my manuscript benefited from Patricia Sterling's careful editing.

And there are two other people but for whom this book would probably have been written years earlier. They know who they are; they know what made the passing time good.

JONATHAN MORSE

Honolulu, Hawaii

Acknowledgments

Permission to quote from the following works has been granted by their copyright holders:

AHARON APPELFELD. From *The Age of Wonders*. Copyright 1981 by Aharon Appelfeld. Reprinted by permission of David R. Godine, Publisher, Boston, Massachusetts. From *Badenheim 1939*. Copyright 1980 by Aharon Appelfeld. Reprinted by permission of David R. Godine, Publisher, Boston, Massachusetts.

JOHN ASHBERY. "Down by the Station, Early in the Morning," from *A Wave*. Copyright © 1984 by John Ashbery. All rights reserved. Reprinted by permission of Viking Penguin, a division of Penguin Books USA, Inc., and Carcanet Publishers, Manchester, England. This poem first appeared in *The New Yorker*.

EMILY DICKINSON. Poems 258, 959, and 1203 are reprinted by permission of the publishers and the Trustees of Amherst College from *The Poems of Emily Dickinson*, edited by Thomas H. Johnson. Cambridge, Mass.: The Belknap Press of Harvard University Press. Copyright 1951, © 1955, 1979, 1983 by the President and Fellows of Harvard College. Poem 601 and an extract from poem 754 are reprinted from *The Complete Poems of Emily Dickinson*, edited by Thomas H. Johnson. Copyright 1929 by Martha Dickinson Bianchi; copyright © renewed 1963 by Mary L. Hampson. By permission of Little, Brown and Company.

T. S. ELIOT. Excerpts from "Burnt Norton," "East Coker," and

"The Dry Salvages" in *Four Quartets*, copyright 1943 by T. S. Eliot, renewed 1971 by Esme Valerie Eliot, reprinted by permission of Harcourt Brace Jovanovich, Inc., and Faber and Faber Limited. Excerpts from "Fragment of a Prologue," in *Collected Poems 1909–1962* by T. S. Eliot, copyright 1936 by Harcourt Brace Jovanovich, Inc., and Faber and Faber Limited, copyright © 1963, 1964, by T. S. Eliot, reprinted by permission of Harcourt Brace Jovanovich, Inc., and Faber and Faber Limited.

ROBERT FROST. From *The Poetry of Robert Frost*, edited by Edward Connery Lathem. Copyright © 1969 by Holt, Rinehart and Winston, Inc. Copyright © 1962 by Robert Frost. Copyright © 1975 by Lesley Frost Ballantine. Reprinted by permission of Henry Holt and Company, Inc., and Jonathan Cape Ltd.

BRIAN GARDNER. From *Up the Line to Death*. Reprinted by permission of Methuen London.

VASILY GROSSMAN. From *Forever Flowing*. Copyright in English translation © 1972 by Thomas P. Whitney. Reprinted by permission of Harper & Row, Publishers, Inc.

CLAUDE LANZMANN. From *Shoah*. Copyright © 1985 by Claude Lanzmann. Reprinted by permission of Georges Borchardt, Inc., and Pantheon Books, a division of Random House, Inc.

ROBERT LOWELL. Sonnet 4 and excerpt from sonnet 1 of "Mexico" from *For Lizzie and Harriet* by Robert Lowell. Copyright © 1967, 1968, 1969, 1970, 1973 by Robert Lowell. Reprinted by permission of Farrar, Straus and Giroux, Inc., and Faber and Faber Ltd.

FRANK O'HARA. Excerpt from "On Looking at *La Grande Jatte*, the Czar Wept Anew," from *Meditations in an Emergency*, by permission of Grove Press. Excerpt from "Personism: A Manifesto," from *The Collected Poems of Frank O'Hara*, edited by Donald Allen, by permission of Random House, Inc. Copyright 1974 by Alfred A. Knopf, Inc.

KATHA POLLITT. "Atlantis" copyright © 1986 by Katha Pollitt.

SIEGFRIED SASSOON. "Blighters" reprinted by permission of George T. Sassoon.

WALLACE STEVENS. Excerpts from "The Idea of Order at Key West" and "Connoisseur of Chaos" from *The Collected Poems of Wallace Stevens* by permission of Random House, Inc. Copyright 1954 by Alfred A. Knopf, Inc.

ALLEN TATE. Excerpt from "Narcissus as Narcissus" by permission of Helen H. Tate, executrix of the estate of Allen Tate. Excerpt from "Ode to the Confederate Dead," from *Collected Poems 1919–1976*, by Allen Tate. Copyright © 1952, 1953, 1970, 1977 by Allen Tate. Reprinted by permission of Farrar, Straus and Giroux, Inc., and Faber and Faber Ltd.

UNIVERSITY OF THE SOUTH. The university seal and the excerpts from Andrew Lytle's "A Christian University and the Word" are reprinted by permission of the University of the South, Sewanee, Tennessee.

KURT VONNEGUT, JR. From *Slaughterhouse-Five* by Kurt Vonnegut, Jr. Copyright © 1969 by Kurt Vonnegut, Jr. Reprinted by permission of Delacorte Press / Seymour Lawrence, a division of Bantam, Doubleday, Dell Publishing Group, Inc.

WILLIAM CARLOS WILLIAMS. Extract from "The Desert Music" from *Pictures from Brueghel and Other Poems by William Carlos Williams: Collected Poems 1950–1962*. Copyright © 1954 and 1962 by William Carlos Williams. Reprinted by permission of New Directions.

YALE UNIVERSITY. The university seal is reprinted by permission of Yale University, New Haven, Connecticut.

Introduction: The Syntax of Time

> Our very speech is curiously historical. Most men, you may observe, speak only to narrate; not in imparting what they have thought, which indeed were often a very small matter, but in exhibiting what they have undergone or seen, which is a quite unlimited one, do talkers dilate. Cut us off from Narrative, how would the stream of conversation, even among the wisest, languish into detached handfuls, and among the foolish utterly evaporate! Thus, as we do nothing but enact History, we say little but recite it.
>
> —Thomas Carlyle, "On History"

Here is an oddity of literary history: there are several biographies of Emily Dickinson, and people read them.

What is odd is that the life of Emily Dickinson would appear to offer nothing to a biographer. Dickinson was a recluse. She lived in her house, she wrote her poems, and then she died. The poems are what she left behind for immortality; to be interested in the life without regard to the poems would be the pettiest kind of gossip; it can't be claimed that the life can teach us how to read the poems; and yet the story of the life is written and written again, and read and read. Readers and writers seem to need the ritual of arranging its words on the altar of memory. I think this preoccupation may be able to tell us something about what we read *for*, and in this book I would like to suggest that what we read for is history.

My definition of the term "history" is specialized. I mean by it an ordering semiotic principle governing the presentation of time in literature. As I use the term here, history is not (or not only, or not merely) a sequence of elections, mass sheddings of blood, grunts and yells; it is a linguistic value arising out of the fact that words are uttered in sequence, one behind another in time, forming time as they form themselves. History is the inherence of time in language. It is the sense of passing which is brought into being by words as they shape their sequence into what readers and speakers perceive as time. On the page, history is present in every text, "historical" or not. It inheres equally in James A. Michener's costume sagas and in Ronald Firbank's tiny *Albumblätter* of remembered sensation.

But of course Ronald Firbank's novels aren't going to be shelved in the public library under "History." History's cultural expression differs from text to text, and likewise from literature to literature, language to language, stage to stage of the Darwinian process. For my purposes, that differential expression is most useful taxonomically. Texts communicate their histories in different ways, and those different ways communicate different senses of the texts' relation to time. The time I am concerned with here is our own. I would like to learn what literature in this century has uniquely been with respect to time: what the great deaths have taught it, where it has gone in search of the words whose speakers have died.

Let me start being specific, therefore, by juxtaposing two well-known sentences from texts that have constituted American history. The first is from the nineteenth century, and it reads:

> It is rather for us to be here dedicated to the great task remaining before us—that from these honored dead we take increased devotion to that cause for which they gave the last full measure of devotion—that we here highly resolve that these dead shall not have died in vain—that this nation, under God, shall have a new birth of freedom—and that government of the people, by the people, for the people, shall not perish from the earth.

The second sentence is from our own time, and it reads:

> And so, my fellow Americans, ask not what your country can do for you; ask what you can do for your country.

Now clearly, this second sentence is ceremonial language for a ceremonial occasion. It has the stately rhythm of a platoon of Bill Moyerses treading down the center aisle of a cathedral, chanting to their stenographers as they come. And what gives the document this effect is in fact a little anthology of selections from the history of language. Here is antithesis: *ask not . . . ask*. The *Oxford English Dictionary* will show you how that trope has been used in the past, and how it now evokes the past for us. Here is inversion: *ask not*. Here is parallelism: *ask not A, ask B*. And we know why those tropes are present at this moment in history. Rhetorically, they serve the same function as the opera hat President Kennedy sported on the dais: they fill our memories with anachronism.

Of course, anachronism is a standard trope of ceremonial language. In 1961, when President Kennedy delivered his inaugural address, people did not ordinarily say "Ask not"; in 1863, when President Lincoln delivered his Gettysburg Address, people did not ordinarily say "Four score and seven." Archaism serves to legitimize the language of political leadership; it assures those who hear the old words that their history is in safe hands. In purely rhetorical terms there is no functional difference between John Kennedy's anachronism and Abraham Lincoln's. But there is a difference in motive and effect, and we can read that difference historically.

Think of the context. By narrating the prehistory of the deaths at Gettysburg in the language of the Bible, the Gettysburg Address is meant to articulate their ethical meaning. Here rhetoric has a cultural function that is directly related to the paraphrasable content of the text. Directing our thoughts forward through history by means of the rarely used future perfect imperative, it promises us that these honored dead shall not have died as we feel so many have died in wars different from this one: separated from us by a timeless void that the words of their epitaphs cannot cross; in vain. Lincoln's is a language that involves us in our own history.

The archaism of President Kennedy's sentence, on the other hand, tells us only that the history it addresses through us must have been completed at some time before the words "Ask not" were actually uttered. The terminated history of that text—what

Benedetto Croce would have called its chronicle—is easy to trace.[1] The words were spoken on a specific date by President Kennedy; before that, they were written down by President Kennedy's speechwriter, Theodore Sorensen; before that, they were composed and uttered, in a slightly different form, by another president with literary talent, Warren G. Harding. If we want to, we can compile a scribal chronicle of this sentence, incorporating first and second and third drafts, secretaries' typescripts, blue-pencilings, retrospective transcriptions into *Bartlett's Familiar Quotations* and freshman speech textbooks—an entire archive, in a degree of detail that will be limited only by the availability of the sheets of paper that we have undertaken to arrange in chronological order. If this chronicle can be completed, it will have a definitive beginning and ending, and when we read it, we will be able to talk about analogues, influences, stylistic cause and effect—all the ordinary stuff of the literary history that arises out of our acknowledged belief in the existence of delimitations, demarcations, beginnings, endings. The name "Warren G. Harding" will introduce complicating ironies into the chronicle, but these too will be reducible to the orderly lucidity of words in a dead language. Volumes can be published, and each of these volumes may legitimately be called a history. And yet, oddly enough, the tropes in President Kennedy's sentence will still have no historical context. Reading them years after the fact, enriched by all the value that history can contribute to our understanding, we still don't know who we fellow Americans are; we know only that we are being asked to do something unspecifiable, by a voice which is speaking backward. The sentence which is realized by the voice has no history. It had no existence until it was said, but in the instant of its utterance, it is.

Politically, this is a major advantage. Because the presidential text has no history, its key phrase "my fellow Americans" subsists for us in a zone of simplification where we can believe we know

[1] "History is living chronicle, chronicle is dead history; history is contemporary history, chronicle is past history; history is principally an act of thought, chronicle an act of will. Every history becomes chronicle when it is no longer thought, but only recorded in abstract words, which were once upon a time concrete and expressive" (Croce, "History and Chronicle" [1921], trans. Douglas Ainslee, Meyerhoff 51).

what it means. Words that come out of history are complicated; they are cluttered with etymology and connotation. And that slows us down when we try to understand them. As we try to assimilate words that have histories, we have to take into ourselves a thick, raw mass of historical meaning. Previousness forces itself between the words and us. But words that make up their histories as they come into existence leap at us unchaperoned. First they are in our leader's mouth, then they are in ours. It is a wonderful gift. We can hum along with the words passing through us; we can clap, we can jump. And as we respond to the music we make, we will feel ourselves coming into our being. We will be wrong, but we will believe that we know at last who we are.

There is an instructive text to go along with the Kennedy address: the poem that Robert Frost wrote for the occasion but didn't deliver, "For John F. Kennedy His Inauguration . . . (With some preliminary history in rhyme)." As its title implies, this poem is full of conscious allusions to a past. In fact, it aspires to the condition of a universal history: a document that reveals comprehensible order in every event, past or future. The founders of the United States of America, Frost tells us,

> by the example of our Declaration
> [Made] everybody want to be a nation.
> And this is no aristocratic joke
> At the expense of negligible folk.
> We see how seriously the races swarm
> In their attempts at sovereignty and form.
> They are our wards we think to some extent
> For the time being and with their consent,
> To teach them how Democracy is meant. (423)

If you find those lines distressing, I suggest that the reason is historical, in the ordinary sense of the word. A generation after the fact, we see how factually wrong those words were, how arrogant. Eleven months after Frost would have spoken, the first American died in combat in Vietnam. The history of events casts its shadow over this verse. But I suggest that with respect to the history of words, Frost's poem is just as ahistorical as Kennedy's speech. The poem addresses posterity through us, but all its historical reference is to a history that exists prior to and outside of the text.

I mean: here is Robert Frost considering the events of Election Day, 1960, within the continuity of American history. On that day, let us recall, Senator John F. Kennedy had defeated Vice-President Richard M. Nixon by a margin so narrow that the outcome was in doubt until the next morning. And yet the transfer of power two months later was smooth and peaceful, as it might not have been in another country. The American political system had worked, and Frost interpreted that as a logical result of the principles of the American Revolution.

> Our venture in revolution and outlawry
> Has justified itself in freedom's story
> Right down to now in glory upon glory.
> Come fresh from an election like the last,
> The greatest vote a people ever cast,
> So close yet sure to be abided by,
> It is no miracle our mood is high.
> Courage is in the air in bracing whiffs
> Better than all the stalemate an's and ifs. (423)

The literary failure here is partly a failure of historical logic. Frost appears to be assuming that the American Revolution, *qua* revolution and act of outlawry, was a unique event—unique in that it has stood apart from its consequences. But of course revolution is about consequences, and it is consequently always *in medias res.* A deconstructionist might say that revolution is the discovery that the law has always already been broken. Handsome President Kennedy was about to be inaugurated that day in part because Richard Daley, a squat and neckless man who held the office of mayor of Chicago, had followed an old American custom and voted the cemeteries. Other departures from strict regularity were soon to follow in Cuba, the Congo, and Southeast Asia, and less than three years later Kennedy was to die at the hands of an American whose rifle had been delivered to him by his U.S. mailman. Frost thought that a revolution based on a written text could start and then stop. That was an elementary blunder in syntax.

If you want to call it hubris, then you can: that swaggering assurance that for *this* country there will never come the day of November 22, 1963. But notice that by articulating that moral term to yourself, you are thinking historically. The bad poem evoked the bad memory. The poem had priority; the moral idea came out of an event in the language. Only through the history of meaning can we know what is.

We can see this by contrast in another historical poem of Frost's. The history in this poem is natural history, the cycle of the seasons; the politics is the politics of our relations with time. The poem is called "Spring Pools."

> These pools that, though in forests, still reflect
> The total sky almost without defect,
> And like the flowers beside them, chill and shiver,
> Will like the flowers beside them soon be gone,
> And yet not out by any brook or river,
> But up by roots to bring dark foliage on.
>
> The trees that have it in their pent-up buds
> To darken nature and be summer woods—
> Let them think twice before they use their powers
> To blot out and drink up and sweep away
> These flowery waters and these watery flowers
> From snow that melted only yesterday.

Now as we read this poem, we are going to be affected by what we might call its institutional history. In its stanza form, its subject, and its mood, "Spring Pools" looks as if it belongs in a genre we have all been familiar with since sophomore lit: the Romantic nature meditation. So we will probably bring a Romantic presupposition to this poem's central idea about time. When Wordsworth tells us that his Lucy grew "three years . . . in sun and shower," the specification of the time is fundamental to his poem's delicate complex of pathos, resignation, acceptance, and affirmation.

> Thus Nature spoke—the work was done—
> How soon my Lucy's race was run!
> She died, and left to me
> This heath, this calm, and quiet scene;

The memory of what has been,
And never more will be.
("Three Years She Grew")

Whatever tragedy there is in this second poem's mood comes to us from what Hugh Kenner calls "Romantic Time . . . time receding, bearing visions away" (*Pound* 554). Time here is something that takes us, as the Romantic Yeats put it, out of nature. But Frost's time is different. Those thinking trees in the second stanza are its sign.

They are not personifications; they are not manifestations of the pathetic fallacy; they are not Romantic. They are something stranger, something seen for what it is without emotional interpretation: the silent reflection of a monitory voice that addresses itself while addressing them: "Let them think twice." And the line with the chiasmus, "Those flowery waters and those watery flowers," is more than a witty mimetic declaration. Here the subject matter and the rhetorical form are inseparable. The meditation has been taken up into its rhyme as the water is taken into the trees. The poem has made itself a history. Like that moment toward the end of Pound's *Cantos* where the things of the natural world begin to resolve the fugue at last and "the light sings eternal / a pale flare over marshes / where the salt hay whispers to tide's change" (CXV, p. 794), "Spring Pools" is an invocation of the words through which we approach the domain of wordless time. The trees and the water take each other up into themselves, and the poem's words take in time. And through those words, time shows itself to us as the real does in the title of one of Wallace Stevens's poems: not ideas about the thing but the thing itself.

Another of Stevens's poems tells us explicitly how time works itself into texts. You recall the conditions of the experiment. The huge entropic plurisignificant sea is washing itself ashore at random and washing itself back out again. On the beach just out of reach of the waves a woman is walking, singing a song. The song and the waves approach each other, but neither sound can make itself a sign.

The sea was not a mask. No more was she.
The song and water were not medleyed sound

Even if what she sang was what she heard,
Since what she sang was uttered word by word.

The ocean is the ahistorical. In it there are only simultaneity and parataxis, not a past or a future or an order. And the song is nothing but order. It exists only as that which has been uttered word by word. The woman and the ocean meet on the shore, at their mutual boundary, but when they withdraw again their *différance* remains: the ocean will still be unsingable.

But you know the ending of the poem. "The Idea of Order at Key West" is a triumph of ending. In it the past tense makes history. The song is sung; the song comes to an end; the emotion is recollected and reconstituted in a text that has its own beginning, middle, and end; and

Ramon Fernandez, tell me, if you know,
Why, when the singing ended and we turned
Toward the town, tell why the glassy lights,
The lights in the fishing boats at anchor there,
As the night descended, tilting in the air,
Mastered the night and portioned out the sea,
Fixing emblazoned zones and fiery poles,
Arranging, deepening, enchanting night.

To enchant is to cast a spell over by means of song. A song is a sound that can come to its measured end. Now that we know it is over, we can sing it in the past tense, as history. We make history of ourselves, word by word. And as that history passes through us on its way to the past tense, we shape ourselves around its words. And that is why readers continue to read the life of Emily Dickinson. They know their history. They know that history can tell us only one thing, but that one thing is enough. History tells us this: At the end of the story, we can begin to mean.

Consider this counterexample.

Gerald Murphy is the name of an American painter who was active in France during the 1920s. His career as an artist was short, and he completed only a handful of pictures; but when they were new, those pictures were acclaimed. Half a century afterward, when the Museum of Modern Art mounted a Murphy retrospective, the art journalists looked at Murphy's outsized still lifes of watches and razors and cigars and began coining phrases such as "the father of pop art." But Murphy's reputation as a painter hasn't grown since then. I look at the reproductions in a contemporary *Newsweek* account (Davis); I enjoy; I think, "But they're about fifty percent Braque and fifty percent Léger"; and I go on to other things. The magazine itself has aged. Its paper is yellow. The cover story deals with the then president of the United States, Richard Nixon, and his apparently unpaid income tax. On other pages I find advertisements for open-reel and eight-track audio tapes and for a secretarial service that was then called Kelly Girl. Times, as they say, have changed. Gerald Murphy is dead.

Sometimes, though, I read *Tender Is the Night*, a novel that was condemned by some reviewers, when it was published in 1934, as excessively nostalgic for the period when Gerald Murphy was a painter, and then Gerald Murphy's name comes back to me. There exist many biographies of the author of *Tender Is the Night*, and in most of them I can read that the principal character of that novel is modeled, in part, on Gerald Murphy. But in the book that keeps alive our memory of the man, Gerald Murphy fails to open the door to his studio. It is not mentioned in *Tender Is the Night* that Gerald Murphy had a habit of making marks with a paintbrush. The text that embodies the man has created a history for us to read, but Gerald Murphy's paintings have not been entered in that history. Gerald Murphy exists for us now, if he exists at all, as something read, but his paintings are not there. They are outside the text; they have been canceled.

What has become of Gerald Murphy?

He died in 1964, managing the Mark Cross luggage store in New York.

What has become of Gerald Murphy?

When he was a painter, he gave a party to which he invited a novelist, F. Scott Fitzgerald.

What has become of Gerald Murphy?

Historical judgment has been passed on him: he has been placed under confinement in a literary category. Periodically he is furloughed to serve as an illustration of the term *roman à clef*.

When he returns to his cell in the dark, what has become of Gerald Murphy?

> Our hysterical patients suffer from reminiscences.
>
> —Sigmund Freud, *The Origin and Development of Psychoanalysis*, lecture 1

What is poignant about the life of Gerald Murphy is the sense it conveys of a struggle for historical substantiality. We all want to believe that we can shape the memories of ourselves that will come into being in other minds, and our coming to terms with our own mortality requires us to learn that that desire isn't enough. When we discover that we have failed to live, we say, "That's life." Gerald Murphy thought he was going to be an artist, but things turned out differently. Instead of a painter, he became the subject of a historical irony.

That irony lies at the heart of the work of F. Scott Fitzgerald, the chronicler of the life that Gerald Murphy didn't live. Typically, Fitzgerald's irony takes a historical form: a frantic nostalgia for the moment that has just passed. "Can't repeat the past?" cries Jay Gatsby at the instant of his greatness. "Why of course you can!" (*Gatsby* 111). The moment when he wrote that sentence was Fitzgerald's instant of greatness too, and that satisfying biographical irony has produced a long shelf of books about Scott and Zelda. But of course Fitzgerald noticed the irony himself, and it occurred to him that he needed to speak about what it must have meant to be the instrument of this perception of time. When he reached the age of forty, he began.

It seemed too late. In 1936 Roosevelt and Stalin and Hitler were contending for the soul of the world; meanwhile, F. Scott Fitzgerald, author of "Bernice Bobs Her Hair" and other chronicles of the emotional life of high school children, was telling his readers in a series of autobiographical essays about the sadness he felt when he looked into the distance from atop the newly completed Empire State Building, saw the green of trees and grass, and realized that his world, the new-found land of life willed into existence through lifestyle, was only a little island of cultivated desire in the middle of a vast biological indifference. Seated before a commanding view of the edge of doom, one of the inventors of the Roaring Twenties had undertaken to remind his readers that he was unique.

Of course, Fitzgerald's record of moments in the growth of a man suffered from context. It was published at the wrong historical moment, in the wrong way: in installments in *Esquire*, a magazine devoted, amid the agony of the Great Depression, to style and fashion, the heedless and the ephemeral. So it is not surprising that when John Dos Passos, a politically committed novelist, saw Fitzgerald *mis à nu* among suitings and shirtings, he was outraged. "Why Scott—you poor miserable bastard," Dos Passos exploded in a letter, "Christ, man, how do you find time in the middle of the general conflagration to worry about all that stuff? . . . We're living in one of the damnedest tragic moments in history—if you want to go to pieces I think it's absolutely O.K. but I think you ought to write a first rate novel about it (and you probably will) instead of spilling it in little pieces for Arnold Gingrich [editor of *Esquire*]" (Fitzgerald, *Crack-Up* 311).

Fitzgerald, an alcoholic who wrote in knowledgeable detail about the nuances of self-pity, inspired many of his friends to that kind of bullying. But in one important respect Dos Passos was registering a specifically literary concern. That concern has little to do with subject matter or with craft; radical though he is, Dos Passos sympathizes in this letter with the bourgeois individualism of Fitzgerald's tragic view. He is concerned to the point of exasperation, however, with one of the consequences of this view. At one of the damnedest tragic moments in history, Fitzgerald is wasting time. Watching the dark fields of the republic recede before the shadow of the giant office building, the author of "The Diamond as Big as the Ritz" has uncharacteristically begun to commit optical errors: errors of magnitude, errors of perspective. In his error, he has become a narcissist. And the tragedy of Narcissus was that as his beauty withered, he failed to see. Observing himself unchangeably in the moving river, he was blinded by time. His blindness, Dos Passos saw, was not a mere individual ailment, to be cured by the method of laying the diseased organ bare to the sight of a healer. No; it was a blindness curable only in the memory. Bearing in his memory the beauty of what he once had been, Narcissus could have arisen from his rock and walked away into the freedom of the unlovely present. But he could not bring himself to remember. Narcissus is always committed to the contemplation of the unmediated present. And in the middle of the general conflagration, Fitzgerald's memory lay dark.

> In me thou seest the glowing of such fire
> That on the ashes of his youth doth lie,
> As the death-bed whereon it must expire,
> Consum'd with that which it was nourish'd by.

This book is about words written by some American writers who have sat with Fitzgerald on the banks of time. The taxonomy of the words, the ordering principle governing what they have said through their writers about time, I will call history. History, for my purposes in this book, is the syntax of meaning.

That is a working definition only. All it can claim as a critical principle is this: it may help us to understand how history words itself into read existence as a mode of textual form. Pushing a similar argument to its linguistic extreme, George Steiner has suggested that the well-nigh universal appeal of *Antigone* may be due to its unique congruence with something in our language sense, as if every human being were born with an Antigone-receptor in her brain. My own position is more modest. I suggest only that the term "history" represents not just an idea about time but a semantic construction *in* time.

Such a suggestion implies that the language of history can be thought of in two ways. In one sense, history is simply the textual record of events that happened before they were put into words, while the words were elsewhere in some unenunciable *là-bas*. That is the ordinary dictionary definition of the term. It is also the paradigmatic instance of *differance*: a body of words enunciating a significance of which they themselves do not partake, separated from the fullness of the unexpressed by the abyss of the instant of utterance. The exhibiting of what we have undergone or seen is one thing; the undergoing or seeing is another. That is what torments Freud's hysterical patients: they perceive with all the exacerbated sensitivity of their disease that they will never be able to bring the having-done and the saying-about together. Because of history, we can never tell the truth.

But the hysteric keeps trying to tell it, and when we think about his words we will find ourselves thinking about a different kind of history: the history that is inherent in textuality, brought into being by the words themselves as they shape their sequence into time. Here too the ontological news is bad. The history of our own lives is a continuous translation of acts into words, and to the extent that acts originate in a part of reality which is preverbal, our translations must be false. Freud's hysterics are tormented by that falsehood. Their ailment is an error of faith; it consists in the belief that words have the magic power to mean in themselves, without the need of any mediating interpretation. The hysteric is overwhelmed by memory because he cannot understand the insignificance of the words he remembers. He cannot believe that anything can be ineffable.

Like the Wordsworth of the Immortality Ode, the hysteric may find consolation in the truth-value of whatever preverbal or supraverbal

> Blank misgivings of a Creature
> Moving about in worlds not realised,
> High instincts (lines 146–48)

he may have experienced. But no originary intuition can heal the latter wound that time makes: the separation of words from the things that were born in our minds with them. Instead of having the thing, we know a meaning: a metaphor whose tenor, because it must take the form of a word, can only be another metaphor.

Let us sympathize with the hysterics. Their illness is the illness of all humanity. But let us be conscious of the problem, as they are not. At its logical boundary the regress of metaphor that we call meaning marks the line of demarcation between the physical entity "brain" and the metaphysical entity "mind." At its semantic boundary it maps the zone where our reading is generated: the nimbus of ordering power that clings, glowing, to words. When the words combine, one after another in time, meaning becomes historical. If the words are made of air, a sentence is created; if they are made of purines and pyrimidines, a body is born.[2] If we know time at all, we know it in this embodied form. Let us read it there.

[2] "In 1942–3 [Roman Jakobson] believed, quite rightly at that time, that he could say that 'language is the only system which is composed of elements which are signifiers and yet at the same time signify nothing.' . . . Since then there has been a revolution in biology with the discovery of the genetic code, a revolution of which the theoretical consequences cannot fail to have a dramatic impact on the human sciences. Jakobson understood this immediately" (Lévi-Strauss xx).

I

The Comic History of This Man Goddard

The infant wants to hear the same bedtime story every night, in the same words and with the same inflections. Her buttons will not stay buttoned, her clothes and toys lie on the floor, and within her there is a distress that she cannot articulate. But for a few moments of a few evenings she can solicit a power that will overcome her disorder. Just before resigning her consciousness to the biological force that is making her into someone who will forget what she now is, she takes into herself an ordered verbal structure, one that does not change. Fearful of the history made by events, she comforts herself with the history made by words.

When we grow older, we believe that we can make the events themselves unchanging. Once we have created it, we believe, the changeless will be a nest for our undying bodies. And so potent is this belief that it has taken political embodiment and given birth to nations. At the heart of the American Revolution lies the dream of a more perfect union with the breast of mother earth. Crèvecoeur's American Farmer, "this new man" (Letter III), is free to enjoy his unfolding life because, like the infant, he knows that underneath its epiphenomena it is all really his mother: unchanging; there.

> Whenever I go abroad, it is always involuntary. I never return home without feeling some pleasing emotion, which I often suppress as

> useless and foolish. The instant I enter on my own land, the bright idea of property, of exclusive right, of independence exalt my mind. Precious soil, I say to myself, by what singular custom of law is it that thou wast made to constitute the riches of the freeholder? What should we American farmers be without the distinct possession of that soil? It feeds, it clothes us, from it we draw even a great exuberancy, our best meat, our richest drink, the very honey of our bees comes from this privileged spot. No wonder we should thus cherish its possession; no wonder that so many Europeans who have never been able to say that such portion of land was theirs cross the Atlantic to realize that happiness. This formerly rude soil has been converted by my father into a pleasant farm, and in return it has established all our rights; on it is founded our rank, our freedom, our power as citizens, our importance as inhabitants of such a district. These images I must confess I always behold with pleasure, and extend them as far as my imagination can reach: for this is what may be called the true and the only philosophy of an American farmer. (Letter II, 25–26)

Exuberancy: from *exuberare*, to bear abundantly; intensive prefix *ex-*, root *uber*, udder. A historian of ideas will see the term "physiocracy" in this paragraph, but what makes it live on after the physiocrats have all died is not, or not just, a matter of terms, ideas, themes, or the psychology of the Oedipus complex. To understand this paragraph, one must not think but listen. For by exclaiming "Precious soil!" in exactly the right prose rhythm, Crèvecoeur has given time and space the definitive verbal form of a story with a name in it. Personifying the land his father has cleared, Crèvecoeur has told us the history of home.

It is a universal history; only its practical applications differ from case to case. Crèvecoeur's Farmer has come to Yonkers from Europe; Tom Buchanan, in *The Great Gatsby*, has come to Long Island from Chicago. But like the Farmer, Tom is grateful for his opportunity and his escape. The Farmer says, "These images I must confess I always behold with pleasure"; Tom says, "Oh, I'll stay in the East, don't you worry. . . . I'd be a God damned fool to live anywhere else" (10). And like the Farmer, Tom pays his meed of reverence to his new-found acres and the past he intends to create there. "I've heard of making a garage out of a stable," he remarks to Gatsby. "But I'm the first man who ever made a stable out of a garage" (119). Gatsby, who has not found it necessary to own a horse (104), is reduced to silence. Shortly thereafter he is obliterated.

The Great Gatsby is the story of a man who emerged from nothingness and tried to abolish time. For that he was crushed to death by the heavy mass of the history of events, the warm breathing phenomenal weight of its horses and husbands. Against these, Gatsby had only rhetoric, etiquette, love, and will. The rhetoric, which the infant Gatsby copied down from the lips of Benjamin Franklin and Horatio Alger—"Practice elocution, poise and how to attain it. Study needed inventions" (174)—was inadequate; in the world of Daisy Buchanan, it failed to provide a grammar of the language that money talks. The etiquette—the Darwinian code of Dan Cody and Meyer Wolfsheim, the code of man against the world—could befit only a solitary, a man who can love no one but himself. And love and will, in the stable cosmos of East Egg, have been superannuated. In Daisy Buchanan's world no one loves, because no one acts. Loving and willing have been accomplished long ago; Tom and Daisy live on their ancestors' harvest. They do not love; they are loved. They inherited the love with their money. Crèvecoeur's Farmer is emotionally sustained in the same way by the land his father cleared, and he knows it; that is why he explicitly names the soil he plows *Alma Mater* (Letter III). But Gatsby cannot read the Farmer's story, because he does not know its language—either its Latin, its French, or its English. The words of Gatsby's language have been omitted from its history.

Tom, on the other hand, not only has a history; he participates in his history, observes its course as it carries him along, *is* it. "Have you read 'The Rise of the Colored Empires' by this man Goddard?" he asks Nick Carraway (13–14). "This idea is that we're all Nordics. I am, and you are. . . . And we've produced all the things that go to make civilization—oh, science and art, and all that. Do you see?"

We do see. Tom knows (it is a part of the education that sleeked his hair and trained up his body) that only those who can speak of themselves as "we" in this way are members in good standing of their history. The elderly citizen of a small town, coming home from a high school football game, will think happily, "We won!"

and his mind will fill with memories of his own youth. His back hurts and he can no longer read the small print on his medicine bottles, but because he lives where he was born, he can forever be a sixteen-year-old quarterback feeling the smooth leather of the ball sliding into his hands. Around that event, before and after, his life has been uniform in its texture and fully coherent. It has confronted him with nothing he could not understand through the language he learned from his mother. The old man has been vouchsafed the contentment of history; he knows that he will comprehend the coming of his death.

Tom Buchanan has been possessed of a similar happy situation in history. Like the Swiss yokels of James Baldwin's "Stranger in the Village," Tom is at one with all the ramifications of his culture through time and space. In his lymph flows the architecture of Chartres Cathedral. Because Tom is a member of the Nordic race, the Gothic towers of Henry Adams's prose shaped themselves into being under his creative fingers. On Tom's behalf, an American thinker of the 1920s described the historical reality this way:

> Where the Nordic establishes himself among other races he is instinctively aristocratic. Feeling himself the ruler and the superior, he prides himself on his race and seeks to guard the purity of his blood. Throughout Europe today the old aristocratic class tends to be of Nordic origin. Even in countries where the Nordic element has been mainly bred out of the population, what little Nordic blood remains is found chiefly in the old upper-class families.

These are the words of Lothrop Stoddard (Tom's "Goddard"), writing in the *Saturday Evening Post* at the time Fitzgerald, another *Post* contributor, was working on *The Great Gatsby*.[1] Tom's pride in this history is understandable; reading it, he has learned the textual code of his own life. Fulfilled in history, the Nordic needs

[1]The *Post* article, "Racial Realities in Europe," was the first of a twelve-part series later published in book form under the same title. Stoddard was a professional racist whose work achieved its greatest influence in the months before the passage of the Immigration Restriction Act of 1924. For a summary of his ideas, see Gossett 390–98; for connections between the ideas of "Goddard" and Stoddard's *Rising Tide of Color*, see Turlish; W. Hall.

to do nothing more; he is as free as any of Fitzgerald's beautiful teenage protagonists only to be.

Still, Tom is unhappy. "As for Tom," says Nick, "the fact that he 'had some woman in New York' was really less surprising than that he had been depressed by a book. Something was making him nibble at the edge of stale ideas as if his sturdy physical egotism no longer nourished his peremptory heart" (21). Mere physical history has something to do with that, of course: the effect of changes in the creator's body on all the modes of his creatures' existence. In the year after he published *The Great Gatsby*, the professionally youthful F. Scott Fitzgerald turned thirty and entered a long sad period of drunkenness and artistic sterility. "Thirty," muses Nick Carraway on his birthday, "—the promise of a decade of loneliness, a thinning list of single men to know, a thinning briefcase of enthusiasm, thinning hair" (136). Tom too is thirty. Yet his depression is not merely a sinking of the animal spirits. The book Tom is reading ("'The Rise of the Colored Empires' by this man Goddard" [13]) was in nonfictitious literary-historical fact taken seriously and reviewed respectfully; it must have articulated an emotion that many Americans were feeling, regardless of their age or their social status. Something primitive was going around. In the summer of 1922 the fictitious Tom Buchanan was worried about being overrun by non-Nordics; within the previous eighteen months, Columbia, New York University, Williams College, Harvard, and Fitzgerald's Princeton had established exclusionary quotas for Jewish students (Gossett 372). "You see I think everything's terrible anyhow," Daisy explains in Fitzgerald's fiction. "Everybody thinks so—the most advanced people" (18). And what the most advanced people were saying in nonfiction was, among other things, this.

> A century ago Europe began to be transformed from an agricultural to an urbanized, industrial area. Countless cities and manufacturing centers grew up, where men were close packed and were subjected to all the evils of congested living. Of course such conditions are not ideal for any stock. Nevertheless, the Nordic suffered more than anyone else. The Nordic is essentially a high-standard man. He requires healthful living conditions, and pines when deprived of good food, fresh air and exercise. So long as Europe was mainly

> agricultural the Nordic usually got these things. In fact in cool Northern and Central Europe an agricultural environment actually favored the big blond Nordic as against the slighter, less muscular Mediterranean, while in the hotter south the Nordic upper class, being the rulers, were protected from field labor and thus survived as an aristocracy. Under modern conditions, however, the crowded city and the cramped factory weed out the Nordic much faster than they do the Alpine or the Mediterranean, both of which stocks seem to be able to stand such an environment with less damage to themselves. It is needless to add that the late war and its aftermath have been terrible blows to the Nordic race.[2] (Stoddard, "Racial Realities")

We read now, thinking: twenty years after this American journalist with his Harvard Ph.D. sat at his desk and mused about skull shape and hair color, his words bore fruit on the plains of Poland. How did the advanced people feel then? From the theory of reception we can learn something about the moral effects of thought. But the prior history that inheres in the words of this text can tell us about something that comes before the morality: the reasons why we think in time.

Consider: at about the time F. Scott Fitzgerald was born, people were noticing that their desires seemed to be changing. The names of Bergson and Freud were taking on importance, the adjective "Victorian" was acquiring negative connotations, and Hardy was writing "An Ancient to Ancients." Feeling itself now seemed to be different.

> Where once we rowed, where once we sailed,
> Gentlemen,
> And damsels took the tiller, veiled
> Against too strong a stare (God wot
> Their fancy, then or anywhen!)
> Upon that shore we are clean forgot,
> Gentlemen!

Changing, the damsel sails away into time and is gone. No man from our world will ever touch her with his body. Thomas Hardy

[2] This idea was an obsession with Stoddard and his audience; here he is substantially repeating a paragraph from his earlier *Rising Tide of Color* (163–64).

smiles. To the man who thinks, life is a comedy. But Tom Buchanan becomes desperate at the thought. He shouts, "Nowadays people begin by sneering at family life and family institutions, and next they'll throw everything overboard and have intermarriage between black and white" (*Gatsby* 130). He is afraid. Other people's bodies will interpenetrate, and he will never get to see.

But for people like Tom there is available a comforting succedaneum: virtual history. Virtual history is history as realist metaphor: history as the lives of changeless, immortal personifications representing Progress, or the Middle Class, or America, or the Nordic Race. In the face of George Washington on the classroom wall, America sees an emblem of the language of virtual history: a body language, silent but understood by all. Its wordless signs reach us through the eye. And America's greatest interpreter of this language was in fact a companion in labor of Lothrop Stoddard and F. Scott Fitzgerald. All three men appeared during the 1920s in the *Saturday Evening Post*: Stoddard and Fitzgerald inside the magazine, the artist of interpretation on the cover. His name was Norman Rockwell.

In virtual history the Platonic forms have real existence and complete explanatory value. They allow us to generalize about ourselves in disinterested abstract terms, as if we were components of a painter's composition. Lothrop Stoddard's Nordics have large cranial capacities; Norman Rockwell's Americans have rosy cheeks and outthrust buttocks. As terms of historical explanation, these two anatomical postulates are equally dispositive. Every pictorial element in a Rockwell is balanced by another element, and what has been excluded from the composition does not exist. There are parents and children in a Rockwell but not husbands or wives; there is a body language in which every posture strains to say, "And they got married and lived happily ever after, The End," but because there is no contact between the bent and yearning bodies, there is no marriage. There is only a virtuality of feeling, forever closed off from consummation by the rules that govern the placement of paint on canvas, and bounded on all sides but the side between you and it by a white space. In that space nothing exists but the date of this week's issue. We come as close as we can to the powerful numbers, but we cannot read our way past them into the picture plane. Protected by time, the picture's subjects live on, doing and being. It is Christmas Eve, and they are singing carols in the snow. The snow will always be falling; the sun will never rise; the bodies will always be those of our fathers and mothers, and they will always be alive. Virtual history is history as Grecian urn: an intercourse of pure forms existing in their own time.

But when he applied its emblematic forms to his own case, Tom confused virtual history with nostalgia. That was a geopolitical error. Before World War II a rare American—say, Henry Adams—could live nostalgically and make creative use of his yearnings, but par excellence nostalgia is a European emotion: the emotion of an individual who has been immersed from birth in a history always already completed. The European, as W. H. Auden says in a discussion of the differences between Americans and Europeans (xxi), is a cultural *rentier*. His ancestors have made the primary investments of direct emotion in action; now the European lives on his inheritance of symbols elaborated once and for all, his to spend but not to augment. For him life matters less than reminiscence. High European nostalgia is a middle-aged Walter Benjamin recalling, without the trace of a smile, the intellectual conversations he had when he was nineteen years old ("Berlin Chronicle" 15–24). The treasurable authenticity of action is not the doing; it is the knowing what one has done. It is Humbert Humbert reaching back through the body of Lolita to the child's body he himself once lived in and loved through, knowing what he is doing and knowing that that knowledge is his only sin.

Now we know why we can write Tom off: he has appropriated capital that does not belong to him. Gatsby has done that too, of course, but who steals my purse steals trash. Tom's offense is more serious. By cherishing horses and reading *The Rise of the Colored Empires*, he has attempted to lay title to nostalgia. He sails under a false flag.

For a moment, it may be useful to think of this historical transaction under the exalted rubric *mentalité*. Some such term, at any rate, can help us understand the power of certain obscure phrases: for instance, T. S. Eliot's suggestive blur of history and aesthetics, "the mind of Europe." After all, that universal-sounding phrase is intelligible in fact—that is, historically—only within the context of a specific political *Weltanschauung*: in the case of Eliot's "Tradition and the Individual Talent," an unstable mixture of Victorian medievalism and *Action Française*. In one important sense, it is impossible to read Eliot without first having read Charles Maurras, just as it is impossible to read Pope without having read Boileau. But in terms of *mentalité*—well, for most of us Eliot is a part of the air we have breathed all our lives. For us, to read Eliot is actually to enter into the mind of Europe. Reading, we undergo an experience that has been internalized by so many minds, for so long, that its existence as an effect of reading is practically independent of our individual lives. This is not to make an evaluative brief for Eliot; it is only to say that for most American readers at the end of the twentieth century, modernism has been a part of real history. That is, it has affected the way we remember in language. We knew there might be a "mind of Europe"; now, with the aid of grammar and syntax, we can understand and articulate how that mind might manifest itself through our own words.

History does work that way. Consider, for example, what the American Revolution did to the grammar of Henry James's language on the occasion of the review of his native culture which eventuated in *The American Scene*.

> I had formerly the acquaintance of a very interesting lady, of extreme age, whose early friends, in "literary circles," are now regarded as classics, and who, toward the end of her life, always said, "You know Charles Lamb has produced a play at Drury Lane," or "You know William Hazlitt has fallen in love with a very odd woman." Her facts were perfectly correct; only death had beautifully passed out of her world. . . . It is some such quiet backward stride as those of my friend that I seem to hear the voice of old Concord take in reference to her annals, and it is not too much to say that where her soil is most sacred, I fairly caught, on the breeze, the mitigated perfect tense. "You know there has been a fight between our men and the King's"—one wouldn't have been surprised, that crystalline Sunday noon, where so little had changed, where the stream and the bridge, and all nature, and the *feeling*, above all, still so directly testify, at any fresh-sounding form of such an announcement.

> I had forgotten, in all the years, with what thrilling clearness that supreme site speaks. (259–60)

The clearness is the absolute grammar of history: the mitigated perfect tense, the thrill of a language penetrated to its heart by time. (*Thrill*: from Old English *thyrlian*, to pierce; cognate with *through*.) The history that resides in texts works its changes through grammar and etymology, and the mind of Europe speaks to us most revealingly through the voice of Browning's Grammarian.

Virtual history, on the other hand, deals with rhetoric and syntax. It is the language of oratory, meant to be heard only with the external ear. Because we are only passive recipients of the language of virtual history, the magic it works in our thoughts is less a communal emotion than a multiplied individual psychopathology: not a shared impulse to speak and understand but a shared dumb yearning pause on the threshold of understanding.

There can be a museum of this virtuality, and what will strike a visitor to this museum, if the visitor is Henry James and the museum is the Richmond mausoleum of a different American revolution, one that failed to survive into the political present, will be a mysterious hiatus. On the one hand, the museum of the Lost Cause will be a monument in itself to its founders' passion for memory. The curators will take their guard over a desire for which men died, believing as they died that they were dying for immortality. But on the other hand, the actual objects on display will appear to have no articulable phenomenal reality. In the present, these gray things in the vitrine are not souvenirs, memories; they are the votive objects of a history that can never be written, because it exists only as a desire.

> The collapse of the old order, the humiliation of defeat, the bereavement and bankruptcy involved, represented, with its obscure miseries and tragedies, the social revolution the most unrecorded and undepicted, in proportion to its magnitude, that ever was; so that this reversion of the starved spirit to the things of the heroic age, the four epic years, is a definite soothing salve—a sentiment which has, moreover, in the South, to cultivate, itself, intellectually, from season to season, the field over which it ranges, and to sow with its own hands such crops as it may harvest. The sorry objects, at Richmond, brought it home—so low the æsthetic level: it was impos-

> sible, from room to room, to imagine a community, of equal size, more disinherited of arts or of letters. These about one were the only echoes—daubs of portraiture, scrawls of memoranda, old vulgar newspapers, old rude uniforms, old unutterable "mid-Victorian" odds and ends of furniture, all ghosts as of things noted at a country fair. . . . The moral of the show seemed to me meanwhile the touching inevitability, in such conditions, of what I have called the nursing attitude. "What on earth—nurse of a rich heroic past, nurse of a fierce avenging future, nurse of any connection that would make for *any* brood of visions about one's knee—wouldn't one have to become," I found myself inwardly exclaiming, "if one had this great melancholy void to garnish and to people!" (James 386–87)

And here the subjective perception coincides with the data of chronicle. It is the fact, for instance, that when James visited Richmond in 1906, he stood closer in time to the end of the Civil War than we are to the end of World War II. If millions of men and women have been driven to enact a great national tragedy, we would ordinarily expect the ideas that moved them to live on for more than forty-one years. *Mein Kampf* is in print today. It is read; it guides the dreams of millions. And yet John C. Calhoun and Alexander Hamilton Stephens, William Gilmore Simms and Edmund Ruffin, Robert Barnwell Rhett and J. D. B. De Bow, all the men who gave a mind and a form to the Confederacy, passed instantly into the void in 1865. Their heirs were, as James said, disinherited: left with nothing but military chronicle, the nursing attitude, the melancholy void, and the hope of a future history.

> Sleep sweetly in your humble graves,
> Sleep, martyrs of a fallen cause!—
> Though yet no marble column craves
> The pilgrim here to pause.
>
> In seeds of laurel in the earth,
> The garlands of your fame are sown;
> And, somewhere, waiting for its birth,
> The shaft is in the stone!
>
> (Henry Timrod, "Ode sung on the occasion of decorating the graves of the Confederate dead at Magnolia Cemetery, Charleston, S.C., 1866," Ridgely 81)

But disinherited—because history doesn't read Plato. As a mode of grammar, history deals in closure; as a bringer of words into meaning, it makes us know that the phrase "ever after" is meaningless unless it is falsified in the text. Thoreau's experience of immortality at Walden Pond is available to us only because it is delimited; because it has a middle term that holds eternity steady between two dates on the calendar: Friday, July 4, 1845, when the moment began, and Monday, September 6, 1847, when it ended. Two years, two months, and two days: we can make an educational mnemonic of that, and then our students will be able to start reading. To understand an idea syntactically, with regard to its historical dimensions, is to know both when it was born and when it died; to know that it was born, to know that it will die. But to practice virtual history is to think outside the grammar of time.

Jay Gatsby thought he knew how to reconcile universals with the concrete delimited reality of his love for Daisy: make a different beginning. He had done that before when he changed Jimmy Gatz of the North Dakota prairie into Jay Gatsby of the yacht *Tuolomee*, bringing his vague diffused ambition to articulable form within bounds shaped by the naval architect. Changed in form, Gatsby cut his way smoothly through the sea. On shore now, reaching out to the green light at the end of Daisy's dock, Gatsby wants to hold Daisy so close that they will both change. New-created, they will part the universe itself before their coming. But of course there is a technical problem: dividing our world from the rest of the cosmos is a zone of dark time that even Gatsby's smile cannot penetrate. That is the shadow of the sixth evening of creation, where the idea of body is shaped. It is there that love and tragedy are born.

But Gatsby wants to do away with evenings and mornings. And just as the young James Gatz took to heart the words of Benjamin Franklin and Horatio Alger, the mature Jay Gatsby has a mentor in his desire: the buoyant young Ralph Waldo Emerson of "Self-Reliance," who looked at the record of time and asked: "Whence . . . this worship of the past? The centuries are conspirators against the sanity and authority of the soul. Time and space are but physiological colors which the eye makes, but the soul is light; where it is, is day; where it was, is night; and history is an impertinence and an injury, if it be anything more than a cheerful apologue or parable of my being and becoming."

Ever being, perennially becoming, we can ignore the impertinences of time and heal its injuries. The idea is, as Emerson says, cheerful. But the young Emerson whose writings gave birth to Christian Science was a man who had suffered, and the reactions of a man who has suffered are always suspect. He may become an Elie Wiesel, a sad recidivist of pain; or he may deny his pain its memory by denying the importunate realities of life in the body: illnesses and hungers, weakness, mortality. Making that denial into a creed ("Can't repeat the past? Why of course you can!"), Gatsby committed an act of literary hubris: a reading of the history of the body as if it were history in a text. That act became his tragic flaw.

Because only Tom in *The Great Gatsby*, muscular Tom, has lived intimately enough on body's terms to understand the language of its history. For him virtual history is a history separate from reality: a body of absolute words, existing only as reading matter, *lisibilité*. And virtual history can be read only that way: purely, without interference from the traces of the body, its warm breath and memory-entangling hair. On the page is where virtual history has worked for men like Tom—on the page and in the mind freed from memory.

Of course, we who know Tom through the pages of *The Great Gatsby* see him and his sense of his place in the world through a filter of irony. *The Great Gatsby* is a novel that has been praised for its verisimilitude, but it is nevertheless a novel: a book one of whose purposes is to reassure its readers that what it shows them of themselves isn't really, you know, like, ah, *real*. The back cover of the paperback text sends us that comforting signal. "A novel of romantic love, infidelity and inevitable violence," it blandly announces, sliding a sheet of explanatory cardboard between the paraphrasability of what goes on in the book's words and the ineffability of what goes on in the reader's heart. Tom is on that side of the barrier; we are on the other. We can afford to laugh. Tom's history, Tom's *storia*, surely pertains to him alone.

Nevertheless, as Emerson says in "Fate," there is complicity. Consider, for instance, Tom's history-word "Nordic," and consider your own reaction to this quotation.

> Nordic Americans for the last generation have found themselves increasingly uncomfortable, and finally deeply distressed. There appeared first confusion in thought and opinion, a groping and hesitancy about national affairs and private life alike, in sharp contrast to the clear, straightforward purposes of our earlier years. There was futility in religion, too, which was in many ways even more distressing. Presently we began to find that we were dealing with strange ideas; policies that always sounded well, but somehow always made us still more uncomfortable. (91)

Here, you will say, is an important word in a fully historicized context. Whatever phenomenal reality the word "Nordic" possesses is attached first, with no mediation save language itself, to the reader's ego. The anthropological term has borrowed emotional expressiveness from your own memories. Your uncertainty in the face of the world has been given a name now, and a specific *floruit* ("for the last generation"). Now you know who you are: the woman confused in thought and opinion, the man who has not known, up until the moment of reading, who he is. Now you know; you have a history because you know a word.

And now I will impart some historical information and a small surprise. This text, with its elegiac overtones of Matthew Arnold's Scholar-Gipsy wandering through the history of Europe in search of psychic unity ("Thou hadst *one* aim, *one* business, *one* desire . . . —what we, alas! have not"), was originally published in 1926—a year after *The Great Gatsby*—in a conservative New England magazine, the *North American Review*. Its author, Hiram Wesley Evans, was the spokesman for an organization that had at the time a membership in the United States of about five million. The organization worked through political action, and in several states during the 1920s it dominated the agendas of both major parties. But as this passage shows, it defined its goals primarily in cultural terms. Because of their belief in these cultural goals, many of its members suffered bravely in the prisons of America.

The organization was the Ku Klux Klan.

As you read that last sentence, the expression on your face

changed. Someone watching you would have been startled. You would have explained, and then something odd might have happened to the two of you: you would have laughed. In a petty way, you would have been sharing the Olympian joke that history plays on us. We enter into complicity with that joke every time we laugh.

Here we are, for instance, watching two long-dead comedians perform on our own television screen. A new world plays itself into being before us, a world in which the cars and the clothes and the voices are subtly different from our own, and perhaps—there, just off the edge of the screen—our own grandparents might be waiting for us, younger then than we are now. We become happy; we have realized that what is happening on the screen before us is definitive. Nothing can fail now, no one can die. All is past. The fat man and the thin man are at one. They love each other. No matter how long we watch, they will always have loved each other.

We know their love is immortal, because they give and receive pain yet do not die. As they hurt, they move closer—closer to each other, closer to us. Soon we have partaken of the language of their pain, and we laugh. At an infinitely debased level, we have been touched by the happiness that lifts Dante free at the end of the *Comedy* from his accepted suffering: the happiness of knowledge revealed, the happiness that is vouchsafed to us at the approach of what George Herbert in "Prayer (I)" calls "something understood."

So that when we smiled at our newly discovered emotional connection with the phrase *Ku Klux Klan*, we were smiling too at our newly discovered complicity in the blood satisfactions of history. We too, we have learned, desire clear, straightforward purposes; we too desire to know without words. Perhaps all that separates us from the Klan is a social accident. "We are a movement of the plain people, very weak in the matter of culture, intellectual support, and trained leadership," admits Evans. "This is undoubtedly a weakness. It lays us open to the charge of being 'hicks' and 'rubes' and 'drivers of second hand Fords'" (100–101). We respond with sympathy. In the land of Goethe and Beethoven the intellectual classes responded similarly in 1933. Deeply desiring to know without words, we are all complicit in helping the words of virtual history recreate us in the image of a new God. The old God brought forth light out of language and created us in the image of a word. We have been feeling inauthentic ever since. The new God will ally himself with our silence, and we will be happy.

That he noisily expresses this yearning of ours for silent peace makes Tom Buchanan a comic figure. A philanderer who cants of moral purity, Tom is obviously vulnerable, like Tartuffe, to the irony of the contrast between what he says and what he does. When we think of him, we can articulate our reactions pretty adequately with a small lexicon of noun phrases: hypocrite, vicious fool. But what makes Tom's particular hypocrisy and viciousness comic on the largest scale is that they exemplify a general human frailty. Fitzgerald's role as spokesman for his age consists largely in mapping some of the loci of that irony: the institutions we have made to shelter ourselves from unmediated reality. Where the ivy grows on the Gothic towers, there is Fitzgerald's irony of the cultural sign.

Consider a character from one of Fitzgerald's other novels. Like Tom Buchanan, Dick Diver of *Tender Is the Night* is a graduate of Yale. The blazon on Yale's coat of arms proclaims *lux et veritas*, and it retranslates the Latin phrase back into its Hebrew original: *urim v'thummim*. To read those words in the spirit in which they were inscribed is to take on oneself the regalia of language, as Moses admonished Levi in Deuteronomy 33:8, 10 to do: "Let thy Thummim and thy Urim be with thy holy one. . . . They shall teach Jacob thy judgments, and Israel thy law." Dick Diver tries to live in the spirit of these words; throughout *Tender Is the Night*, in almost every conversation he enters, he becomes a teacher. But his most potent memory of Yale itself is Tap Day, and as Freud's student in Vienna "he could not feel that [his mental processes] were profoundly different from the thinking of [his roommate] Elkins—Elkins, who would name you all the quarterbacks in New Haven for thirty years" (116–17). Something is missing from the lesson plan: a word, a clarifying reference to what has gone before.

It was missing for Fitzgerald too. Even at the end, knowing that he had failed to learn some important things, Fitzgerald still had trouble deciding just what *was* important. "The old dream of being an entire man in the Goethe-Byron-Shaw tradition," he mourned in *The Crack-Up* (84), ". . . has been relegated to the junk heap of the shoulder pads worn for one day on the Princeton freshman football field and the overseas cap never worn overseas." Familiar legends fill in the details that the penitent assumes we know: freshman Fitzgerald, five feet seven and 140 pounds, cut from the team on the first day of practice; Lieutenant Fitzgerald leading his platoon onto a troop ship on the morning of November 11, 1918, and leading it off again that afternoon. In the life of the young man, the two events once possessed a high and equal value; now, in the life of a man as old as he will ever become, they are equally junk. Older than Fitzgerald, we might say that the ending of a war is a more important crisis for a man than the beginning of a football game. But when Hardy's Victorians vanished into history, they took with them their genius for making such distinctions. To Fitzgerald, a son of the Victorians, events presented themselves as a bewildering succession of single happenings, bringing with them no contexts but those he was painfully able to discover for himself, by himself.[3] In his work and his life, he shows us that. That is his importance. Fitzgerald is the spokesman for an age which has just discovered the terrible truth that things and their symbols are sometimes hard to tell apart.

To Lothrop Stoddard and his readers this discovery took the form of a passionate will to believe in the reality of the symbolic—for example, in a real presence inherent in the word "Negro." We needn't be surprised at the fear engendered in them by such words; if even a sensitive writer like Fitzgerald could be confused about the difference between word and thing, there could be no hope at all for the Tom Buchanans of his world. It probably matters, therefore, that at the same time Tom was reading Stoddard, T. S. Eliot was formulating the doctrine of the dissociation of sensibility. The two ways of viewing history, Tom's and Eliot's, have at least this in common: each bespeaks a loss of the ability to understand. Tom's loss is a loss of the ability to make

[3] "My father . . . as a boy during the Civil War was an integral part of the Confederate spy system between Washington and Richmond. In moments of supreme exasperation he said, 'Confound it!' I live without madness in a world of scientific miracles where curses or Promethean cries are bolder—and more ineffectual" (Fitzgerald, "My Generation" 121).

words ("Daisy," "love") mean; Eliot's loss is of the ability to respond with the body to the cries of words heard in the mind's ear. Each loss is a historical one: I mean a loss of the history which begins by assuring us of our names and makes us real, word by word, from there. That loss, working itself through Western culture during the next twenty years, was to lead to terrible things. Many people paid with their lives for Dr. Evans's friends' feelings of discomfort. But here in the text, at least, that historical discomfort has a comic aspect too. Tom, we see, is a man exasperated by a specter: Mr. Hardy, say, chasing himself and Mr. Laurel noisily through the house in pursuit of a strange sound. Mr. Hardy has made the sound himself, but his house cannot tell him that; it can only permit Mr. Hardy to bounce his body off its solid surfaces. We laugh; all around Mr. Hardy the laws of physics are abetting the kinetic energy of his furious life, but he is unconscious. He is at home, but he doesn't know it. He has become nothing but a moving body. He has, as Eliot could have put it, escaped from emotion.

For Jay Gatsby, the situation is reversed. Among the inessential houses at the end of the book, he alone is real. He has become the history of his desire. All the rest is virtual. The words around him and around us—his library of unopened books, the motto on the stationery of Dr. Diver's alumni association, the captions under photographs which tell us that these bodies once had names and were loved—have been transcended. It is a bleak enough happiness for Nick and us to bear witness to, but in a world of words it is sufficient. In any event, it is the only one available.

2

Coat of Arms: The Virtual History of the Undivided Mind

Because it lived by images . . . loosely gathered from the past, the South was a profoundly traditional European community. The Southerners were incurable in their preference for Cato over the social conditions in which he historically lived. They looked at history as the concrete and temporal series—a series at all because they required a straight line back into the past, for the series, such as it was, was very capricious, and could hardly boast of a natural logic.

—Allen Tate, "Remarks on the Southern Religion"

The design of Yale's coat of arms is simple: an open book displayed in a shield. The Hebrew words *urim v'thummim* occupy the pages of the book; around the shield, running up the left side, across the top, and down the right, are the three words of the Latin translation, *lux et veritas*. In a circular band around the coat of arms run words that locate it in the law and the history of this world: *Sigil* : *Coll* : *Yalen* : *Nov* : *Port* : *Nov* : *Angl* : (Seal of the College of Yale, New Haven, New England). This is the mark of a school that certifies the word for the use of man.

The escutcheon of the University of the South bespeaks a different mission. It is in the shape of a mandorla, the almond-shaped *vesica piscis* which, according to James Hall's *Dictionary of Subjects and Symbols in Art*, "has no intrinsic significance. . . . but in time came to be used as a kind of 'glory' or aureole, the light that emanates from a divine being." In Christian art, the mandorla usually glows in the air around the Virgin, visually protecting:

protecting her from an impure world, protecting the world from too close contact with the supernal. It is the illumination that follows on the discovery of difference. Here in the coat of arms, however, the shape of light mediates, delimiting and translating an allegory made of words and symbols.

The words are there from the beginning, immediately available to us, in a belt around the inside of the shield, alternating with crosses: "+ + + SEAL + OF + THE + UNIVERSITY + OF + THE + SOUTH + + + 1858 + + + +." But then comes the light. Penetrating past the zone of words, diving from the mandorla's pointed upper tip, a haloed dove representing the Holy Ghost descends, blazing, on a circle. Inside the circle is another circle, this one consisting of an unbroken chain containing twenty-four links, representing the unity of the text of the universe: twelve tribes of Israel and twelve Apostles, the Old Testament and the New, the world and the spirit. At the center of this circle, its arms extended equally to the four corners of the earth, is a Greek cross, sign of the Church (Ferguson, s.v. "cross"). Within the cross's four quadrants are its empowering words, the Greek symbols $\overline{\text{IH}}$ $\overline{\text{XP}}$ A Ω: Jesus Christ, the first and the last. Below the circle and slightly overlapping it is a banner inscribed *Ecce quam bonum*: the first words of Psalm 133, "Behold, how good and how pleasant it is for brethren to dwell together in unity!" The words are emblematized by a picture of two hands locked in a (Masonic?) handshake. The arms attached to the hands are dressed in business suits. The hands themselves are white.

The escutcheon teaches us an image of silent cyclical history interrupted by words, then shaping those words into historical forms. Set down on paper within the conventions of iconography, the light and the words have been enrolled within the conventions of a genre. Restrictions have been imposed on the ways in which we may interpret their significance. The mandorla was once a shape in which we could invest our own powers of mind, but now it has been historicized into a specific associational meaning. There will be no more prophets. The university seal testifies to the institutionalization of epiphany: light restricted to the short depth of field that we call history. But the history existed prior to the light. First comes the flesh, then comes the word. The wordless handshake testifies to that. Before the word came to celebrate and interpret it, it was. Through words, it may be again. At any rate, I am looking at it on the title page of a book.

The book is a publicity volume called *Sewanee: The University of the South*. Its object is to depict in words and photographs (it is mostly a picture book) the uniqueness of the school. Sewanee, of course, is famous for being visually unique among American universities: its students wear jackets and ties to class, its faculty wear cap and gown. That dress code is consciously intended as a sign of homage to the past, for Sewanee is built on a consciousness of its own history. Other schools too hire alumni fund-raisers who specialize in appealing to the emotion of nostalgia, but only Sewanee, perhaps, speaks to nostalgia in the tone of elegy. Look in Sewanee's book, for instance, at this photograph of a grave. The tombstone is small, lichen-covered, undistinguished in appearance; what is important about the ground it rests on, the image tells us, lies within. The words under the image are modest too; they assume we know without having to be told what they really mean. "Kirby-Smith gravestone in cemetery," say the words, and if we can read the textbook of Sewanee, we will understand how that word "cemetery" fits into its vocabulary. "Kirby-Smith," says the word, and the communicant knows: Edmund Kirby-Smith, CSA; professor of mathematics; the last Confederate general to lay down his arms.

Beside the photograph is an elegiac poem. "Be thou still /

Among us," it prays to the spirit of the grave: "A man . . . of war if need be and of peace / To whoso peace ensueth." And surrounding this pious artifact of image and verse, typographically an enfolding and unifying part of it, is the text of a commemorative address titled "A Christian University and the Word." The address was originally delivered in 1964 (Polk 98). The speaker was the novelist Andrew Lytle, one of the twelve southerners whose manifesto *I'll Take My Stand: The South and the Agrarian Tradition* had required its first readers, thirty-four years earlier, to rethink their ideas about the connection between history and the language of culture.

On first thought, the fact that this rethinking is still going on seems strange. If it is an economic tract, *I'll Take My Stand* has long been out of date. In the desperate year 1930 its twelve authors exhorted the South to reconstitute itself as an agrarian region outside the capitalist system, but by 1936 their best-known spokesman, John Crowe Ransom, had conceded that "the farmer needs income . . . he should not be expected to live as a self-subsistent primitive" (qtd. in Singal 217–18). Perhaps the book's economic ideas were never much more than a pretext for cultural revolution, but as a cultural critique too *I'll Take My Stand* is not much more today than a museum of obsolete ideas. In the display to your right can be seen John Gould Fletcher, the only poet who was both one of the original Imagists and one of the original Fugitives, expressing his desire to close down (his actual word is "destroy") the public schools (120). On your left a young Robert Penn Warren suggests[1] that separate but equal ought to mean separate but *equal* (252–54). As you step out the door into the sunlight, it occurs to you that *I'll Take My Stand* was superannuated by the mechanical cotton picker.

The book is a wholly idiosyncratic mélange of Confederate nostalgia and economic fantasy. Yet it continues to be read. And there is a reason: *I'll Take My Stand* offers its readers a powerful schooling in the mental technique of making virtual history. From this education they can learn the essential quality of virtual history: that it is history as image.

[1]In an essay which at least two of the other contributors considered too radical for inclusion (Singal 348–49).

Here, for instance, are two dates, the raw material of history, from "A Christian University and the Word": in October 1860 the cornerstone of Sewanee was laid; in March 1866 the rebuilding of the ruined school began. Between these dates occurred a terrible period that Lytle evokes in the ordered incitements of nineteenth-century narrative history. Like Macaulay or Carlyle or Parkman, he marshals his data to serve the purposes of the pictorial.

> The endowment gone, the few buildings burned down, the cornerstone blown up by enemy soldiers and carried away in their pockets as souvenirs. . . . The South was beaten, exhausted, tromped upon. Whole counties in Alabama and Mississippi didn't have even a needle. Houses burned, stock and cattle gone, some women pulled plows while men pushed to keep their children from starving. For ten years the ex-slaves led by carpetbaggers and scalawags combed the South for anything left by armies, levying taxes, bonding states for their private gain, selling counties of plantations under the hammer, dragooning and humiliating the defeated population. But [*Here something happens. His chronicle is finished, but the historian keeps writing*] still something remained, intangible, incomprehensible. The South was still undefeated in spirit. [1][2]

And with this the historian has found his subject: the invisible workings of the word. The dates have been learned; now we will begin to know what they signify. For that, pictorialism is insufficient. The practitioner of virtual history is faced with a different technical problem: communicating the significance of the intangible. For an audience of human beings reading between earth and heaven, the virtual historian will have to say what he has to say mediately, with reference to both zones of significance. That is, he will have to speak in metaphors.

Lytle's chief metaphor is one of the traditional tropes of narrative history: personification. Sewanee was reconsecrated to learning at specific times by specific men, men with names and bodies, but such data in themselves are merely the stuff of chronicle.

[2] The pages of *Sewanee* are not numbered; my page [1] is the first in Lytle's four-page address, and so on. In quoting from this book, I have silently corrected a few typographical errors.

Their real significance must be evoked by interpretation. In Lytle's interpretation, the bishops and generals who recreated the University of the South were personifications of a holy force which saw the light brought down to us from heaven and captured it in Sewanee's coat of arms.

> It is very moving even now to read about these Cincinnati who once ruled in great affairs, living on short rations, in rough but beautiful surroundings, knowing however that the salvation of the South lay in the kind of thing they were doing. Out of the clear faith of a Christian view they knew that the Northern secular education relates to Christendom only in so far as it has for patron that old adversary, that fallen light which shines in darkness but does not illuminate. The lie we live today is that a secular society and a carnal world is the whole of life. It used to seem tedious to you gentlemen to come to chapel, but remember this. Only there could you feel yourselves belonging to a whole body, not just individuals engaged separately in a common end. [2]

The key phrase here is "rough but beautiful surroundings." Had Lytle's purpose been homage to the heroism of Sewanee's refounders, he would have said "beautiful but rough," but the point of this passage is that the heroism was only a means to an end. Only at the beginning of our enterprise must we traffic with Cincinnatus, with the rough flesh. That must be placed in a subordinate position, before the "but."

Especially since it is still all too present to our memories, still able to wrestle with the force of virtual history for control over what the prophet Ezekiel called our chambers of imagery (8:12). It was "the Romans of the early Republic, before land speculators and corn laws had driven men from the land to the city slums, who appealed most powerfully to the South," says Frank Lawrence Owsley, another contributor to *I'll Take My Stand*, and proceeds to draw a counterimage: "These Romans were brave, sometimes crude, but open and without guile. . . . They reeked of the soil, of the plow and the spade; they had wrestled with virgin soil and forests; they could build log houses and were closer to many Southerners than even the English gentleman in his moss-covered stone house. It was Cincinnatus, whose hands were rough with guiding the plow, rather than Cato, who wrote about

Roman agriculture and lived in a villa, whom Southerners admired the most" ("The Irrepressible Conflict" 70).

This passage evokes the image of an antebellum southern history fully realized and vigorously lived through. But the locus of that history is the semifeudal frontierland depicted in 1861 by Frederick Law Olmsted in *The Cotton Kingdom*. For Lytle's purposes, that history is not useful. Allen Tate would have said that Owsley draws our attention away from Cato to the social conditions in which he historically lived. Lytle's object was to draw our attention the other way: from dust-covered Abraham, say, to Archbishop Laud; from the chronicle of the first founding to its legend.

> The South in all its parts, plain man, mountain man, planter, slave, man of affairs—all are here out of common respect for what was being done. . . . This was October 1860. [1]

And we readers can take our choice. We can think, "My mistress' eyes are nothing like the sun," or we can pay grateful tribute with Lytle's slaves to the spirit of higher education. Either way, reading either for the persons or for the personifications, we will profit historically. For legend too has a historical function: it shows us how to look for the beauty in the roughness, and how to value it once we think we have found it.

Now valuation is fundamentally metaphoric. My dollar bill is only a vehicle whose tenor is purchasing power. If the Federal Reserve has been well managed, I may take the metaphor so far for the reality that I will employ it as the tenor of another metaphor—a second-order abstraction from the reality. "Sound as a dollar," I will say, thinking that the dollar is the fundamental thing. But my senses will check me after a while. The bill, I will realize, is after all only a piece of paper. In enunciating the terms of *his* metaphoric valuation, Lytle has the advantage of appealing to a much less arbitrarily chosen tenor. Lytle's chain of linked metaphors originates in a reality that actually is fundamental: the body.

Discussing the power of the Sunday service to change us, Lytle metaphorizes the body by focusing our attention on its context. We enter the chapel, and there our individual bodies are subsumed by the category of a body of men. In a body, as a body, we partake of the body of Christ. Changed from what we were, we eat fine bread, rule in great affairs, and go forth to do battle with our old adversary. That adversary's name is legion, but in our new bodies we have been strengthened in the knowledge of names. We are no longer people; we are personifications: living words, metaphors that can move off the page and effect consequential action. The word is made flesh and dwells among us, full of grace and truth. Henceforth we will not read words as we read before.

> Let us take the word honor, since it involves the whole action of man and not merely his profession. In Mississippi, Colonel Dabney, who had been a rich planter before the Civil War, afterwards found himself ruined. A white-haired old man, he did the family wash, because Sherman had said he would bring every Southern woman to the wash board. Also, in his prosperous days, he had put his hand to a note, promising to pay. In the reversal of fortune, which any one of us might expect, he found his obligation increased a hundredfold. He paid every penny of it, working only for this, and then died. He did not bemoan the turn of fortune that made of a simple matter a heroic act. His name was on that note. It was the symbol [of] himself. It defined him, himself to himself and to others. That signature meant that he would deny himself, his total being, if the note remained unpaid. It also meant submission to another, so long as the promise to pay was not paid. To redeem his word was to make him free. About the same time Jim Fisk tried to corner gold. When he failed, he said, "Nothing lost save honor." So, gentlemen, you have your choice.
>
> That statement is the core of Yankee triumph over the South and its European inheritance. [4]

In Lytle's last two sentences, the story of colonel Dabney is fully moralized: that is, rendered fully understandable in historical terms. We know what it means, all of it. It will support no further interpretation; for it, the words "The End" are absolutely terminal. Allen Tate's straight line into the past has reached its origin. Life has been completely converted into history.

Of course, chronicle will tell us that there were lawyers in the South as well as the North, and suits among gentlemen for breach of contract. But we are obviously not intended to think about this passage in chronicle terms. For the chronicler, words are merely referential; they are labels attached to things, not the things themselves. Their only purpose is to help us locate the things in time and space. "What is honor?" asks Falstaff in the skeptical spirit of chronicle. "A word. . . . a mere scutcheon." In the chronicle of a battle, the purely symbolic escutcheon is not to be confused with a real shield. But in virtual history, power is only a realized word. Honor, reified, washed the clothes, paid the note, and drove Pickett's men up the hill at Gettysburg against Meade's guns. Honor is what we learn to read at Sewanee; honor is what we are.

Or rather, it is what we have become. That is the ground of Lytle's conservative optimism. But not everyone can convert memory so easily into hope. Matthew Arnold, remembering the story of the Scholar-Gipsy, wants it to make him new but knows it cannot. "To the just-pausing Genius we remit / Our worn-out life," he moans, "and are—what we have been." Historical guilt has imposed its heaviest sentence on him: to remember the past without being able to change it. The nineteenth century suffered much from this morbid nostalgia and searched hard for cures. When Freud said, "Where id was, there shall ego be," he was proposing to replace retrospect with prospect by reinterpreting the words of his patients' histories. Lytle too found historical power in words. He had been aware all along that *I'll Take My Stand* was economically a fiction, in that "if you destroyed the industrial set-up, then we would be slaves."[3] But the modal distinction between fiction and truth doesn't concern Lytle's enterprise. Lytle's business is with the absolute magic of the words themselves, not the secondary authority of their generic context. Unlocking his word-hoard, the poet sets out his treasures in order to heal us. They are words: the words of a liturgy, the words of a folk song.

The liturgy comes to us from two sources: chronicle and the wordless earth. They combine into an ideal history.

> The South [before the Civil War] was a Christian society, but an incomplete one. It had as many puritans as New England. And they

[3] Lytle in conversation at the 1956 reunion of the Fugitives, qtd. in Lucas 33.

> were fine people, but communion between Heaven and earth is bound to be uncertain, so long as you have only a pulpit and no sacrificial table before which to worship. Yet Southern people were believers as are all people who are constantly at the mercy of nature and its laws. The seasons turn for a farmer (when there were farmers) and his welfare and even life depends upon this turning. The rough laws of nature may be defined, but nature is finally a mystery as it acts upon man. It is the very ground of a religious state of mind. [2]

"Natural piety," Wordsworth called it, in a pastoral poem. Culturally, at least, the rough laws of nature follow the rules of literary convention. When we think about the world through the medium of words, we have no choice but to subjugate it to the laws of grammar and genre. Interpreting, we engage in a rule-bound struggle against the silence of phenomena. We can obey the rules ourselves according to different grammars: altar or pulpit, liturgy or sermon, southern dialect or northern. Once we have chosen our grammar, however, we may legitimately use it for only one purpose: to appropriate the power of the phenomenal. Our world of words must live and move, with the light of a rising and a setting sun. We must seize that light for ourselves out of the silent sky.

Or, perhaps, we must become aware that the light has already been seized for us. To Tom Buchanan, the news that he is a Nordic comes as a revelation; it gives him the power to make coherent sense of his world. A word has brought him into his inheritance. But Tom remains unsatisfied. He doesn't know why, but we do. We know that only Adam, naming the world anew, understood it through words in a completely authentic, completely unambiguous way, through a language whose only history came solely from himself. Sons and daughters of Adam, we have borne his curse of history ever since. But if we can only bear that curse unselfconsciously, putting mind and words on in the morning and putting them lightly off again in the evening, it will not enter into us. Our bodies will dwell in the dust of the earth, but our souls will remain in Eden.

That is the hope and the theory. The Romantic enterprise sought practical examples, and it found children, noble savages, and sturdy Scottish yeomen. Walter Scott was a collector of folk songs; so was Andrew Lytle. Here is Lytle, watching his beloved Tennessee farmers at a square dance. The time is shortly after the end of World War I. Electricity and paved roads are about to change this world forever, but the farmers dance on. They do not know. Quietly, sadly, Lytle takes us aside and writes us a note:

> This and other games, "Fly in the Buttermilk," "Shoot the Buffalo," "Under the Juniper Tree," will fill an evening and break the order of their lives often enough to dispel monotony, making holidays a pleasure; and not so frequent nor so organized that they become a business, which means that games have become self-conscious, thus defeating the purpose of all playing. As they play they do not constantly remind one another that they are having a good time. They have it. ("The Hind Tit" 231)

Sadly, because this moment of unified sensibility is the last. Soon the money economy will come to the valley, bringing with it mind and the sin of the Serpent. "Throw out the radio and take down the fiddle from the wall," Lytle pleads. "Forsake the movies for the play-parties and the square dances. And turn away from the liberal capons who fill the pulpits as preachers. Seek a priesthood that may manifest the will and intelligence to renounce science and search out the Word in the authorities" (244). Clearly, Lytle shares with T. S. Eliot the perception that the rustic dance on the cusp of time is an utterance in body language of "the agony / of death and birth":

> Lifting heavy feet in clumsy shoes,
> Earth feet, loam feet, lifted in country mirth
> Mirth of those long since under earth
> . . . .
> The dancers are all gone under the hill.
> (*Four Quartets*, "East Coker")

But he shares with the Romantics Shelley and Coleridge a desire to realize this perception here on muddy earth through the positive disciplines of politics, economics, and sociology. Lytle was a working farmer; like Scott, he knew his subjects at first hand and conceived of his writing as an authentic articulation of the grounds of their lives. He writes and they shout, but metaphysically, Lytle and the farmers are at one: proud, tender inhabitants of a little universe with a unique and treasurable cosmology.

> Industrialism is multiplication. Agrarianism is addition and subtraction. The one by attempting to reach infinity must become self-destructive; the other by fixing arbitrarily its limits upon nature will stand. An agrarian stepping across his limits will be lost.
>
> When the farmer, realizing where all this is leading him, makes the attempt to find his ancient bearings, he discovers his provincialism rapidly disintegrating. The Sacred Harp gatherings, and to a less extent the political picnics and barbecues, have so far withstood the onslaught; but the country church languishes, the square dance disappears, and camp meetings are held, but they have lost their vitality. Self-consciousness has crept into the meetings, inhibiting the brothers and sisters and stifling in their bosoms the desire to shout. ("The Hind Tit" 241–42)

But Lytle's own shout seems at first to ring false. Working with ease in the difficult dialect of the college-educated class, Andrew Lytle wrote on clean sheets of typing paper, quite probably by electric light, words praising the simple folk: Andrew Lytle of Sewanee, Vanderbilt, and Harvard, spokesman for Episcopalian higher education. One is reminded of Marie Antoinette at the Petit Trianon, playing farmer. Or, more charitably, one is reminded of Walter Scott dying of the strain of living like a laird.

Still, one does remember. Lytle's evocation of this vanished life refuses to be dismissed. We feel its poignancy much as Lytle intended us to: that is, as an evocation of the ideally good, ideally exotic, and definitively absent. After all, Lytle does not pretend to be one of the folk himself. Like us, he only watches the dance. And he knows why he does not take part. "Make no mistake about it," he tells his Sewanee audience, "this kind of education is aristocratic. It can't be democratic" ([3]).

But if we know that we are separate from the others, how do we make contact with ourselves? History has walled us round with a deep moat.

> We've never had a democracy in this country. We once had a Republic. Since the Civil War we've had a plutocracy. . . . How

> can a gentleman function and be himself in an ochlocracy, towards which we are moving? [3].

How can we be what we are, any of us? In that general form, this is the question that sent Lytle off to the rural slums, Wordsworth and Scott in his hamper. His reports of the expedition suffer from xenophobia, myth-mongering, and the idiom of a debased romanticism. These are faults, of course. But they are literary faults. On its own terms, the terms of virtual history, Lytle's homage to the authentic remains authentic. When he requests us to honor the self-subsistent primitive, it turns out that he is not primarily talking about economics, or sociology, or even (*sensu lato*) culture. No, he is asking us to look at some men and women who once were themselves. They were not ladies or gentlemen, and they did not function as ladies or gentlemen; they were folk, and they functioned as folk. They were not able to do so for long, of course, and that was sad for them. But if they could have articulated the cause of their sadness, their situation would not have been just sad; it would have been tragic. As Tiresias tells Oedipus, it is better to be blind to inescapable destiny.

But the artist is the one who dares not be blind. Tiresias, Cassandra: the one who shapes the truth into words comes to know tragedy all too well in his or her own body. Some tragic heroes die of hubris; others die of consciousness. The conscious ones are the more bitter at the end. That is Andrew Lytle's situation here. A representative minor intellectual, he is a representative failed tragedian of our age, a man who casts the incantations of history but cannot escape from his own magic circle. Virtuality has him in thrall: the beautiful personification who rises from the ashes of the past and persuades us that she is real because we have dreamed her so. C. Vann Woodward, a professional historian of the South, briskly dismissed the Agrarian idea as "a second lost cause" (Lucas 30), but virtuality is not a ghost who can be laid by mere fact. She lives on in us, and the stories she tells us are convincing because we confided in their truth long before we became conscious. Because she knows us, she knows that we want to hear of Oedipus going blind from learning. We want lost causes and the memory of failure; we want to believe that in remembering the past we have regained the touch of our parents' bodies. We want to be within the sound of the dead voices; we want to dress ourselves in our fathers' and mothers' words and pretend. And when we are done pretending, we want to feel sad and start pretending again. With the Hart Crane who wrote "Passage," we weep to ourselves, "I was promised an improved infancy." We need truth, but we would rather have tragedy. That is our own comic failure.

Sometimes, though, virtual history speaks to us clearly in spite of ourselves. That is an uncanny experience. We are surprised to discover just how much she has mattered to us all along, and how much of our minds she does partake of.

Consider, for instance, what happens when a clear text suddenly becomes unclear. That happens to Lytle. Speaking on October 10, 1964—Founders' Day at Sewanee—Lytle goes uncharacteristically euphemistic at one point:

> The South was struck down, unformed, before it knew itself. It had many diverse elements, but it had one institution which outlasted the destruction, which in this country and in Europe is the Christian unit, and that is the family. . . . The recent attacks against the South are actually against the family, for so long as it thrives a dictatorship will have trouble. [3]

What recent attacks against the South, what dictatorship? Chronicle notes the date, observes that Lytle's speech falls neatly between the passages of the omnibus civil rights bill of 1964 and the Voting Rights Act of 1965, and deduces that we are reading an analogy here, or rather a metaphor in the classic form of an analogy:

$$\left.\frac{\text{The South resists}}{\text{integration}}\right\} \quad \text{as (or because)} \quad \left\{\frac{\text{the family resists}}{\text{dictatorship}}\right.$$

So the attacks and the dictatorship are euphemisms. But they are also mere code phrases, easily decipherable with the help of newspaper files. The phrase "the family" is a euphemism too, but it has to be read differently. Ordinary euphemisms, such as "passed away" or "differently abled" or "dictatorship," can usually be traced back to a single originating term with strong primary emotional content: dead, crippled, would-you-want-your-sister-to-marry-a-nigger. But "the family"—well, it means "Southerners." And it means "we who have always lived this way." And it means shared memories of Clark Gable and the Ku Klux Klan outwitting the Yankee soldiers in *Gone with the Wind.* So that when Lytle talks about "the family" as if the phrase actually meant something, he is not being diplomatically vague about, say, endorsing George C. Wallace three weeks before a presidential election. For Lytle the term "family" is never vague. It is precise, but it is also uncontrollably rich. Unlike other euphemisms, it has a diachronic dimension. Its meaning extends far beyond the topicalities of 1964. It is historical.

And to read historically is to read the history of our own reading minds. Here, for example, is one text from the history of an important term in literary criticism.

> It appears to me from my own observations, from those of the selected persons who have aided me, as well as from the history of the Jews, that their minds work in a somewhat different manner from our own. Our habit is to separate the fields of action so that we have a limited field for preliminary intercourse with men, another for business relations, yet another wherein the sympathies may enter. With the Hebrew all the man's work is done in one field and all together; he is at the same time friend, trader, and citizen, all of his parts working simultaneously. There is a basis for much friction in this diversity of mental habit. (119–20)

The text is Nathaniel Southgate Shaler's *The Neighbor: The Natural History of Human Contacts*; the year of publication is 1904; the critical term, as it was to be formulated in 1921, is "dissociation of sensibility." And our reaction is probably something like what Melville called the shock of recognition. It is worth our while to ask why.

After all, we have known for some time that the idea of dissociation was circulating long before Eliot reduced it to a phrase (see, e.g., Menand 133–34, 146–48). One more confirmation is probably supererogatory. But if we consider that Eliot's strictly rhetorical analysis is a text in virtual history, we may understand why Shaler's natural history has the effect of immersing us in a radically different context. For Shaler, the context is the naked wordless idea and its mute containing body; for Eliot, it is the word.

The differences follow from that. For Eliot, and generally for readers in the modernist tradition, dissociation is deprivation, the sad consequence of a primal sin of language. For Shaler, dissociation is simply a given. Jews don't experience it; everybody else does; hence everybody else hates Jews. The arguments about "Gerontion" and Ezra Pound's radio broadcasts don't matter, never did matter. We have passed through the integument of words to the idea at their heart. In the presence of that immense, unguessed-at, and wordless significance, we are shocked into silence.

Theatrical people, actors and directors and producers, were taking dramatic advantage of this silence long before Bertolt Brecht worked out his theory of the alienation effect. After all, the existence of the silence speaks to something fundamental in our relationship with words. There, in the silence, virtual history comes into being. We need words to explain why our words have failed us, and if we cannot believe that the words have content, we still have the form. Hence, perhaps, Andrew Lytle's rhetoric. "The Agrarian South," he exhorts his fellow southerners in *I'll Take My Stand*, "should dread industrialism like a pizen snake" (234). Industrialism had settled into the South well before 1930, but Lytle could still cry his defiance in the southern tongue. It was all he had. If she lives at all, personification lives in her emblems. Chronicle holds the capital of reality, but virtual history holds the terms of its valuation.

Like a banknote, it works through promises. Lytle's note, for instance, assures us that there can exist a human life occupying its world so fully that nothing in it is not full of human significance. That is a fiction, no doubt, but it serves as a standard to hold reality up to. And that, perhaps, is why we feel estranged from Shaler's reading of the human soul. Shaler probably knew dissociation as deeply as his fellow southerners Lytle and Eliot; the son of a slaveholding Kentucky family, he fought on the Union side in the Civil War. But in locating the source of dissociation in the brain cells or the germ plasm, he was placing it out of the reach of words—that is, out of the reach of history, out of the reach of the possibility of change. Shaler's Hebrews and non-Hebrews are

Platonic types. They will never die, but they were never born either.

We can't desire that immortality. We want to be human, even if we know we can't be: that is what the personifications of virtual history have to teach us. By figuring life to us, they show us how to hope, and whether that hope looks forward or back, to progress or nostalgia, matters little enough to our life in language. For the words, all that matters is that we do hope. Virtual history, hope considered as a mode of language, is therefore an inescapable part of our lives in time. It and we have gone through terrible epochs together, lying and being lied to. But the stories we tell must continue.

Wallace Stevens explains why, in a poem suggestively called "Men Made Out of Words." Mindful of their need for virtual history, Stevens's word men sing "the terrible incantations of defeats." That song is a preliminary to the human work of language. For Andrew Lytle, however, nothing follows the song but the silence of death. That is why Lytle is a minor writer. For him, words stopped being able to mean in 1865. But Stevens possesses the power to finish the story. His men are able to transcend history altogether and live their story in an eternal present tense.

> The whole race is a poet that writes down
> The eccentric propositions of its fate.

Stevens's men move forever through time, naming. They live in Eden. But the rest of us, those who live on amid the confusions of the real, have to find our propositions in the words of virtual history. The locus of *our* history is not Eden but Atlantis. Katha Pollitt wrote a poem about us there, and for that we must be grateful. We and our wordless realia cannot continue to live, but in virtual history we live on.

Atlantis

Dreaming of our golden boulevards and temples,
our painted palaces set in torchlit gardens,
our spires and minarets, our emerald harbor,
you won't want to hear about the city we knew:

the narrow neighborhoods of low white houses
where workmen come home for lunch and an afternoon nap,
old women in sweatstained penitential black
ease their backaches gratefully against doorways

and the widow who keeps the corner grocery
anxiously watches her child dragging his toy
who was sickly from birth and everyone knows must die soon.
You won't want to know how we lived,

the hot sun, the horsetraders cheating each other out of boredom,
in the brothels the prostitutes curling each others' hair
while the madam limps upstairs to feed the canary,
the young louts smoking in bare cafes

where old men play dominoes for glasses of cognac—
and how can we blame you?
We too were in love with something we never could name:
we never could let ourselves say

that the way the harbor flashed like bronze at sunset
or the hilltowns swam in the twilight like green stars
were only tricks of the light and meant nothing.
We too believed that a moment would surely come

when our lives would stand hard and pure, like marble statues.
And because we were, after all, only a poor city,
a city like others, of sailors' bars and sunflowers,
we gave ourselves up to be only a name,

an image of temples and spires and jewelled gardens—
for which reason we are envied of all peoples,
and even now could not say
what life would have to be, for us to have chosen it.

3

The Joke about the Man from the East

"Well, what do you think makes him act that way?" asked the cowboy.

"Why, he's frightened!" The Easterner knocked his pipe against a rim of the stove. "He's clear frightened out of his boots."

"What at?" cried Johnnie and the cowboy together.

"Oh, I don't know, but it seems to me this man has been reading dime-novels, and he thinks he's right out in the middle of it—the shootin' and stabbin' and all."

"But," said the cowboy, deeply scandalized, "this ain't Wyoming, ner none of them places. This is Nebrasker."

"Yes," added Johnnie, "an' why don't he wait till he gets *out West*?"

The traveled Easterner laughed. "It isn't different there even—not in these days. But he thinks he's right in the middle of hell."

—Stephen Crane, "The Blue Hotel"

Part of the appeal of Katha Pollitt's poem lies in its evocation of a special emotion: ideal nostalgia, the attribute of an Atlantis that has passed directly from the never seen to the never-to-be-seen-again. Pollitt's Atlantis is pure chronicle: it has traversed the passage from fable to memory without having touched, even for a second, on the drab shore of reality where we readers pass our merely real lives. From that shore we see the fable as it vanishes into mythic time, shining on the rising water as it eludes the historian's clumsy grasp.

But once it has become a myth, Atlantis is rebuilt every day. It subsists on the page of its written history as independently as the background detail from Fra Angelico's *Descent from the Cross* subsists on the cover of the paperback edition of Paul Veyne's *Comment on écrit l'histoire*: a tiny city, five centimeters by six, complete in all its castellated details, surrounded by a blank space on which is inscribed the explanatory words of a theory of retrospect. There on the page full of words, scissored free of the image of the Cross which once gave it an origin in our lives and a reason for existing there, the city has become a myth in its own right, like the little town embossed on the curving wall of Keats's Grecian urn: a reality forever a part of and yet forever separate from the words with which we attempt to explain its presence in our lives.

One thing we do when we read is to effect that isolation of the phenomenon from its place in the continuum of time. As Veyne says:

> Madame Bovary truly believed that Naples was a different world from our own. There happiness flourished twenty-four hours a day with the density of a Sartrean *en-soi*. Others have believed that in Maoist China men and things do not have the same humble, quotidian reality that they have here at home; unfortunately, they take this fairy-tale truth for a program of political truth. A world cannot be inherently fictional; it can be fictional only according to whether one believes in it or not. The difference between fiction and reality is not objective and does not pertain to the thing itself; it resides in us, according to whether or not we subjectively see in it a fiction. The object is never unbelievable in itself. (*Did the Greeks Believe in Their Myths?* 21)

No; but until they have accumulated memory around themselves, objects are invisible to believability. Their having become believable is a sign that they have acquired history; that is, that they have become entrained in the sequence of encoding in words which we call memory. To be at a loss for words is sometimes a historical problem, a symptom of having dropped for a moment out of a sequence of meanings. And if such a sequence extends longitudinally, through time, from an origin perceived to be a past, the loss for words becomes a loss of contact with a culture.

Consider the central incident of "The Blue Hotel": the tragicomic story of a stranger who disrupts the communal life of a little group of men with a few sentences of paranoid fabulation. The stranger fears death, and says so; the stranger is crazy, and says so; and no matter how explicitly he says what he says, the men of the blue hotel cannot understand. Everything they hear bewilders them. But they honor the stranger's words by attempting to interpret them, and in time they arrive at the plausible explanation I have quoted at the beginning of this chapter. They think they know: the stranger must be suffering from the symptoms of literature. The stranger, they suppose, would be normal like them if his vocabulary hadn't assimilated itself to the idea of the Wild West. The stranger misunderstands what they say, they suppose, because his traveler's phrase book was manufactured under substandard conditions, in a literature factory too far from its suppliers of words. And they begin to understand their interpretive *agon* as a conflict between two vocabularies; merely between two vocabularies.

There are vocabularies and vocabularies, of course. The stranger's vocabulary is literature and hallucination; the vocabulary of the men in the hotel is the social ritual of the game of poker. Unable to reconcile his vocabulary with theirs, the stranger rises from the card table, beats one of the men, staggers out of the hotel, tries to make one more man understand him, and is stabbed to death. Dying in a saloon, at the hands of a gambler, he has triumphantly succeeded in becoming a part of the dime novel. He has entered genre at last, and become lost in translation. And after death and retrospect have extended the stranger's genre into their language, the men in the blue hotel can take part in the historical irony of learning at last what the stranger meant.

The words of "The Blue Hotel" in fact record an alienation in time, from time. Within the hotel but outside its interpretive community, the stranger takes his meanings from the timeless lexicon of archetype. He thinks that the Wild West manufactured in the literature factories of the East exists, and will exist forever by virtue of geography. Meanwhile, in an actual hotel in an actual town in Nebraska, isolated from the rest of the world by a driving blizzard, is a little world of alternative explanations. In that world, things obey Aristotelian convention: they are amenable to logic; they have beginnings, middles, and ends. The men of the hotel, with their regular schedules and their predictable ideas, think in terms of the culture of which they are members. Unlike the stranger, they live in the history from which they draw their conventions of meaning. And this is the terrible conclusion that Stephen Crane forces us to draw: because they live in their history, therefore they cannot understand it.

The terrible question then arises: what *do* they understand? One answer is suggested by Henri Bergson's essay "Laughter." There, discussing the nature of the comic, Bergson hypothesizes that "Were you asked to think of a play capable of being called *le Jaloux* . . . you would find that *Sganarelle* or *George Dandin* would occur to your mind, but not *Othello*: *le Jaloux* could only be the title of a comedy. The reason is that, however intimately vice, when comic, is associated with persons, it none the less retains its simple, independent existence, it remains the central character, to which the characters in flesh and blood on the stage are attached" (70). By this test, it appears that we can think of "The Blue Hotel" as comic, and understand the stranger's dilemma accordingly in terms of comic irony.

It is possible, after all, to agree that another title for "The Blue Hotel" could well be something like *Le défiant* ("The Mistrustful Man"). What has led the stranger to his death is, in fact, a Bergsonian principle: the coming into being of a self-subsistent semantic entity. If irony consists in a perceived contrast between a reality and its representation, the stranger's code of representation is a comic mechanism that works by automatically ironizing every communication it processes. Its insane lexicon, unlike any merely social communication, is perfectly unambiguous. The stranger, unlike anyone else in the blue hotel, knows exactly what he means. By contrast with his undeconstructible code of absolute meaning, the words of the men of the hotel are comically imperfect. When he walked into the hotel, therefore, the stranger inserted into its history a fragment of the timeless rhetoric of absolute representability. "He thinks he's right in the middle of hell," laughs the Easterner, as the human language of the men in the hotel dashes itself against the stranger's archetypal code and shatters. But of course the joke is that he really *is* right in the middle of hell, and so are we. The stranger's hell is the comic character's imprisonment in his own Bergsonian archetype. Our hell is different. It is not an imprisoning presence in an idea but an absence: an ironic distance that separates us from the reality of every representation we speak.

To the great masters of modernist literature in this century, the stranger's hell of archetypal perfection has been an imaginative resource, a warming Dantean fire. As they rethought the complicated relationship between lived history and its verbal record, such artists as Ezra Pound and James Joyce found themselves looking with the stranger's liberating perspective of alienation at some of the imperfect old epistemological conventions by which we know time. Wyndham Lewis's entire oeuvre, for instance—the novels, the paintings, and *Time and Western Man*—can be read as an aesthetic model of a desire to supplant one way of thinking in time by another: linearity, say, by simultaneity. Other authors elaborated other models, and of these *The Waste Land* is probably the most comprehensive and certainly the most influential. But T. S. Eliot wasn't content merely to build models of his ideas; he wanted to touch them at first hand, as if they were real. So he built himself a social structure, his journal the *Criterion*, and peopled it with a coterie of his followers: so many strangers in the hotel, all speaking about time in a new way. Their immediate purpose was to carry out the historiographic program of Eliot's "Tradition and the Individual Talent" (*Selected Essays* 3–11): the program of subordinating the time-bound exigencies of human history to the immortal abstractions of "the mind of Europe" and "impersonality." But their larger purpose was to make those abstractions capable of explanatory power, as if they were as human as history. Eventually—this seems to have been the hope—the abstractions were to have made their entrance onto the stage of the historical drama raging outside the covers of the journal, and decisively changed its outcome.

Changed its outcome, that is, to something like a realization of the Idea on earth. When it came to practical politics, as William M. Chace has observed, Eliot was possessed of a "lifelong scorn of any practice that found an easy way to function in a world so lost" (145). What in fact was going forward in the commentaries and book reviews of the *Criterion*, issue after issue, was a social drama. *The Waste Land* was among other things a political poem, with a specificity of reference which isn't always appreciated, and the *Criterion*, considered as a whole, is probably best read as a political document. Its political purpose, however, was not a matter of parties or topical issues, but something larger and more abstract. If the term "politics" can be applied to the *Criterion* at all, it refers chiefly to a desire to intervene in the language in which history is made. Other political documents deal in analogies, personifications, and metaphors: iron curtains, uncle sams, kinder americas. The *Criterion* did too, but with this difference: it didn't begin its drama of figuration with names. For Eliot the poet there were indeed emblematic names to conjure with: Sweeney, Bleistein, Rachel *née* Rabinovitch. But the Eliot of the *Criterion* proceeded in a different way. He and his collaborators took nameless chthonic fear as the tenor of a series of political metaphors and then located that fear in a specific place, on this specific planet. Considered as a single work of art elaborated over a period of years, the *Criterion* is a geography of Bergsonian reifications. It shows us fear in a handful of dust and gives the dust a place in time and a history.

By the waters of Leman I sat down and wept . . .
—T. S. Eliot, *The Waste Land*, "The Fire Sermon"

Politically speaking, the history begins in Germany. There, in the aftermath of World War I and the Russian Revolution, readers of all levels of sophistication found themselves retracing the eastward path that Rainer Maria Rilke had opened just before the war. For Rilke the journey ended in Russia, on the banks of the Volga, in an image of a white horse in whose pure and wordless breath was unified Leo Tolstoy's universe of absolutely represented morality.

Der fühlte die Weiten, und ob!
der sang und der hörte—, dein Sagenkreis
war i n ihm geschlossen.
Sein Bild: ich weih's.

He felt the spaces, oh, how great!
He neighed and listened—*in* him was invested
your saga.
His image I dedicate. (I. 20)

But Rilke made his Russian journey in 1899. For the German petite bourgeoisie during the next thirty years, representability required more exciting images. Therefore, over the emblematically dwarfed childhood of Oskar Matzerath, the hero of Günter Grass's *The Tin Drum*, there hung the family adults' humid fantasy of Rasputin, the mad monk. And a popular book in Germany during the 1920s was Count Hermann Keyserling's *Travel Diary of a Philosopher*, with its solemn meditations on the sexual wisdom of the Japanese woman. White nights in St. Petersburg and a warm quilt on the floor inside the little paper house: the defeated nation escapes en masse into the world of might-have-been and with salvaged pride nods in agreement as Keyserling proclaims:

> If we modern Europeans regard East and West as a fundamental opposition, we do not in fact oppose the East so much to the West as the classical and mediæval ideal to that of modernity, which is essentially Protestant; and this means that we oppose the ideal of perfection to that of progress. Thus I would appear to have found the key to the problem [of my antipathy toward the West]. I prefer Orientalism to Occidentalism because I value perfection in any form higher than success. (2: 262)

Keyserling set out accordingly to study the Orient.

Meanwhile, however, some other intellectuals were studying the Keyserling-Rasputin enterprise and finding in it a symptom of a geographical malady of the spirit. In Switzerland, Hermann Hesse was so distressed that he wrote three essays about the phenomenon and collected them in a little pamphlet, which he called *Blick ins Chaos*: a glimpse into the chaos. And there in Switzerland at the end of 1921, undergoing psychotherapy and revising the manuscript that was to become *The Waste Land*, T. S. Eliot read it.

Eliot cited Hesse's meditation on *The Brothers Karamazov* and the Bolshevik Revolution in his notes to "What the Thunder Said."

He also wrote Hesse about "votre *Blick ins Chaos*, pour lequel j'ai conçu une grande admiration" (*Letters* 509, 13 March 1922) and asked him to contribute an article to the first issue of the *Criterion*. The article duly appeared, under the title "Recent German Poetry." In substance it is a translation of the third essay of *Blick ins Chaos*, "Gespräch über die Neutöner," and in form it is an ordinary essay in literary history. The translation, however, conceals an interesting Bergsonian datum: "Gespräch über die Neutöner" is written in the form of a Platonic dialogue between an academic and a war profiteer. The nostalgia of defeat here takes the form of historical irony. "Recent German Poetry" is written as an ordinary academic essay, but there too Hesse chooses his texts Platonically, as expressions of Idea.

The idea that specifically concerns Hesse is the idea of authority, what might be called the semantics of compulsion in language. Concerned with creating a *catalogue raisonné* of the language of culture, Hesse reads the poetry of his time in proto-Foucauldian terms:

> All these different groups [of linguistic conservatives and radicals] close up immediately again into one uniform whole so soon as the rather fruitless search after new forms is abandoned and the spiritual content only is examined. This is always exactly the same. Two principal themes are everywhere dominant: rebellion against authority and against the culture of that authority in process of downfall; and eroticism. The father thrust against the wall and condemned by his son, and the youngster, hungry for love, who endeavours to sing his sexual passion in new, free, lovelier and truer forms: these are the two figures that are everywhere to be found. They will too constantly recur, for they indicate, in fact, the two central interests of youth.

Too constantly now, the Oedipal contest rages where the trenches once ran with blood. And the specific agency of this psychic tragedy is historical, for all that has afflicted the *Neutöner* and their fathers is what Keyserling called progress; that is, the historical circumstance which forces us to think that we must change. Hesse continues without a break:

> The experience and impetus behind all these revolutions and innovations are clearly discernible in two powerful forces: the world-

> war, and the psychology of the unconscious founded by Sigmund Freud. The experience of the Great War, with the collapse of all the old forms and the breakdown of moral codes and cultures hitherto valid, appears to be incapable of interpretation except by psychoanalysis. Europe is seen by the youth of to-day as a very sick neurotic, who can be helped only by shattering the self-created complexes in which he is suffocating. ("Recent German Poetry" 90–91)

Hesse's valetudinarian imagery must have meant a great deal to Eliot, whose letters from the time he settled in England to the time of *The Waste Land* are one long cry of physical and mental distress. Hesse's pessimism, too, accords with the *Criterion*'s cultural analysis. "Neither the experience of the war nor the advent of Freud has led as yet to any very fruitful results," Hesse proclaims (91). But by the time the first subscribers to the *Criterion* read these words, what the youth of Europe desiderated and Hesse feared had already come to pass. For there in volume 1, number 1, of the *Criterion*, thirty-nine pages earlier, for the first time, men and women read the words "April is the cruellest month." That too was a critical thesis, with a bibliography going all the way back to Chaucer. The trenches and the couch underlie the words of both authors equally, but the difference between Eliot's text and Hesse's is this: Hesse has chosen to write literary history, and Eliot has chosen to invent a new form of historiography. Specifically, what Eliot did in *The Waste Land* was to elaborate a method for making chaos into an archetype: a chaos delimited and made representative of an entire language which had up until then existed only virtually, as a potential language waiting for its vocabulary to be born out of history.

Consider, for instance, the historical locus of the notes to "What the Thunder Said": the Bolshevik Revolution, personified as a faceless horde shambling out of the East. The East is the direction of the exotic and the uncanny, the direction out of which, in time, something will come to change our sense of who we are and how we live. That time is always *not yet*, one of the domains of historical irony. As they watched from their city walls, the last defenders of Constantinople undoubtedly had plenty of time to speculate on the nature of the change they saw coming, and they wrote their eschatologies accordingly. But sooner or later their speculations reached the point at which *not yet* means *too late*, and then they were ready to read *The Waste Land*. Eliot's readers in 1922, like Hesse's, must have felt that they too were ready to understand—to understand, for instance, what a word like "London" must mean now that the Zeppelin bombers had called into question the idea of "London" itself. The first readers of *The Waste Land*—those readers like the college students in Evelyn Waugh's *Brideshead Revisited*, chanting Tiresias's words through a megaphone on the long spring evenings—understood one thing, at least: that they were reading historically. The first condition for their reading was that all the conventional eschatologies had come due. The ending they foretold had come about, and they had accordingly passed into the domain of mere archive. To the first readers of *The Waste Land*, the old language was now as perfectly incomprehensible as the stranger's in the blue hotel: the tongue of an angel now bewilderingly redescended into time.

And there, in time, they read this passage from "What the Thunder Said," the cry of a man who realizes that his language and his history alike have become only a play of signifiers without significance.

> What is that sound high in the air
> Murmur of maternal lamentation
> Who are those hooded hordes swarming
> Over endless plains, stumbling in cracked earth
> Ringed by the flat horizon only
> What is the city over the mountains
> Cracks and reforms and bursts in the violet air
> Falling towers
> Jerusalem Athens Alexandria
> Vienna London
> Unreal (lines 367–77)

Under their hoods, the faces of the hordes are undoubtedly the faces of monsters—monsters with a specific cultural physiognomy which we can identify on other pages of Eliot's *Complete Poems and Plays*. There will be names associated with those faces, too: the Bleisteins and Sweeneys and Grishkins. And the names and the faces will have political significance. They are personifications of a collective id, and the vocabulary by which they mean what they mean is to be found in the American political iconography of Eliot's childhood (Morse 137–40) and the eugenic literature that Eliot and his friends were reading during the early 1920s (Leon 170–74). We can locate these monsters' origins on any ordinary political map. But what Eliot did to teach his readers here was to locate them too on the map of meaning. They occupy a place of their own there: a place the *Criterion* coterie was to call East.

Eliot's collaborator Herbert Read, for example, is concerned primarily with the East as a mode of consciousness. Read's East may have a specific locus on the globe, but in its impenetrability to the mind it is an ageography: a zone outside thought like the Marabar Caves of Forster's then recently published *A Passage to India*. All that matters geographically is this: somewhere some amorphous thing takes up words into itself, eviscerates them of their meaning, and returns nothing to consciousness but an empty sound. For Herbert Read, *that* place is East. "The one tendency that emerges from all Count Keyserling's observations and experiences," he explains in his 1926 *Criterion* review of *The Travel Diary of a Philosopher*, "may best be expressed by the word *orientalism*" (191).

Against orientalism, Read articulates a plea on behalf of a self-consciously Western epistemology. Read calls by name on Saint Thomas Aquinas, but the actual words he invokes to save his readers from peril are those of a contemporary scholastic: Henri Massis, a right-wing social theorist whose xenophobic *Defence of the West* was shortly to be serialized in the *Criterion*. In *Defence of the West* Massis would warn that "it is the soul of the West that the East wishes to attack, that soul, divided, uncertain of its principles, confusedly eager for spiritual liberation, and all the more ready to destroy itself, to allow itself to be broken up by Oriental anarchy, because it has of itself departed from its historical civilising order and tradition" (231). The sentences which Read quotes from another Massis text, however, put the matter in terms less apocalyptic and more specifically sociological. Analyzing his culture for Read as if it were a comparative grammar, Massis concludes:

> The chief characteristic of the Occident is that it *makes distinctions*, and the program of Western thought from antiquity to the present

> can be gathered from Anaxagoras's classic sentence, "In the beginning all was mingled together; Mind came and set each thing in order." What strikes one from the very first in the history of the Occident is that this power, and more particularly its development as *fully human life*, originates—by a process simultaneously rational and natural—in a conception of that ordering force and the intellectual hierarchies to which it gives rise: the ideas of resemblance and difference, of identity and discrimination. (My translation)[1]

"All this Keyserling ignores," Read tries desperately to explain.

And in his desperation he offers a historiographic proof of his thesis: an etiology of Keyserling's blindness. Demonstrating that Keyserling's symptoms are a hereditary taint descending from Kant and Rousseau, Read is able to venture a prediction of their outcome; a terrible prediction:

> It is perhaps the seeming hopelessness of our opposition that adds bitterness to these observations on Keyserling's book. A revival of the scholastic attitude seems very remote, especially in England, where there is not even the promise of a corresponding art, as in France. [*Read is presumably thinking of such artists as Rouault and Claudel.*] One thinks, finally, of the worldly fate of Keyserling's book, of its immense popularity in Germany. It does not seem destined for popularity in England: in France it will meet with sufficient opposition. Nevertheless, it is a portent. But before we could venture to interpret it, we should need a very intimate knowledge of the components of its popularity in Germany. It might reflect either of two opposed moods. It might reflect the hunger and desperation of those material forces which endow modern Germany with its indefinite vitality. Or it might indicate how deeply and how widely the subjectivism of German philosophy has permeated into the mentality of the German people. Only the second eventuality need induce despair. (192–93)

[1] "Le caractère de l'Occident, c'est la *distinction*; et le programme de la pensée occidentale est assez bien rassemblé, dès les hautes époques, par la sentence classique d'Anaxagore: 'Au début tout était confondu; l'intelligence vint et mit chaque chose en ordre.' C'est de la vue de cet ordre, des hiérarchies intellectuelles qu'il comporte, de la vue des rassemblances et des différences, des identités et des distinctions, que resulte, par un processus à la fois rationnel et naturel, ce mouvement general, et, en particulier, ce développement de la *personne humaine* qui frappe, dès l'abord, dans l'histoire de l'Occident" (qtd. in Read 192).

The review ends there. And only now, we realize, can it be read.

That is, only now has it acquired historical meaning. The horrors of the twentieth century have at least left us with some retrodictive confirmations. Sitting very still in front of the microfilm reader, staring at a page of the *Criterion* as it glows on the screen, we seem suddenly to be midway in the river of blood that has flowed between its words and us. We may almost permit ourselves to believe that something in Eliot's poems knew the flood was coming. There is in our reaction, at any rate, something we may recognize in retrospect, with the right poems to help us—something, let us say, like the beginning of an understanding of what history might be in its relation to the words by which we know good and evil.

For consider: the death camps that Read almost foresaw in Keyserling's imperial egotism were intended to enact—to be a part of, to *be*—an invisible history. Military action made them visible. Before that happened, they had existed only in words—in the words, for instance, of *Mein Kampf*. Those words were history in potential, waiting through time to be read into living breath and converted into action. To read them with regard to their later realization in events is therefore to see history embryologically, as a body of words shaping time around themselves, forming time into a past tense which then, and only then, can be understood.

By definition, those originating words can be understood only in retrospect. In themselves, with regard to any diachronic evidence beyond the temporal boundaries of the culture in which they originate, they are meaningless. And therefore, the same history that teaches us to read Read better than he wrote has emptied Massis's words of any sense referable to the world we live in. For better or worse, it is impossible now for readers acculturated by education to understand a phrase like "the soul of the West," or to know a priori, as Eliot did, that they belong to the most superior race of all.[2] The distinction between *écriture* and

[2] "There will probably always remain a real inequality of races, as there is always inequality of individuals. But the fundamental identity in *humanity* must always be asserted; as must the social sanctity of moral obligation to people of every race. All men are equal before God; if they cannot all be equal in this world, yet our moral obligation towards inferiors is exactly the same as that towards our equals" (qtd. in Kojecký 88–89). One takes the point of *Scrutiny's* gibe that the *Criterion* was always solemn but not always serious.

meaning turns out to be a historical one: a matter of the presence or absence of a social context in which words may be allowed to give rise to their own significance. In Stephen Crane's story and in Henri Massis' alike, men come out of the east to tell us, in words we cannot understand until too late, that history is made out of words in a forgotten language.

Nevertheless, of course, we continue to understand the words of the stranger in the blue hotel, meaningless as they are at the moment of their utterance. In the cultural retrospect that is reading, certain connotations remain constant across different frames of historical reference. In the rhetoric of the proto-Fascist Henri Massis, East = Bad; in Adolf Hitler's anti-Bolshevik rhetoric too, East = Bad; but, as Alvin Rosenfeld has entertainingly demonstrated, East = Bad also for the chief mythographer of the Hitler legend in the English-speaking world, the unquestionably antifascist Hugh Trevor-Roper. There are Lord Dacre's terms, spread out across two pages of Rosenfeld's *Imagining Hitler* (22–23): "oriental court," "oriental sultanate," "the new Pharaoh." The condemnatory connotations have been emplaced long before by our culture; we know exactly how we are to react to Adolf Hitler when we read in the words of Hugh Trevor-Roper that

> when he envisaged himself against a historical background, when his imagination was heated, and his vanity intoxicated, with flattery and success, and he rose from his modest supper of vegetable pie and distilled water to prance upon the table and identify himself with the great conquerors of the past, it was not as Alexander, or Caesar, or Napoleon that he wished to be celebrated, but as the reembodiment of those angels of destruction—of Alaric, the sacker of Rome, of Attila, "the scourge of God," of Genghis Khan, the leader of the Golden Horde. (Qtd. in Rosenfeld 22)

In fact, it takes a positive effort of the imagination to defamiliarize the connotation that East = Bad; to recall, for instance, that Alexander or Caesar might not have been regarded by a Persian or a Gaul as they are by a product of a British classical education. For Trevor-Roper, for Hitler, for Read, and for us, the ordinary sense of this metaphor is stable under all conditions. East = Bad.

In Western literature's ordinary grammar of meaning, the notion is not susceptible to parsing. What it means, it means absolutely, without regard to any history which might occur off the page.

That is, it is a term of virtual history. And it comes, like the speaker of Robert Lowell's sonnet sequence "Mexico," to inform us that virtual history is the last penetralia of the wordless primary communication of infancy: that which lies incommunicable at the heart of narcissism. The effects have all taken place by now, the history of events informs us; the ashes are cool, the dead are dead. Ah, replies virtual history; but I can still write poems to myself in words.

> South of Boston, south of Washington,
> south of any bearing . . . I walk the glazed moonlight:
> dew on the grass and nobody about,
> drawn on by my unlimited desire,
> like a bull with a ring in his nose, a chain in the ring. . . .
> We moved far, bull and cow, could one imagine
> cattle obliviously pairing six long days:
> up road and down, then up again passing the same
> brick garden wall, stiff spines of hay stuck in my hide;
> and always in full sight of everyone,
> from the full sun to silhouetting sunset,
> pinned by undimming lights of hurried cars. . . .
> You're gone; I am learning to live in history.
> What is history? What you cannot touch. (Sonnet 4)

Before we had read Lowell's sonnet or thought about the metaphor of the East, we could have said this about history:

When it is in language, history is a set of rules for ordering ideas and sense impressions into a syntax. It operates by retrospective comparison, forming subjects out of memories arrayed against one another in an invariant past tense. History's nouns are time terms, nominalized by their relation to having acted or having been acted upon. An ordinary characteristic of history's verbs is irony, which can be defined in terms of historical grammar as a sort of past optative: the verbal construction indicating that things might have been otherwise but weren't.

As it extends from language into the nonverbal universe around it, this irony allows us to perceive ourselves as selves, functioning among other people but at a distance from them. By ironizing perception in this way, history allows imagination to come into being. From the sense of what might have been flows the sense of what could be, or ought to be: all that we know of wonder. That is history's news: that time changes us, day by day and word by word. If we speak, we tell that story. Bergson's mechanical men, however, devote their comical lives to denying this truth that their own words tell. For them, the words of modal logic—words like *possibly* and *perhaps*—are a foreign language. Having rejected history's invitation to mean ironically, in a language bound unstably to ever-passing time, they can no longer mean at all. Their language has lost its base in the human. It has become a mere verbal construction: a virtual history.

When virtual history clashes with a history containing time, therefore, the rhetorical effect is describable in Bergsonian terms. In fact, one of the most useful critical terms we could employ comes to us directly from the mechanical men. In its connotations of impotence, after all, the Watergate conspirators' word for their own chief difficulty is a whole compendium of moral criticism. When words cross over from speech into memory, the language of virtual history is indeed inoperative. Asked a few days before his 1989 inaugural to comment on his campaign rhetoric of the previous fall, President-elect Bush replied, "That's history. That doesn't mean anything any more" (Hoffman).

But when speech takes the place of memory, when the Bergsonian metaphor is all that takes part in the speech act . . .

Robert Lowell's sated lover, who begins the love affair chronicled in "Mexico" as a fifty-year-old poet "humbled with the years' gold garbage, / dead laurel grizzling my back like spines of hay," ends it with a vaunt in the classical tradition. The woman is gone, but the poet does not mourn. The woman has obliterated the poet's sense of his origins and his culture, Boston and Washington, but she has occasioned a poem: a poem into which she cannot enter. Only the poet lives in the poem's words, and there his culture is solely his own. There, in the timeless state that Lowell calls history, the woman exists as a facsimile made of words. Her immortality is the poet's gift, held at his sufferance. Or, as Shakespeare put it in sonnet 18:

So long as men can breathe, or eyes can see,
So long lives this, and this gives life to thee.

And Horace (*Odes* III.xxx) read over the words he had written and ecstatically realized: *non omnis moriar*, I shall not altogether die. The poem of virtual history subsumes life itself into itself. It transforms the mortal body into an imperishable lexicon.

That, at any rate, is the claim and the desideratum. Only the word is capable of evoking memory, is the claim; only the word can become history. Some real, living human beings, generations of them, have failed history's entrance examination, which is administered in the language of virtuality. They live now only insofar as the bard has recreated them in his own grapholect. For Walt Whitman, for reasons we will see toward the end of this book, the primal inhabitants of America belong only to that history of the creative ego. "Yonnondio," the archaeologist of memory translates for us, reconstructing for a single brief instant the words that have passed away into silence: "The sense of the word is *lament for the aborigines*."

I see swarms of stalwart chieftains, medicine-men, and warriors,
As flitting by like clouds of ghosts, they pass and are gone in the
    twilight,
(Race of the woods, the landscapes free, and the falls!
No picture, poem, statement, passing them to the future:)
Yonnondio! Yonnondio!—unlimn'd they disappear;
To-day gives place, and fades—the cities, farms, factories fade;
A muffled sonorous sound, a wailing word is borne
    through the air for a moment,
Then blank and gone and still, and utterly lost.
("Yonnondio," lines 5–12)

The prophetic cry is also a hymn of triumph; the bard's lament is also a vaunt like Horace's. The author of "Song of Myself" has succeeded in creating words out of silence, out of that which has been without form, and void.

Nevertheless, Whitman's Indians, Shakespeare's young woman or man, Lowell's nervous poet, Horace's priest and silent vestal climbing forever to their temple on the Capitoline Hill are also parts of a history which extends beyond the words on the page. The silence that Whitman commemorates is a product of money, railroad engineering, and a body of human thoughts and actions which eventuated in the rifle and the large, uniformed army. That is a part of Whitman's power, and Horace's: this evoked sense that there is a wonder and a terror in time which language can reach to and touch but not comprehend. The future that Whitman envisions in "Crossing Brooklyn Ferry" is populated with men and women speaking a tongue different from the poet's, yet capable of realizing a past with the help of the poet's translation. That language is the performative of history. As it is read and acted upon, it enacts a sense of the wonder we know when we remember. Remembering, we realize why "Yonnondio" is a magic word: it is a word of a dead language. It has grown into our speech as a part of speech's historiography of the real.

The *Criterion*'s eastern power, on the other hand, is a manifestation chiefly of virtual history. It originates not in the mind's political connections with other minds but in its power to shape dream, fear, and cliché out of itself. It commemorates a fanciful geography, therefore, but it does so without irony. It is a traveler's tale, with all the power of that genre to appeal to our own dreams. In the dream it makes for us, virtual history tells the tale of a land where there is no time. There, in that East, there are only words.

4

Outtakes: Virtual History, Genre, and the Dissociation of Sensibility

Among words, on a stage, stand a man and a woman, facing each other in the costume of London ladies and gentlemen, ca. 1914. They are wearing wigs and makeup and reading the lines written for them by a playwright. The woman—her name while the stage lights are up is "Mrs Higgins"—recites from memory the words, "I'm afraid youve spoilt that girl, Henry. I should be uneasy about you and her if she were less fond of Colonel Pickering." After she has reached the end of her second sentence, the man recites back, "Pickering! Nonsense: she's going to marry Freddy. Ha ha! Freddy! Freddy!! Ha ha ha ha ha!!!!!" Several miles away, on a shelf in the dark of an empty house, is a closed book containing all those sentences, followed by one more in brackets: "[He roars with laughter as the play ends]." But we are not in the house, reading those words; we are elsewhere, experiencing them. Where we are, actors and actresses now stand in front of a curtain, smiling and bowing. A bouquet is handed to one of the women. Her smile flashes in the circle of brilliant blue-white light that holds us away from her, in darkness. Soon she will walk behind the curtain and change. We too will change. Lights will come up on us, and we will be seen to be seated on red plush, in clothes intended to be looked at and remarked upon, inside a building that has been watched from the outside, through the snowy night, by policemen and parking valets and men who eat out of garbage cans. It is time now for us to remember our bodies and go back out the door into the dark. But for a moment that briefly lingers here, we have been made happy. The play has ended; we have achieved termination.

But the actors haven't; they will be back tomorrow night to say their words again. And while they are working their way all over again from their first sentence ("I'm getting chilled to the bone") to their last, we will be elsewhere, doing something else: at home, perhaps, reading the words we remember. Because the actors repeat the play's action, their experience doesn't terminate; because we recall, our experience is remade. Our entrainment in the recursion of time is similar to the actors' reduction of time to a repeatable segment, but it is not identical. For the actors, memory is a means to an end; for us, it is the end. The actors deal with one part of the dramatist's speech act, the performative of being; we deal with the other part, the words.

Here we are then, rereading. We are hoping to recreate last night's pleasure, but we would also like to solve a puzzle. Shaw's comedy *Pygmalion* has done violence to our expectations with a surprise ending: Eliza has decided to marry the dim Freddy Eynsford-Hill rather than the brilliant Henry Higgins. We wonder why, and the text is there with an answer: fifteen pages (in the Penguin edition) of analytical epilogue. "As our own instincts are not appealed to by her conclusion," Eliza's creator proposes, "let us see whether we cannot discover some reason in it" (135). And he sets us to work. A disinterested literary and social critic, he reads along with us, taking no obvious advantage of his privileged knowledge of the characters.

A close reading of the text allows him to deduce, for example, the probable nature of the relationship between Higgins and his mother. Further consideration reveals the existence of lines from a yet unwritten text of the play. "Pleas as to Freddy's character, and the moral obligation on him to earn his own living," the dramatist explains, "were lost on Higgins. He denied that Freddy had any character, and declared that if he tried to do any useful work some competent person would have the trouble of undoing it: a procedure involving a net loss to the community" (140).

Shaw speaks of this future event in the past tense; he comprehends what he has read both prospectively and retrospectively. In the historical present tense, he has heard the lines that will fill a yet unbuilt theater far from the cold, dark world of physicality in which we now sit, holding the limited, necessarily partial text of the play we watched during the three little hours when the actors freed us from time. And there, at last, the author separates his reading from ours. In the weakness of our mortality we have to read and be in the zone of time, but the man on the other side of the page we are holding doesn't. A part of the text, its author speaks its full performative history, past and future; but we can make contact with him only in the present, at the barrier of words he has erected. There he is, drawn by Feliks Topolski on the last page, just where the book ends for us: a man in a tweed suit walking down a path. The man's back is turned to us, but we can see that he is thin and elderly, with a bushy beard. The path meanders off away from us, into the virtual space created for it by the mental discipline of perspective. We cannot walk it; it and we exist in different dimensions. But there on the path just ahead of George Bernard Shaw, token of a promise waiting only to be fulfilled in us, are three written words. They read, "Many happy returns."

We do return. The history of text has made it possible for us to accept the invitation. Rereading, we seem to have begun walking on a circular path, treading step after step through a world from which time has been excluded. Texts that we read in linear sequence, word following word, are little riddles of the Sphinx, mimetic approximations of the course of our mortality: beginning, middle, and end. But to reread, to reread any text at all, is to experience a little rebirth; and to be allowed to feel that our reading need never come to an end is to experience immortality. *Pygmalion* is not *Oedipus Rex*, but it does make us feel that the reality attributed to its characters exists independently of the portrayals on the stage or the words on the page. *Exegi monumentum aere perennius*, says Horace of his words, I have built a monument whose bronze is everlasting; and here among the archetypes it appears that the monuments of plot and character outlast performance, publication, language itself. They partake of the numinous. Shaw's text—"the total speech act in the total speech situation" (Austin, 52)—seems to have created something that speech cannot express. And of course this is a general phenomenon. When we say that so-and-so is a good writer, we usually mean, one way or another, that we seem to be able to see through his language to something stable beyond time.

Here we are, then, wordlessly believing: believing in the extratextual or supratextual reality of men and women made of words. Propositionally, in terms strictly of words, we cannot explain this faith. It would be irrational (cf. Austin 48–49) to say, "I know Shaw's characters don't exist, but I believe they do."[1] All we can say by way of justifying ourselves, perhaps, is that Eliza and her father and Henry and his mother do partake in ordinary literary terms of some of the phenomena of existence. Just like our flesh and blood acquaintances, they can be discussed in words. We can make assertions about them that are strictly factual ("Henry Higgins, a character in George Bernard Shaw's play *Pygmalion* . . . "). In fact, they differ from our flesh and blood acquaintances only in the wider range of verbal reference that they can support. We can responsibly speak only fact about our acquaintances, but we know Henry Higgins and Eliza in the same way as we know George Washington; that is, we can assert a plausible fiction equally well about any of them and think of that fiction as a sort of Platonically true nonfiction. George Bernard Shaw does that about Henry and Eliza in his epilogue to *Pygmalion*; Mason Locke Weems does it in his story about George Washington and the cherry tree. Such stories are a kind of creative criticism: explications of what we know must be true, even though we have only faith to tell us so. They are pragmatic

[1] Not that people don't believe in the reality of verbal propositions *qua* verbal propositions. Consider this transcript of a conversation which once took place in my office.

SYLVIA: You don't give A's to girls, do you?
PROFESSOR MORSE: Yes I do.
SYLVIA: No you don't.
PROFESSOR MORSE (taking gradebook out of desk drawer): Well, Sylvia, let's take a look. . . . Here's a girl who's getting an A. And here's a girl who's getting an A. You're not getting an A, sorry. But here's another girl who's getting an A.
SYLVIA: But in *my* opinion, you *don't* give A's to girls.
PROFESSOR MORSE (beginning to feel out of his depth): Well, your opinion is wrong.
SYLVIA (with exasperation, as one explaining to a slow learner): But it's my *opinion*!

effects: not texts at all, strictly speaking, but events produced by textuality. And of course they result from many sorts of mental activity, not just the reading of history or literature. In action as well as in words, a theory of meta-truth was the fundamental working principle of the Reagan administration.[2]

But if it can compel belief, every such story will possess one identifying verbal characteristic: while it cannot exist as told without the words it is made of, it seems to remain independent of them. We can talk about the story and believe what it has helped us to say, but the more we talk, the more conscious we become that there is a part of the story we haven't yet told right. The story means more than its author can tell. "There is, then," says C. S. Lewis in *An Experiment in Criticism*, "a particular kind of story which has a value in itself—a value independent of its embodiment in any literary work. The story of Orpheus strikes and strikes deep, of itself; the tact that Virgil and others have told it in good poetry is irrelevant. . . . If some perfected art of mime or silent film or serial pictures could make it clear with no words at all, it would still affect us in the same way" (41).

We call such stories myths. Giving them a name and a place in the taxonomy of aesthetic effect, we testify to their perceived reality. Every society that ever existed seems to have done the same thing. And yet the very existence of myth seems impossible on historical and verbal grounds. Historically, we are forced to realize that our sense of the numinous in myth is constrained by time, place, class, culture, and economics. The Confederate flag means more to Andrew Lytle than it does to me.[3] And if that flag

[2] "When shown that Reagan had cited a nonexistent British law to disparage gun control, press secretary Larry Speakes responded, 'It made the point, didn't it?'" (Green 10).

[3] "Not all stories which an anthropologist would classify as myths have the quality I am here concerned with. When we speak of myths . . . we are usually speaking of the best specimens and forgetting the majority. If we go steadily through all the myths of any people we shall be appalled by much of what we read. Most of them, whatever they may have meant to ancient or savage man, are to us meaningless and shocking; shocking not only by their cruelty and obscenity but by their apparent silliness—almost what seems insanity. . . . Conversely, certain stories which are not myths in the anthropological sense, having been invented by individuals in fully civilised periods, have what I should call the 'mythical quality.' . . . Since I define myths by their effect on us, it is plain that for me the story may be a myth to one man and not to another" (Lewis 42, 45).

means anything at all to anybody, it means only instrumentally, by way of its stars and bars, just as the myth means only by way of its words. "The sense in which saying something produces effects on other persons, or *causes* things, is a fundamentally different sense of cause from that used in physical causation by pressure, &c.," says the author of *How to Do Things with Words* (Austin 113 n.1). "It has to operate through the conventions of language." And yet myth doesn't so much operate through those conventions as it subordinates them. As they transmit a myth's significance to us, words impede it. Meaning and words are related, but antagonistic. Between them there is a disjunction. When we try to express one in terms of the other, we bog down in nostalgia, the fantasy of memory reconciled with desire.

> There's the moment years ago in the station in Venice,
> The dark rainy afternoon in fourth grade, and the shoes then,
> Made of a dull crinkled brown leather that no longer exists.
> And nothing does, until you name it, remembering, and even then
> It may not have existed, or existed only as a result
> Of the perceptual dysfunction you've been carrying around for years.
> The result is magic, then terror, then pity at the emptiness,
> Then air gradually bathing and filling the emptiness as it leaks,
> Emoting all over something that is probably mere reportage
> But nevertheless likes being emoted on. (Ashbery 14)

The title of John Ashbery's poem, "Down by the Station, Early in the Morning," is the first line of a children's song. Recalling, thinking of baby John singing his song, we feel the tenderness of nostalgia. But nostalgia is not merely an emotion arising from color and texture and odor and shoes, a purely private objective correlative, a fiction based on edited memories of the days that are no more. It is a mode of history, a means of uniting individual perception with the mythic. We know we wore those shoes; we know that buying them and wearing them and doing things while wearing them had more meaning than any fact can signify to us in retrospect. So we seek for the numinous in the nimbus of memory that quivers around the event.

Historical nostalgia loiters at the margins of events that are rich in little details. On its lips is a sentence beginning "If only . . ."

But it is not interested in the big, crude *if onlies*. It wants to feel itself in possession of the little shoes, the tiny ugly frog princes of memory, the things no one else has loved enough to know. It likes thinking about the loss of the *Titanic*, for example, precisely because the big *if onlies* of that disaster are so unambiguous that emotion can disregard them. The *Titanic* would not have collided with the iceberg if her master had exercised ordinary prudence. After the collision, few lives would have been lost if the ship had carried enough lifeboats. It really is that simple. But we turn the pages of the official report discontentedly. The proof doesn't feel satisfying. Something is still missing from what we want to think. The big *if onlies* turn out to offer us a merely pragmatic solace: stop crying and get busy on the redesign. But if only—oh, if only the *Titanic*'s radio operator hadn't asked the nearby *Californian*'s radio operator, just before the collision, to shut his transmitter down;

or if only First Officer Murdoch, with lookout Fleet's shriek of horror ringing in his ears, had thrown the rudder over *or* reversed the propellers *but not both* (but he did both);

or if only the *Californian*'s watch officer had been able to understand the *Titanic*'s rapid agonized SOS when he turned the radio back on a moment later . . .

The list of inexorable little precatastrophes lengthens. Reading it, we discover that we are excited and happy. It is serving us as a framework on which to construct emotion. Building there, pathos by pathos, we are experiencing the heightened consciousness of connoisseurship. We savor, we prolong from second to second, the moment when the glass reaches the lip and *not yet* shudderingly becomes *now*.

We are enjoying dramatic irony, as we were not when the only questions were of establishing the facts, doing justice, and saving lives. All ships must now carry enough lifeboats for everyone on board; all ships must now be equipped with radio, and their radios must be in operation twenty-four hours a day. These are some pragmatic legacies of the *Titanic* disaster. But we would rather think—would we not?—of the single watertight bulkhead that would have saved the *Titanic* if only it had been extended one deck higher. We aren't interested in the reports devoted to preventing future disasters, but we will read with pleasure "The Convergence of the Twain," Hardy's poem about the cosmic irony of 1503 human beings crushed, drowned, and frozen to death. Given the choice between thinking about tragedy and thinking about tragedy averted, we will think about tragedy.

The reason is simple enough, psychologically if not aesthetically. "The intense feeling, ecstatic or terrible, without an object or exceeding its object," says Eliot, "is something which every person of sensibility has known" ("Hamlet," *Selected Essays* 126). The artist, in Eliot's famous formulation, seeks to realize this feeling by finding for it "an 'objective correlative'; in other words, a set of objects, a situation, a chain of events which shall be the formula of that *particular* emotion; such that when the external facts, which must terminate in sensory experience, are given, the emotion is immediately evoked" (124–25). Weeping in the library, the teenager sees on the table a book about the *Titanic*. He opens it, and the mighty ship becomes the expressive metaphor for one more wordless glandular sadness. The book has revised his history of himself. His perceptual dysfunction has been given a vocabulary, a thesis, a critical criterion, and a characteristic choice of objects. To the extent that the *Titanic* will figure henceforth in this young man's thoughts, he thinks in genre.

Let us suppose him at home there for a few years: a member of the Titanic Historical Society (there is such an organization), a collector of memorabilia and memoirs. He and we have grown apart, he with his objective correlative and we without. Now he and we are about to watch a film together: *A Night to Remember*, the 1958 British docudrama based on Walter Lord's 1955 best seller about the *Titanic*. The film unrolls on the TV screen before us, its status as memory icon only made more poignant by the commercials that yank us back moment by moment to the present, away from the irrecoverable past. And now here it is at last, the great shot, the scene we have been waiting for. The ship's stern, surprisingly small now just above the surface of the water, tilts up, grows erect in the night sky. People cling to it, struggling to keep their footing. Their lives are over, but they cannot know that. Above their heads flaps the flag of England, stirring lazily at the rail. Nothing can help. Now, on the transom, raised up for the last time above the water, we see words:

TITANIC
LIVERPOOL

And then there is a sliding forward and down and down, and it is all gone. The lifeboats pull away. We sit back on the couch together, shaken.

And then we begin talking about matters of historical detail. Looking beyond the optical illusion achieved by twenty-four frames per second to its evoked historical content, the keeper of the *Titanic*'s chronicle will tell us which scenes of the sinking are accurate depictions, which are conjectural, which fictitious. He will know what he has seen. We, on the other hand, will be less certain. We have been reading Andrew Lytle, and we know that life and art are not always closely related. In the habit of looking at documents first as collections of words on parchment and only later as communications from the realm of the speechless, we looked first at this film's formal features, and there we noticed some odd things. *A Night to Remember* is a spectacular, with a huge cast and magnificent special effects, and yet—a strange false economy—the print's aspect ratio is that of the old pre-1950s narrow screen, and the film stock is black and white. The actor who portrays bandleader Wallace Hartley sings "Nearer, My God, to Thee" with a foreign accent. The acting style in general is inconsistent: restrained and modern by the major actors, broad and antiquated by the supers, as if the two-shots and the crowd scenes had had different directors. And at one point somebody speaks a few sentences in German.

The man who lives in genre has seen one document: a chronicle illustrated with moving pictures. We have seen another document: a film. Thinking afterward about the images we have seen, we and our friend will construct different histories of the event we shared in front of the television set. But now something else happens to both of us: we read David Stewart Hull's *Film in the Third Reich* and discover (226–32) that our seeing has an additional history, independent of the film as such: a political history. The magnificent special effects in *A Night to Remember*, it turns out, were lifted without credit from a 1943 Nazi propaganda film, *Titanic*. In the scene we remember, the director's intent was to make an educational point: as with the *Titanic*, so with England.

A long pause ensues.

The film we saw has changed. It was an objet d'art; now it is the artifact of an entirely unsuspected history. Now that we have read this history, its subject will have to be read as a parable with a double purport. Read according to the known history of its makers' intent, *Titanic / A Night to Remember* signifies that the British Isles are about to sink into the sea, mortally freighted with hubris; read in conjunction with the military history of World War II, it explains that the population of Germany was taught well to gather itself around Adolf Hitler and defend him to the end. Either reading is suffused with historical irony. Little did they know, any of them: the cinematographers who made the film, the audiences who watched it.[4] And of course that irony extends to us too. We have to consider that the source of this film is an artifact of the history of propaganda and policy: that is, of fiction claiming to be truth and secret metafiction denying its own reality. The historical event comes to us asking, with jesting Pilate, "What is truth?" Francis Bacon and the Gospel of John point out that Pilate did not stay for an answer. That is the purport of every historical record.

Our friend the collector is also concerned with fiction, but in a slightly different way. For him—a man who is obsessed for reasons of his own with the realia of legend—the film's antecedents are a fascinating new education in the techniques of fantasy. Reading about what he saw, he has learned that outtakes lie all around us, waiting to be viewed in ever changing combinations. Any time he wants to, he can write himself a new history. Yeats's poem about the purpose of revision can serve, it turns out, as an ontological program: "It is myself that I remake." The *Titanic* was getting a little boring anyway. Maybe he will start a Hitler collection.

The classic collection text is that most cinematic of modernist works, *The Waste Land*. Its embedded quotations are the realia of

[4] These earlier audiences (the ironies multiply) saw the film only in occupied France. *Titanic* was banned in Germany, first because its director had had to be murdered by the Gestapo, second because "the terrified actions of the ship's passengers reminded [Propaganda Minister Goebbels] too clearly of how the German people were reacting during the increasing bombing raids" (Hull 229).

literary and cultural history; its subtext deals with a poet accumulating the body of experience that will eventuate in a poem called *The Waste Land*. Or rather, its subtext deals with a body of experience that *has been* accumulated before the poem begins. For the narrator of *The Waste Land*, life is history: the document of actions that took place before we were able to talk about them. Now that we can talk about them, they can no longer take place; the word has taken over from the thing, pushed it back into the silent past, robbed it of its power to change and live.

Eliot's poetic enterprise, from beginning to end, is a long struggle to reconcile words spoken about life with life itself. "It is impossible to say just what I mean!" mourns J. Alfred Prufrock at the beginning, knowing that the mermaids' song of invitation is not his to accept. And at the end, in *Four Quartets*,

> My words echo
> Thus, in your mind.
> But to what purpose
> Disturbing the dust on a bowl of rose-leaves
> I do not know. ("Burnt Norton")

And cannot know, at least not here, not now. "Human kind," the bird warns the poet, "cannot bear very much reality."

Remembering what human kind has borne throughout history, we may be inclined to protest. In art and memory, we may say, we are presented daily with images of life lived in the real, images ranging from the almost wholly fictitious to the almost wholly true. Here in the article in *Time* is the Republican politician, walking soulfully along the beach, working twenty hours a day, speaking words uniquely able to inspire happiness in his constituents' pinched little lives. Or here is the statue by Praxiteles. Or here in the Warsaw Ghetto is Simon Dubnow, seeing and remembering and charging us to remember. We respond to such images, and not just out of wish-fulfillment. Seeing some truth in a life, we dare to hope that we recognize ourselves. Furthermore, Eliot was personally familiar with an instructive counterexample: the actual history of the politician and man of letters George Wyndham, a man who lived his multifarious life as a single deed, whole and entire in body and mind and soul.[5] Was Wyndham, could Wyndham be imagined to be conceivable as, unreal?

Yes, says Eliot. "His literature and his politics and his country life are one and the same thing. They are not in separate compartments, they are one career. Together they made up his world: literature, politics, riding to hounds. In the real world these things have nothing to do with each other" (qtd. in Kenner, *Invisible Poet*, 113). Reality—Eliot is quite firm about this—is fragmentation. The real, Bradleyan, world is a world of sensations separated from one another by time. Each sensation takes place in its own time and accretes to itself the words of its own history. The histories remain after the sensations have vanished, but we cannot recreate the life from its record in words. We live our life in words outtake by outtake, assembling and reassembling the fragments of memory, knowing that the central image is gone and can never be found, but knowing too that we can never stop looking.

Which is why George Wyndham's life is unreal, mere biographical fact to the contrary. It is full of Keatsian palpabilities, passion and weather and muscle, but the real world is the world of separate compartments. Wyndham's ability to unscrew the locks from the doors, unscrew the doors themselves from their jambs, is at best a lucky accident, at worst a historical fraud, because Wyndham's apparent unity of soul has been illegitimately won. It is grounded in physiology, social class, and the history of events: timebound things all of them, subject like Gerontion to invasion and subversion by unreality. As Hugh Kenner says, speaking for Eliot against Wyndham, "The romantic allows some catalyst to fuse in his life the ingredients only art should be allowed to bring together" (*Invisible Poet* 113). That catalyst may be love or health or any other good thing, but when it makes us believe that our lives have been reconciled with time, it leads us into suffering. Art can heal, because art exists for the purpose of absorbing our

[5] "Wyndham (1863–1913) had a passion for literature which survived Eton, Sandhurst, the Coldstream Guards, 'the Season,' and the House of Commons. . . . There are times, reading about Wyndham, when it is hard not to believe that he was invented by an Edwardian novelist. The family estate with the improbable name ('Clouds'); the subaltern in barracks teaching himself Italian; the best-dressed man in the House of Commons—it all seems a little too good to be true" (Gross 156).

broken fragments of individuality into the continuum of time. Eliot discusses this thaumaturgy in "Tradition and the Individual Talent." But the real world, the world of *The Waste Land*, is so shattered that nothing can make it coherent: not time unmediated, not time mediated through art.

That is why April is cruel when it mixes memory with desire. Desire is wordless, but memory is of the word: the word spoken with breath, through time. To admit in words that we love is to proffer an outtake: a statement in art, with grammar and syntax and rhetoric, which separates itself from us in the moment of saying. It is a lie in history: a statement, in the present tense, about a part of us that ceased existing a moment ago. Changing that lie into the truth of art, the Romantic poets made it into the program of a revolution. Keats's nightingale, bearing the knowledge of truth away while the poet remains behind, darkling, with the text of his poem, made changes in the world. By and by, in Eliot's time, other poets realized that those changes were not final. The perceived truths left with us by the passage of time remained, and would always remain, without definitive utterance. This bleak truth about words had to be put into words.

One of Eliot's partners in history, Wyndham Lewis, tried to do so by obliterating the historical content of his discourse. Here is one of his spokesmen, the protagonist of the autobiographical novel *Self Condemned*, realizing that history falsifies language by telling the lie of presentational realism.[6]

> At this point René would go no further [in *Middlemarch*]. This sodden satire, this lifeless realism, provoked him into saying, "Why am I reading this dull nonsense?" . . . He continued to ruminate. "The historic illusion, the scenes depicted, and the hand depicting them, could be preserved in some suitable archive; but should not be handed down as a living document. It is a part of *history*"—and with this he dismissed it.

[6] I am employing the distinction between realism of presentation and realism of content made by C. S. Lewis in *An Experiment in Criticism*, chap. 7: "The two realisms are quite independent. You can get that of presentation without that of content, as in medieval romance; or that of content without that of presentation, as in French (and some Greek) tragedy; or both together, as in *War and Peace*; or neither, as in the *Furioso* or *Rasselas* or *Candide*" (59–60).

> He went out on to the deck and swinging his arm back hurled the heavy book out to sea. (156)

History, in this view, is what went down with the *Titanic*. It is nostalgia and sentimentality—neither archive nor living document but something undesirable in between. Lewis's own attempt to write a prose void of history yielded some remarkable descriptions of machinery and of people acting like machinery, ahistorical because inhuman. The mechanisms function as they have been designed to function, and sometimes two mechanisms function together to assemble words into a plot.[7] This laboriously contrived style has an object: to prevent its creator from becoming "the historical writer, [who,] in every case, is distracting people from a living Present (which becomes dead as the mind withdraws) into a Past into which they have gone to live" (Lewis's *Time and Western Man*, qtd. in Kenner, *Wyndham Lewis* 76).

In the service of the living Present, Lewis projected the swashbuckling image of his ego, several times larger than life, onto the surface of his entire oeuvre: soldier, polemical journalist, artist against the philistines, fighting philosopher, Cellini redivivus. His project had been impractical since the days when men carried swords, but the author of *Time and Western Man* was the last man to be deterred by the thought of historical precedent. Besides, as an artist he was used to thinking spatially. For him, the problems of being were to be solved by taking action in space. Nothing moves in Lewis's vorticist pictures; there exist only states of completed movement. Time is that which arranged the composition before the image assumed its completed form on the canvas. Eliot was readier than Lewis to work with time *in* time and to seek his ontological solutions there. But Eliot shared with his fellow modernist a desire to depict the subjects of his art synchronically, in their entirety at the present instant, not in outtake but in the fullness of reality. That desire entailed the definitive formulation of one of the most potent historical ideas of this century: the hypothesis of the dissociation of sensibility.

[7] "It is a style composed of phrases, not actions. The verb, inexorably the *time*-word, is where possible reduced to impotence . . . or else simply omitted" (Kenner, *Wyndham Lewis* 15).

Much has been said about the hypothesis, and I shall say more later. It is unprovable, arbitrary, historically incoherent, contradicted in many instances by fact. We know all this now, but we continue acknowledging its influence. And that is so for a reason which has little to do with T. S. Eliot the poet, T. S. Eliot the critic, or modernism in general. No, the reason is a fundamental one. It is this: like Shaw's retelling of the legend of Pygmalion and Galatea, or the folktales of the sinking of the *Titanic*, the hypothesis of the dissociation of sensibility comes to us in the authoritative form of virtual history. That, more than anything else, gives it its power. In common with those other stories, dissociation tells us more about ourselves than about its ostensible subject.

Consider, for example, how the idea of dissociation helps us understand our reaction to a premodernist text, *Pygmalion*. Here is a play about the dissolution and reconstitution of a human being: a comic *Frankenstein* with a socialist moral about language and social class. What we used to call the author's intent is explicit throughout; this is one text which, as our sophomores like to say, definitely makes you think.

> LIZA: You see, really and truly, apart from the things anyone can pick up (the dressing and the proper way of speaking, and so on), the difference between a lady and a flower girl is not how she behaves, but how she's treated. (122, Act V)

It is a didactic play, and in retrospect Shaw claims that his entire purpose in writing it was to teach us. "I wish to boast that Pygmalion has been an extremely successful play," he says in the penultimate paragraph of his preface. "It is so intensely and deliberately didactic, and its subject is esteemed so dry, that I delight in throwing it at the heads of the wiseacres who repeat the parrot cry that art should never be didactic. It goes to prove my contention that great art can never be anything else" (9).

And yet, the spirit of modernism points out, there is that fifteen-page epilogue. *Pygmalion* doesn't end with a simple moral *happily ever after*; in fact, it doesn't end at all. The action continues on the page after the curtain comes down in the theater, and after the political point has been made and accepted and forgotten. Liza and Freddy get married, the Labour Party becomes an important political entity, George Bernard Shaw bequeaths his estate to alphabet reform—and we still want to hear about Henry Higgins. The educational point has long been lost in the static of chronicle; only the text of the myth survives. It has become a virtual history: the continuing denouement of one of our dreams. The dream text tells us that when we wake up we will be all better. Here and now we struggle in our dark beds for words, but when the curtain finally goes down at the end of the epilogue to the epilogue to the epilogue, we will be able to walk out of the theater into daylight and say—at last, for the first time in our lives—what we mean and how we feel. There will be an end.

In the terms of Eliot's hypothesis of dissociation, we might say that as we read a comedy of wish-fulfillment, we yearn to experience a "mode of feeling [which can be] directly and freshly altered by [our] reading and thought" ("The Metaphysical Poets," *Selected Essays* 246). We want to be Elizas touched on the lips with a burning coal and changed. Perhaps that is why Eliza cannot be allowed to marry Henry Higgins. Perhaps we want to believe—perhaps Shaw wanted us to believe—that there will always be a Henry Higgins waiting somewhere, at some time, now and forever after, with a word for us to speak. The word will be ours alone; and our own Higgins, like Kafka's guardian of the law, will teach us to speak it once we ask him. Because we are allowed to imagine the existence of such an angel, *Pygmalion* is a comedy. Because *Pygmalion* is a comedy, there is no question that we will be able to recognize the angel, to approach and begin speaking. But in real life—that is, in Kafka—things are less certain. The guardian bars our access to the law because we don't know that we should have spoken.

So we insist, not quite knowing why because we lack the words to say what we know, that something always remains to be said. The *Titanic* collector wants to add just one thing to his amassment: a word with the power to make him know that the history it tells is true. We want to exhaust the meaning of the words of the story, but we come back only to limitation and irony. Writing about the ship before it was launched, somebody in an engineering journal used the word "unsinkable"; later, somebody on the *Californian*'s bridge saw the distress rockets and assumed that the people on the unsinkable ship were having a party. The transmission was successfully completed; only the content of the communication, only the hope and terror, only the distress, failed to make themselves understood across a few miles of calm darkness.

J. L. Austin's catalog of ways to fail in speech gives us a linguistic vocabulary for the historical sequence of events: Nonplays, Misplays, Miscarriages, Misexecutions, Non-executions, Non-fulfillments, Breaches . . . (18 n.1). But the hypothesis of dissociation does that and more. Dichotomizing, the hypothesis of dissociation says: on this ship were the emotion and the symbol; on that ship were the cerebration and the word. The two modes of communication were incommensurable. And that incommensurability is not a unique event; it is the characteristic genre of communication in our time. Therefore, we respond with tragic emotion to the sinking of the *Titanic* because we receive its historical data under the literary category of tragedy. To reality we cannot respond, but to the story, if it belongs to the proper genre, we will respond with our pity and our terror. When it has become words, we will be able to assimilate the knowledge of the *Titanic* and turn it into an emotion of our own: a private metaphor, unavailable to the men and women and children actually on the ship; a way of speaking about ourselves.

So in *The Waste Land* the historical agony of the modern world and the personal agony of the speaker become indistinguishable. Each agony becomes the vehicle of a metaphor about the other. There are no fixed terms, of magnitude or of time or of value or of language; there is only synchronicity. In this encompassing ahistory, everything is equivalent to everything else. The corpse in the English garden in the main text near the beginning of the poem means one thing; the millions of Russian and German corpses in the German footnote near the end of the poem also mean one thing; and we cannot give that thing a name. But thanks to the hypothesis of dissociation we can give it a history, complete with cross-references to other histories. It will be a virtual history, a history whose readers continually separate themselves from the writer in the text. In the text, memory will change and be rewritten, and words will vanish. But the theory of dissociation will help us become Stevens's Connoisseur of Chaos, saying,

A. A violent order is disorder; and
B. A great disorder is an order. These
Two things are one. (Pages of illustrations.)

We will have fitted the chaos into a genre: the genre of dissociation. And we will know what the illustrations are: outtakes, real pictures of the nonexistent. "These fragments I have shored against my ruins," says the scholiast at the end of *The Waste Land*, in an image that might come from one of Piranesi's melancholy etchings of illiterate shepherds squatting uncomprehending among the ruins of Rome. But Piranesi's pictures are also full of words, and a confidence that the words can tell us, on down the ages, what the ruins signify. On the world of *The Waste Land* a greater destruction has fallen: the words are in ruins along with the buildings. But we still have their grammar to read: a virtual history of the incommunicable. The outtake has become a guidebook: a lexicon of picture words.

5

Picture Words (I): Aharon Appelfeld, Vasily Grossman, John Dos Passos, and the History of the Image

We have been reading the lyricism of history: a play that retells an ancient story of love and creation, an allegory of hubris with regard to time and nature, a poem about change and the loss of value. Each of these texts works its magic on us through images: Eliza transformed, the *Titanic* going under, rain stirring the lilacs' dull roots. Historical texts do that; a paleontology of virtual history would take us first through words, then down through rationalization, sentiment, and primary emotion to the memory of an image. That memory is the origin; all history, virtual or real, partakes of the eidetic.

And of course the eidetic is there to be exploited. It is largely responsible, for instance, for the prodigies of sententious force achieved by the great historians of the nineteenth century. In this passage from chapter 8 of Francis Parkman's *Oregon Trail*, for example, pictorial description becomes the basis of a claim for the reality of empire.

> At noon, we reached Horse Creek; and, as we waded through the shallow water, we saw a wild and striking scene. The main body of the Indians had arrived before us. On the farther bank, stood a large and strong man, nearly naked, holding a white horse by a long cord and eyeing us as we approached. This was the chief, whom Henry called "Old Smoke." Just behind him, his youngest and favorite

> squaw sat astride of a fine mule: it was covered with caparisons of whitened skins, garnished with blue and white beads, and fringed with little ornaments of metal that tinkled with every movement of the animal. The girl had a light clear complexion, enlivened by a spot of vermilion on each cheek; she smiled, not to say grinned, upon us, showing two gleaming rows of white teeth. In her hand, she carried the tall lance of her unchivalrous lord, fluttering with feathers; his round white shield hung at the side of her mule; and his pipe was slung at her back. Her dress was a tunic of deerskin, made beautifully white by a species of clay found on the prairie, and ornamented with beads, arrayed in figures more gay than tasteful, and with long fringes at all the seams. Not far from the chief, stood a group of stately figures, their white buffalo robes thrown over their shoulders, gazing coldly upon us; and in the rear, for several acres, the ground was covered with a temporary encampment; men, women, and children swarmed like bees; hundreds of dogs, of all sizes and colors, ran restlessly about; and close at hand, the wide shallow stream was alive with boys, girls and young squaws, splashing, screaming, and laughing in the water. At the same time a long train of emigrant wagons were crossing the creek, and dragging on in their slow, heavy procession, passed the encampment of the people whom they and their descendants, in the space of a century, are to sweep from the face of the earth.

This description was first published in 1849. Two years later, Frederick Scott Archer invented the collodion negative, and modern photography was born (Taft 118–19). And when Americans viewed T. H. O'Sullivan's great stereographs of the West after the Civil War, Parkman's perspective etude left the printed page and became pure image. We have been living with that image ever since. It has seized primacy from the word.

That is largely because the image partakes directly of the kinesthetic sense. A written paragraph is the historical record of something that has taken place. It is a translation of movement into movement's static trace. Because it cannot make us feel the event moving through time, it is inherently a falsification of what it purports to represent. Insofar as a pictorial image appeals to memory rather than to the immediate *eigentlich gewesen*, it too partakes of *differance*. It too requires us to seek reality at second hand, in ourselves rather than in the event. But insofar as it is able to record motion *in* motion, the image can at least show us the trace of the event as it changed and was changed. The image brings us closer to time than the word can.

Compare Parkman's evocation, for example, with this paragraph.

> In *Birth of a Nation*'s famous iris-shot, Griffith begins tightly on the weeping mother's face and then irises out to reveal the awesome army below her, the cause of her sorrow. This use of the mask-shot to reveal cause and effect is only one of many in the picture. (Mast 62)

We are intended to understand the significance of the image by imputing a word to it: awe, or sorrow. Gerald Mast's technical analysis is a form of literary criticism, of the kind made familiar to us by Sergei Eisenstein's classic exercise in aesthetic history, "Dickens, Griffith, and the Film Today." First came Dickens: that is, nineteenth-century realist prose. In the beginning was the word. But in fact, naturally enough, we now think of scenic description not as a source but as an imitative effect. Parkman's vista seems obviously copied from a John Ford film: establishing shot (the creek), closeup of character actor (the Indian maid), pan with follow focus (the Indian encampment and the wagon train). So much does the motion entrain our perceptions.

It does more; it entrains our moral sense. We enjoy Parkman's description chiefly as an exercise in the aesthetics of mood, just as we would enjoy a movie, because the Sioux have indeed been swept from the face of the earth, just as Parkman predicted. They are static now; creatures of the written word only. Genocide has bestowed on us the freedom to think of them that way, as items in a historical lexicon. The history that Parkman was trying to tell has become an objet d'art made of words, and we have become a part of it ourselves: the part of the composition which lies above the picture plane. Because we no longer need to see the Indians, we can create our images in memory as afterthoughts made of words. The moving has been made still; now we can sit still ourselves, read the words recording its stillness, and partake in our own stillness of a factitious memory. Because the encampment on the banks of Horse Creek no longer matters to our lives, we can pay attention to it. If there were a collective aesthetic conscience, literature would have much to answer for.

But of course literature does claim to answer for morality. Here, for instance, is a novel about our ways of living with evil: Aharon Appelfeld's *Age of Wonders*. The evil occupies a special place in this novel: a void between Book 1 and Book 2, filling no pages at all. Around it there appears to be no plot, only a pair of bitter anecdotes about an unhappy family and its legacy. If they bespeak tragedy, the words of this story seem to bespeak only a lyric tragedy: the tragedy of the single sadness. But this tragedy has a historical setting, and that requires us to read it in a special way. We have to understand it in the way Sophocles's audience understood *Oedipus Rex*: as a representative account of our culture. Its psychology may or may not be important for us to know, but its geography is fundamental.

Book 1 of *The Age of Wonders* begins:

> Many years ago Mother and I took the night train home from the quiet, little-known retreat where we had spent the summer. The coach was new, and on one of its rounded walls was a poster of a girl holding a bunch of cherries in her hand. Our places were reserved, the seats solid and comfortable with embroidered white antimacassars on their headrests. (7)

It ends:

> By the next day we were on the cattle train hurtling south. (132)

These two journeys demarcate a space in time through which the protagonist and his family move ceaselessly. The journeys are long and short, on foot and by carriage and by train, in every direction. But they have only one destination, for the place and time are Austria in the late 1930s, and the protagonist and his family are Jews. They have been placed. We readers know their history, but only we can say it in words. We have chronicle and geography; the others have only fear and hope. The protagonist's father is a man of modernist letters who idolizes the prophetic words of Franz Kafka, but not even he—especially not he—is able to utter the words of his own history. Back and forth across Austria go the trains. Their travel is circumscribed by the border, just as a writer's words are circumscribed by the political boundaries within which they can be understood.

> To this place his father had brought Stefan Zweig, Jakob Wassermann, and Max Brod. . . . In the last year the writers did not come and his father spent many hours with the priest Mauber. Mauber thought that the Jews should get out as quickly as they could and go to Palestine to make a new life for themselves there. . . .
>
> The last conversation, the worst of them all, took place here, too, on this hill. Everything all around them was already infected with hatred, rejection, and renewed discrimination. Of course, no one yet knew where these things would lead. But the bitter smell was already everywhere. Mauber begged his father, "Why don't you leave? Why don't you return to Palestine?" The tone of his voice was both ardent and practical. And while the priest persuaded and coaxed, his father took off his hat and said, "I, for one, will not emigrate. I would rather be persecuted and disgraced than emigrate. I've done nothing wrong. I am an Austrian writer. No one will deny me this title." (196)

So the cattle train comes, and passes the frontiers of human thought just as easily as it has passed the frontiers on the map. The language of the Austrian writer was insufficient to tell the truth. It was lacking in a simple image, specifically an image of a railroad train: first in the mind of Adolf Eichmann, as proleptic history; then, as a part of afterhistory, in the mind of Aharon Appelfeld. Appelfeld evokes the image of the train, but by necessity he must do so in words, and that is why his history of the event is only a *post facto* epiphenomenon. The primacy of this history will always be with the wordless: lines on a blueprint, steel rails in the Polish snow.

This causes literary problems, of course. After history has changed us to wordless clouds in the air, how can we speak of what it has done? The narrator who spoke Book 1 of *The Age of Wonders* in the first person discovers how difficult that can be. Having survived what followed his journey in the cattle train, he now returns ("Many Years Later When Everything Was Over"—that is the subtitle of Book 2) to the small Austrian city where he spent his youth. Physically, it has not changed. But it has become incomprehensible. He cannot make himself understood by the few people there who remember him; he can only make them unhappy. The language he speaks with them has died. There are no more Jews in Austria; there is not even a Jewish history; there is only an emptiness. At the end of the novel the protagonist is alone on a station platform, waiting for the train that will take him away from Austria for the last time. His home is now Jerusalem. And this part of *The Age of Wonders* is narrated from a great distance, in the third person.

There in the third person, receding from its subject as it advances toward its reader, the history named Bruno A. can be read as an ordinary fictional narrative. Unlike the history of events, after all, it possesses a section to which the words "The End" seem to attach themselves. Furthermore, we can place it in any one of a number of well-established genres: Holocaust literature, say, or Zionist parable. But this move somehow seems wrong. It accounts for situation, incident, and characterization, but something seems left out. We can try to think about that absence in literary-critical terms—for instance, by saying (and meaning) something like, "*The Age of Wonders* is vitiated by Appelfeld's recourse to the simplifying formula of *galut* deracination vs. *yishuv* authenticity." And we will not be wrong to do that. But we know what that literary criticism cannot take into account: the silent image which occupies no written pages at all between Book 1 and Book 2. What began to happen, how can we say what happened, when the door of the cattle car closed on Bruno A. and his family?

For Appelfeld there can be only silence; silence and a parable about the foolishness of words in a lifeless language. Here, moving toward the end of Appelfeld's earlier novel *Badenheim 1939*, for instance, are the members of an Austrian Jewish community, walking under police escort toward what they cannot know. The time is the early morning of their last day in Austria, and they are approaching a building whose history and function they all know: a railroad station. The ordinary way of understanding still exists; things are still seen for what they are; words are still spoken. But a change is taking place. Words are still spoken, but they have become detached from their meanings. Words are still spoken, but things are no longer understood.

> The fields grew greener and greener. The pasture was cut into squares; they looked as if they had been measured with a ruler. A horse grazed in the field and a farmer's wife stood at her door. That

> was the way it had always been and that was the way it was now too.
>
> "How strange it is," said the waitress, and tears came into her eyes. (170)

The artist has a practical problem here: he must make us understand this failure of comprehension. Fortunately, he has available for symbolic purposes a historical datum: the destination of these men and women is to be reached by way of a railroad station. They are about to become a part of the history of transportation: a history which has up to now always symbolized liberation from boundaries. "Type of the modern," Whitman exults in "To a Locomotive in Winter,"

> Roll through my chant with all thy lawless music, thy swinging
> lamps at night,
> Thy madly-whistled laughter, echoing, rumbling like an earth-
> quake, rousing all,
> Law of thyself complete, thine own track firmly holding,
> (No sweetness debonair of tearful harp or glib piano thine,)
> Thy trills of shrieks by rocks and hills return'd.

For the old glib language has been abolished, and now we speak with the tongues of rocks and hills. The word and the thing have become one: the subject is fully incorporated into language, and our memory of it will henceforth reveal to us everything that can be known. For Whitman, the modern is fully transparent to meaning. It is paradise restored. But Appelfeld's image of the train imparts a different story: a story of transport away from memory, name, word, the power of knowing and remembering, and the mode of existence which consists of being known and remembered. In this story, some Jews step onto the platform of a railroad station, and then the earth forgets them.

> And suddenly the sky opened and light broke out of the heavens. The valley in all its glory and the hills scattered about filled with the abundance, and even the trembling, leafless trees standing wretchedly at the edge of the station seemed to breathe a sigh of relief. (174)

At the terminal, a history has ended.

From here to the end of the line, therefore, language can be spoken only provisionally, in the subjunctive mood. It too is in transit; it is on its way to silence.

> An engine, an engine coupled to four filthy freight cars, emerged from the hills and stopped at the station. Its appearance was as sudden as if it had risen from a pit in the ground. "Get in!" yelled invisible voices. And the people were sucked in. Even those who were standing with a bottle of lemonade in their hands, a bar of chocolate, the headwaiter with his dog—they were all sucked in as easily as grains of wheat poured into a funnel. Nevertheless Dr. Pappenheim found time to make the following remark: "If the coaches are so dirty it must mean that we have not far to go." (175)

We want to hear what happened to Dr. Pappenheim's *if-then* logic, but we are never going to; those are the last words of the novel. Brimming with all the foolish horror of dramatic irony, they hang in the air, spoken with one of their speaker's last few breaths. The air, still warmed by the words, is now a different air, one unbreathed by the men and women who up to a moment ago were standing still, looking and thinking and breathing, on the platform of the railroad station. This air possesses the chemical property of causing people to rise off the ground like smoke and disappear. It will not sustain the breath of Aharon Appelfeld if he tries to tell us the history of this mysterious change. But if he draws us a picture of something moving onward through time—say, something remembered from childhood, an antique means of transportation, a railroad train—he may be able to help us make a counterfeit memory of a passage from motion to motion, and then to the final stillness.

But under some extreme conditions, that stillness can be studied *in situ*. It takes the form of a suspension of history.

Consider, as Vasily Grossman does in *Forever Flowing*, what happens to an inmate of the Gulag—someone who has been eradicated from the history of the world outside his prison. He is never to be mentioned there again, by anyone; he has become an unperson. But somewhere, in a dossier in a file cabinet in a police agency, is his history; and somewhere else, because of that history, his body lives on, feels cold, eats food, speaks words with its mouth. Within limits mapped out clearly by lines of barbed wire, it exists. But its existence in time has been affected. Inside the zone of penal history, the historian observes:

> There was one profound difference in emotional makeup between people who were in prison and those in freedom. Ivan Grigoryevich could see that in camp people remained faithful to their own particular period. Various epochs of Russian life lived on in the character and thoughts of each. Here were men who had taken part in the Civil War, with their favorite songs, heroes, books; . . . here were officials of the Comintern of the twenties, with their own pathos and vocabulary, with their own philosophy and way of bearing themselves and pronouncing their words; here were very old people—monarchists, Mensheviks, SR's—and all of them preserved within themselves an entire world of ideas, manners, and literary heroes that had existed forty and fifty years before. . . .
>
> In contrast, elderly people in freedom did not display the obvious signs of their past; in them the past had been erased, wiped out, and they merged easily into the landscape of the new era. They thought, suffered, and experienced the world in a contemporary way. (108–9)

The inhabitant of the Gulag has been mummified. Forever after, he will be a citizen of one particular tract of time. The elderly person in freedom, by contrast, inhabits space; he lives in a world through which history, forever flowing, moves him steadily on his way from memory to oblivion. That is his freedom: the passivity of an aggregate of physical properties borne into consciousness and back out again, unresisted. It is the freedom of silence. In Grossman's universe, the ability to interpret—the ability to mean—is the ultimate punishment. It reminds us that we once had a history.

> [W]hen, in the light of the setting sun, she was going back to the camp, near the lumber warehouse, the Magadan radio station began to blare out.
>
> Masha and the two other women who were dragging their way along, squelching through the mud, put down their spades and stopped.
>
> Silhouetted against the sky stood watchtowers, and the sentinels

> in their black sheepskin coats perched on them like great enormous flies, and the low flat barracks looked as though they had once started to grow out of the ground and then reconsidered: perhaps they ought to grow back into the ground.
>
> The music was not sad but gay: dance music. And Masha wept when she heard it as she had never wept in her life. The two women standing next to her wept too. . . .
>
> Nor did Masha herself understand why her heart was suddenly filled with anguish and desperation. It was as if everything that had ever happened in her life had come together all at once. . . . Masha just didn't understand why suddenly, when she heard the gay dance music, she had begun to feel the dirty undershirt on her body, her shoes as heavy as irons, the sour stink of her pea jacket, why, suddenly, the question slashed her heart like a razor blade: To what end, for what, why, for her, all this endless cold, all this spiritual degradation, all this submissiveness that had developed within her toward her fate at hard labor?
>
> Hope, that had always pressed its living, vital weight upon her heart, had died.
>
> To the tune of the gay dance music, Masha lost once and for all the hope of ever again seeing [her daughter]. . . .
>
> In a year's time Masha left the camp. . . . The morgue assistants placed Masha Lyubimova in a rectangular box made of boards rejected by the lumber inspectors for any other use. For the last time they looked upon her face. On it was an expression of gentle, kind, childish triumph and dismay, that very same expression her face wore at the lumber warehouse when she heard the gay dance music—when she had first felt joy and then had understood there was no hope for her. (135–37)

To interpret is perilous. But we can understand the nature of peril only by interpretation. Grossman's Masha Lyubimova died of her interpretation, but to listen to the song on the radio and understand its purport was a task she could not escape. The remembered words of her history have followed her with a fidelity as deadly as the Fury's.

Marsha Lyubimova is, in short, a tragic figure. But Grossman's depiction of her tragedy is dependent, in a way Greek tragedy isn't, on pathos: Masha's memories, recreated in detail, of her warm apartment in Moscow, her living room full of plants, her happiness in marriage and motherhood. In postclassical narrative that has been the ordinary way of communicating a sense of the human: by induction, through the accumulation of details until they assume the form of a personality. But any such narrative convention requires something that the world of the Gulag calls into question: a stable system of objective correlatives, like the ones so insistently called into existence by an eighteenth-century classicizer during a time of change:

> Dear lovely bowers of innocence and ease,
> Seats of my youth, where every sport could please,
> How often have I loitered o'er thy green,
> Where humble happiness endeared each scene;
> How often have I paused on every charm,
> The sheltered cot, the cultivated farm,
> The never-failing brook, the busy mill,
> The decent church that topped the neighboring hill.
> (Goldsmith, *The Deserted Village*, lines 5–12)

The pathos of Aharon Appelfeld's characters is that they assume their feelings, their culture, and their lives have a significance as completely understood, because just as conventional, as Goldsmith's adjectives. Educated people, they have committed the error of thinking of themselves, their desires, and their destinies only in terms of the limited possibilities conceivable through conventional language. Of course they are wrong; the language they have thought in was an inaccurate translation of themselves all along, and they pay with their lives for their misreading. Their dependence on other people's words imbues their situation with pathos. But pathos is not understanding. It is a merely human condition, and the novelist who hopes to make us understand historically may need to learn a language of the inhuman: of what happens not during the loss of meaning but after.

Consider, for example, the event of our time which most demands to be recorded in tragedy: the mass exterminations of the Hitler era. Writers have tried to record the significance of that event, but so far they have all failed. Their own ways of thinking in words have subverted the effort. We think we want to speak tragedy, but so far we have been able to utter only sentimentality, pornography, and lyricism. We are trapped in literature, with its clutter of associations extending across time and space; that is, insofar as we write in language we are a part of the culture which enacts and is enacted by that language. The Holocaust, however, belongs to no culture. It was a definitive rejection from culture: a decision, made within a history, to draw a terminus at that history's edge and say, *Beyond this there will be no more.* Tragedy demands an ideal elemental form, but the Holocaust has deprived the ideal of its light and air. There are no words to write its history.

But consider what happens when we find one of its texts in a state of wordlessness. We will find it in a strange place: Grossman's panoramic novel of World War II, *Life and Fate*, which depicts the lives and loves of some two hundred wooden characters in 880 pages of wooden prose. The technical problem is easy enough to identify; as *Life and Fate*'s translator, Robert Chandler, says, "The novel is . . . a remarkably old-fashioned one. . . . its faults are typical of Socialist Realism: an occasional tendency towards sententious philosophizing, a certain long-windedness and lack of sparkle" (12–13). As a communication in words, *Life and Fate* is less efficient than, say, a lyric poem by Paul Celan. But the numb Dreiserian inefficiency of Grossman's narrative communicates a verbal history of its own: a history of the way language can roll over the human, forcing each individual sign into contiguity with its neighbor, crushing it into a purely relational term. We speak our language, go on speaking it *in extremis* as if the words meant something in themselves; meanwhile, time is directing our listeners' attention away from the words we say and toward the wordless approach of the end.

So, for instance, on the one hand, Grossman piles up his effects by multiplying his characters, each with one defining characteristic: the unthinking Communist who learns in the Gulag who he is; the decent German sucked into the Nazi war machine; Marshal Paulus, gloomily contemplating the imminent surrender of his German army at Stalingrad. Marshal Paulus receives special treatment in *Life and Fate*: an asterisk carefully reminds us that *he* is real, actual, genuine, historical. And it all counts for nothing. For most of its length *Life and Fate* is nothing but American Legion literature: the material of human life placed at the disposal of a set of preexisting responses.

But when there are no preexisting responses; when any human response would have been inconceivable before the moment when the depicted historical fact occurred?

> The interior of the building [housing the gas chamber] corresponded perfectly to the epoch in which it was built, the epoch of the industry of mass and speed.
>
> Once life had entered the supply canals, it was impossible for it to stop or turn back; its speed of flow down the concrete corridor was determined by formulae analogous to that of Stokes regarding the flow of liquid down a tube (a function of its density, specific gravity, viscosity and temperature, and of the friction involved). (474)

Here the referentiality of prose takes on the communicative power of a subject in itself. The merely human has been subsumed into mechanism, and with it any possibility of a conventional narrative appeal to what is called human interest. Now we are in the realm of the history that operated through this epoch: a history of power, one that caught up the old literary-historical conceptions of ego and character and obliterated them. We are ready to understand a history within the text.

Other novelists have brought us to that point and abandoned us there, and so, usually, does Grossman. The next chapter of *Life and Fate*, for example, serves only to restore the barrier between us and understanding. We want history, and right at the beginning of the chapter we get a portentous single-sentence paragraph full of it: "Liss [one of the German officers] met Eichmann that night" (476). We are intended to respond with a reaction based on our knowledge of who Adolf Eichmann was. But that aestheticized reaction can't tell us anything about history, or about ourselves in relation to history. Like D. W. Griffith in *Birth of a Nation* or Abel Gance in *Napoleon*, Grossman is about to stop the action, present us with a freeze-frame tableau from "real" history, and insist that *here* he is telling us the truth, *wie es eigentlich gewesen*, without fiction. The implied claim is that we are partaking of a historical Mystery of the Eucharist: a representation in which the signifier communicates to us the totality of the signified, in perfect clarity and with perfect understanding. It seems unlikely. Elsewhere in *Life and Fate* we are told we are within the mind of Adolf Hitler, but we don't believe Grossman's psychology as we believe, say, Dante's.

We believe Dante, perhaps, because *his* epic depicts a historical situation in the grandeur of its own terms—terms requiring that everything in the human which is merely individual be subordinated to the depiction of all humans' moral geography. Entering into that geography, under the control of the abstract forces of grammar, syntax, and rhetoric, we become entrained in an extended metaphor, one whose tenor extends outward from the printed page into the domain of the history of events. We see ourselves there as we are under the eye of heaven. If the event itself can be conceived in sufficiently inclusive terms, the enabling technology of those terms—be it Scholasticism or Socialist Realism—will cease, for the moment, to matter. As Dante ceases to hear Virgil at the gate of Paradise, we cease to hear our author. We have arrived without him at the intersection of two histories: the history of our times and the history of the deep structure; the history of the death camps and the history of the Indo-Europeans, speaking words in their beech forests. The two cultures have occupied roughly the same tract of ground; now they occupy the same time. Here, long ago, air passed into the human body and became thought and words; now the process is being reversed.

And here, with Grossman, we are at the *locus classicus* of this intellectual process. Brought to where we are by what T. S. Eliot called the mind of Europe, we are in the gas chamber.

> Taking short, slow steps, he walked into a concrete box with a low ceiling. . . . People who had always stayed together now drifted apart, began to lose one another. . . .
>
> This wasn't how people moved. It wasn't even how the lowest form of animal life moved. It was a movement without sense or purpose, with no trace of a living will behind it. The stream of people flowed into the chamber; the people going in pushed the people already inside, the latter pushed their neighbours, and all these countless shoves and pushes with elbows, shoulders and stomachs gave rise to a form of movement identical in every respect to the streaming of molecules. . . .
>
> The door seemed very far away; you could guess its position by the particular density of the white human bodies; they squeezed through the entrance and were then allowed to spread out into the

> chamber. . . . The crowd grew steadily denser; people began to move more and more slowly, their steps shorter and shorter. No one was controlling the movement of people in the concrete box. The Germans didn't care whether the people in the chamber stood still or moved in senseless zigzags and half-circles. The naked boy went on taking tiny, senseless steps. . . .
>
> David had been caught by a sub-current which, thrown back by the wall, was now flowing toward the door. . . . David watched the door close: gently, smoothly, as though drawn by a magnet, the steel door drew closer to its steel frame. Finally they became one. (551–53)

At its terminal point, human existence has been made into the substance of pure thought: simplified to a problem in rheology. The sentences that depict this process are themselves a simplification: a representation of one thing in terms of another, the other being unknown. We in the chamber are the vehicle of a metaphor for that which flows. The tenor of the metaphor, that which defines the flow, lies outside the chamber: outside our view, therefore; outside our ability to understand, outside the ability of our language to represent. The history of Grossman's sentences here entrains the history of his subjects. An image of motion becomes the only adequate way of representing cessation. When the door has finished closing in its steel frame, it will have separated speech from understanding and left us only the speech. There, in speech, meaning dwindles to a few last fragments of order—say, the grammatical order of the sentences in which we call for help. No one listens. That is what history's words tell us.

No one listens; perhaps no one can listen. Doing or suffering, we cannot understand. That verdict doesn't require to be spoken in words; its authority derives from the artifactual evidence. Poland has been essentially *judenrein* since the anti-Semitic campaign of 1968 and Yiddish is virtually a dead language, but Auschwitz is still a tourist attraction. It is *there*, and Grossman, like Tolstoy before him, grows strong in his words from telling us so. Narrative must always be subordinate to the subject it realizes. The title of a work of fiction no longer has to begin, "The True History of . . . ," as it did in the Elizabethan era, but every novel nevertheless seeks its ultimate recourse in the comforting fact that its language is ultimately to be understood in reference to an independent source of meaning. For the most radical twentieth-century experimentalists as for Tolstoy, a line of history-words extends backward from text to text until it reaches truth in the extratextual. In this respect, experimentalist practice has been unique only in its choice of paradigms: *Thom's Dublin Directory*, say, or the famous sentences from *A Farewell to Arms* in which the hero, sickened by the consequences of his comrades' belief in the necessary truthfulness of patriotic rhetoric, concludes with the force of revelation that "certain numbers . . . and certain dates and . . . the names of places were all you could say and have them mean anything" (185).

Hemingway's Lieutenant Henry yearns for immediate meaning, transparent words absolutely coextensive with the entities they label. Under less tragic circumstances he might have been one of the wise men of Laputa, carrying on his conversation with the aid of a backpack full of things. As it is, he cannot afford the luxury of conversation at all. He is an exhausted man, expressing his exhausted century's need to hold fast to the minimum of sense. The Renaissance ideal of *copia* was one of the casualties of the Great War; after Verdun and Passchendaele had sunk beneath their oceans of blood and mud, we were ready to understand the shocked purity of Malevich's *White on White*. We were able to understand, that is, that though the artifact and its associated word are not separable, their mutual meaning is separate from either the word or the thing as such. As with paint and subject or event and history, word and thing are elements in a pattern—a pattern of grammatical elements having little or nothing to do with the putative extraverbal reference of words. And that, precisely, was the goal and the distinctive achievement of modernism in the novel: to recognize that pattern for what it is and to put its purely formal properties to work in narrative.

Gertrude Stein described the procedure in historical terms this way:

> Remembering is repetition anybody can know that. In doing a portrait of any one, the repetition consists in knowing that that one is a kind of a one, that the things he does have been done by others like him that the things he says have been said by others like him,

> but, and this is the important thing, there is no repetition in hearing and saying the things he hears and says when he is hearing and saying them. And so in doing a portrait of him if it were possible to make that portrait a portrait of him saying and hearing what he says and hears while he is saying it and hearing it there is then in so doing neither memory nor repetition no matter how often that which he hears is heard and said. This was the discovery I made. . . . I said what I knew as they said and heard what they heard and said until I had completely emptied myself of all they were that is all that they were in being one hearing and saying what they heard and said in every way that they heard and said anything. ("Portraits and Repetition" 106–07)

That is, approximately: what we say is rendered less than meaningful by *differance*. To understand *in esse*, we have to disregard the words and listen instead to their formal relationship with one another. Meaning is not lexical; it is grammatical. Saussure might have said that it is a system of differences without positive terms.

> People if you like to believe it can be made by their names. Call anybody Paul and they get to be a Paul call anybody Alice and they get to be an Alice perhaps yes perhaps no, there is something in that, but generally speaking, things once they are named the name does not go on doing anything to them and so why write in nouns. (Stein, "Poetry and Grammar" 125)

Vasily Grossman does write in nouns, most of the time; that is why the history he writes is different, most of the time, from the history his subjects lived. Grossman's history is in fact full of terms, things named Progress and Communism and Freedom; meanwhile, the subjects of his history live and breathe and fight and die, and the language they live in is connected only in a vague and unspecifiable way to the nouns that swirl through heaven above them. A modernist would write a different kind of history of their lives: a relational history, one without positive terms. This history's semantic core would be not the noun but the grammatical system.

Here, for instance, are three excerpts from one of the "nonfictional" biographies intercalated in John Dos Passos's historical trilogy *U.S.A.* (*The 42nd Parallel*; *1919*; *The Big Money*).[1] The subject of the biography is Thomas Edison.

> Whenever he read about anything he went down cellar and tried it out. . . .
>
> To find a filament for his electric lamp that would work, that would be a sound commercial proposition, he tried all kinds of paper and cloth, thread, fishline, fibre, celluloid, boxwood, coconutshells, spruce, hickory, bay, mapleshavings, rosewood, punk, cork, flax, bamboo, and the hair out of a redheaded Scotchman's beard;
>
> whenever he got a hunch he tried it out. . . .
>
> Thomas A. Edison at eightytwo worked sixteen hours a day;
>
> he never worried about mathematics or the social system or generalized philosophical concepts;
>
> in collaboration with Henry Ford and Harvey Firestone who never worried about mathematics or the social system or generalized philosophical concepts;
>
> he worked sixteen hours a day trying to find a substitute for rubber; whenever he read about anything he tried it out; whenever he got a hunch he went to the laboratory and tried it out. (*42nd Parallel* 308, 310, 311)

In the ordinary sense of the word, this text is history. We can verify Dos Passos's names and dates from other sources, and if we are in the vicinity of Dearborn, Michigan, we can walk through the physical basis of Edison's achievement: his Menlo Park laboratory, transplanted complete with its topsoil and garbage dump from New Jersey to the grounds of the Henry Ford Museum. In 1929, on the fiftieth anniversary of his creation of light, Edison reenacted the crucial experiment there, and when he had finished, Henry Ford built a fence across the front of the laboratory and gave orders that everything behind it was henceforth to be left untouched. We can see the apparatus there still: sooty glassware touched by Thomas Edison's fingers. It is as close to the experi-

[1] Dos Passos's masterpiece is now available only in a mass-market Signet paperback (three volumes, 1969) to which I refer for lack of anything better. Much of the earlier Dos Passos scholarship is keyed to the one-volume Modern Library edition (n.d.), but this has been out of print for years.

ence as we will ever get, and it comes to us as legendary truth, unmediated by textuality.

Dos Passos's chronicle has likewise an origin outside its text. Aside from the biographical data, it probably comes to us from an essay in literary history: Van Wyck Brooks's discussion of Edgar Allan Poe in "America's Coming-of-Age" (1915). There, anticipating one of *U.S.A.*'s main themes, Brooks says:

> No European can exist without a thousand subterranean relationships; but Americans can so exist, Americans do so exist. Edison, for example, resembles Poe as a purely inventive mathematical intellect, and with Edison, as with Poe, one feels that some electric fluid takes the place of blood; one feels that the greatest of inventors cannot be called a scientist at all, that his amazing powers over nature are not based in any philosophical grasp of the laws of nature, that he is in temperament a mechanic rather than a philosopher. . . . Poe is a mechanic of the same sort. He has discovered in literature the chemical secret of life. He has produced chemical men, chemical emotions, chemical landscapes. (50)

We understand Brooks's point by analogy and generalization: to respond to Poe is to respond to the radical inauthenticity of American culture. But the only way Brooks can tell us this is, as Stein would say, with nouns: by way of such reifications as "subterranean relationships," "philosophical grasp of the laws of nature," and "chemical secret of life." The metaphors lead us, despite Brooks's intentions, back to a comfortable ground of knowable physicality outside the text, where laws of nature are available for the grasping and relationships are rooted deep in terra firma. But Dos Passos writes his interpretation in a different language. Brooks's words refer; Dos Passos's words repeat, obliterating old meanings by shaping themselves into new patterns.

He tried it out: a sentence of ordinary language, repeated. Read mimetically, it shows us that Edison's life was a paratactic series: he invented . . . and then he invented . . . and then he invented. . . . From the lowly "he went down cellar and tried it out" to the exalted "he went to the laboratory and tried it out," Edison's life has been only a single experience, repeated. Dos

Passos uses this anaphoric trick for mimetic purposes elsewhere in *U.S.A.*, notably in his description of Henry Ford's assembly line:

> fifteen minutes for lunch, three minutes to go to the toilet, the Taylorized speedup everywhere, reach under, adjust washer, screw down bolt, shove in cotterpin, reachunder adjustwasher, screwdown bolt, reachunderadjustscrewdownreachunderadjust until every ounce of life was sucked off into production and at night the workmen went home gray shaking husks. (*The Big Money* 75)[2]

That is mimesis as analysis. But in the Edison biography the repeating phrase *he tried it out* has a synthetic property too. It is the constitutive unit of a history.

This history is small and simple; that is why it is terrible. It is made of just one thing: trying it out. The edifice rises, but we cannot find its foundation; below each *trying it out* there is only another *trying it out*. In the description of Ford's assembly line, the words call up an image from memory and ask us to interpret it in a new way. Those pictures of the assembly line in your eighth-grade history book? You weren't told this at the time, but they were pictures of something bad. First came the image, then came the words to help us interpret it. But in the Edison description, the image *is* the words. Edison doesn't exist as an entity independent of the text; he (it) is only that which tries it out, and the trying-it-out exists only as some words on the page. When it stops, there is no more Edison. The sentence beginning "Thomas A. Edison at eightytwo worked sixteen hours a day" and ending "whenever he got a hunch he went to the laboratory and tried it out" is the last sentence of the biography. No rhetoric has been imported into this life from outside the text; there is only a pragmatic bustle of grammar without introduction, body, or conclusion. There are words inside the boundaries of the document, and outside the words there is nothing at all.

The Edison biography is a short, unrepresentative part of a very long novel. Writers and readers usually find it hard to make

[2] The telescoped words in this passage are spelled according to the Modern Library text (3: 55), which differs materially from the Signet version and seems clearly better.

pictures in Dos Passos's way out of words; much easier to evoke the picture from a preexisting lexicon of images in memory. But what if the images themselves are so terrible that we dare not remember them?

Aharon Appelfeld doesn't try to solve the problem. His histories are the words spoken before and after the images were made—only before and only after.

Vasily Grossman pretends, for the most part, that the problem doesn't exist. He parses nouns and pretends that he is describing events. But when he came to see the gas chambers at Treblinka with his own eyes,[3] he was able to interrogate the silent dead by working his way down through language to the unchanging, wordless truth of number.

> Each chamber [of the ten] in the new building was eight meters long by seven wide, for a floor area of 56 square meters. The total floor area of the new chambers was therefore 560 square meters. Counting the 75 square meters of the three original chambers, Treblinka possessed an industrial death surface of 635 square meters. Into a single chamber were packed 400 to 500 persons. (*Enfer* 52–53)

The calculations continue. Grossman, who was educated as a chemical engineer, was familiar with the techniques of mathematical induction. We determine the number of murder cycles per day (two or three on the average, but sometimes as many as five); we determine the number of days per week that the chambers were in operation (seven, during a period of thirteen consecutive months, but let us reduce those thirteen months to ten by allowing ninety days for unavoidable interruptions of the cycle); and

> at the rate of 300,000 victims per month on the average, we obtain, for those ten months, the horrible figure of three million. This confirms our initial conjecture of three million, which was based on a similarly minimized calculation of the number of incoming convoys. (53–54)

[3] According to Robert Chandler's introduction to *Life and Fate* (7), Grossman's 1944 article "The Hell of Treblinka" was "the first journalistic account of a German death-camp in any language." The passages I quote from that article are my own translation of an anonymous French translation, *L'enfer de Treblinka*, first published in 1945. For a discussion of "The Hell of Treblinka" in relation to *Life and Fate*, see Markish 70–73.

John Dos Passos, far in space and time from Treblinka, couldn't conceive that his history book would have to take into account in Grossman's way the history of the unspeakable. In that respect, he was a representative figure of modernist literature in English. That is why modernism in English died of its limitations after World War II.

Modernism is dead, but its historical occasions remain. We still require, even more than we did between the world wars, a way to speak certain numbers and certain dates and the names of places and have them mean something. Right now, in the raw historical record, we have only their mechanical memory, uninterpreted and therefore incomprehensible. If we are ever to learn to speak of them, we will need to enter into the record and learn its secret of a language wholly passive. That will be the language of picture words: words recording their data without connotation, words as wholly devoid of prior significance as the silver halide crystals that make up a photographic image. Those crystals may serve us as the only productive metaphor of a historical language for our time: a language whose own formal properties organize the chaos of light and dark into significance. In any event, if we aren't yet ready to read the words, we will have to look at the pictures.

6

Picture Words (II): Roman Vishniac, Claude Lanzmann, and the Abolition of History

But of course we read the pictures with words too. What we see in a picture of the sinking of the *Titanic* turns out to depend on our politics—or, more generally, on our place in history. "Tell me that a man despised Pope and admired Ossian," says C. S. Lewis (105), "and I shall make a good shot at his *floruit*."

Which means that our answers to the questions "What am I reading?" and "What am I seeing?" will always be subject to change. But this change is saltatory, not continuous. The frontiers of the community of interpretation are stable during certain periods, and in fact those periods of stability are generally perceived as distinct historical entities: semesters, say, or administrations, or eras, depending on scale. If the scale is large enough and we are reading in the vicinity of its midpoint, we will naturally think that the way we are reading now is the only way to read. But that will be a false consciousness. Semantics is always under cultural control.

> Within the literary community there are subcommunities (what will excite the editors of *Diacritics* is likely to distress the editors of *Studies in Philology*), and within the community the boundaries of the acceptable are continually being redrawn. In a classroom whose authority figures include David Bleich and Norman Holland, a student might very well relate a text to her memories of a favorite aunt, while in other classrooms, dominated by the spirit of Brooks

> and Warren, any such activity would immediately be dismissed as nonliterary, as something that isn't done.
>
> The point is that while there is always a category of things that are not done (it is simply the reverse or flip side of the category of things that *are* done), the membership in that category is continually changing. It changes laterally as one moves from subcommunity to subcommunity, and it changes through time when once interdicted interpretive strategies are admitted into the ranks of the acceptable. (Fish 343–44)

Stanley Fish is talking about literary criticism, but of course the context of what he describes is not just literary. Interpretive communities are a part of social life in general, and our membership in them entails social action. "To understand . . . contradictions correctly," writes a Marxist poet, "we must first be clear on what is meant by 'the people' and what is meant by 'the enemy'" (Mao 45). And when we have become clear—

"In Nationalist Turkey," explains Lothrop Stoddard,

> the determination to eliminate the Greeks and Armenians was motivated mainly by political and economic considerations. In Nazi Germany [which Stoddard visited during the winter of 1939–40], the resolve to eliminate the Jews is further exacerbated by theories of race. The upshot, in Nazi circles, is a most uncompromising attitude. If this is not oftener expressed, the reason is because they feel that the issue is already decided in principle and that elimination of the Jews will be completed within a relatively short space of time. So, ordinarily, the subject does not arise. But it crops up at unexpected moments. For instance, I have been stunned at a luncheon or dinner with Nazis, where the Jewish question has not been even mentioned, to have somebody raise his glass and casually give the toast: *Sterben Juden!*—"May the Jews Die!" (*Into the Darkness* 287–88)

I am looking at the introductions to two histories of that toast: Roman Vishniac's *A Vanished World* and Ulrich Keller's *The Warsaw Ghetto in Photographs: 206 Views Made in 1941*. Keller's introduction is that of an academic; it begins, "An official German document of 1941 offers the following information about the Warsaw ghetto," and concludes, eighteen pages later, with sixty-seven endnotes. There is passion in this account, but it is the passion of chronicle: the passion of Simon Dubnow, urging us to write it all down. The passion of Elie Wiesel's foreword to *A Vanished World* is of another sort. After some perfunctory ringing of changes on the cliché "a picture is worth a thousand words," Wiesel bursts out:

> Dear Roman Vishniac, where did we first meet? Somewhere in the Carpathians, a timid Jewish boy waved you away, for it was dangerous for an outsider to venture along the brink of the abyss: was that me? was that you? . . .
>
> I am walking—we are walking—behind Roman Vishniac, and we are caught by a thousand glances which enliven the alleys of the little Jewish villages. Our eyes . . . see two things at once: living beings yesterday, a void today.

And what speaks in Wiesel's words is the sound of the void: a voice crying to itself. For Wiesel, nothing has existed since 1945 but himself. He is alone, crying to himself. His cry is futile because it is heard by none but himself, but he cries anyway. Around him, however, in the dark silence, little bright eyes see and little furry ears hear. The last human being wails. Uncomprehendingly, Elie Wiesel's readers read the words of the wail, take the words into themselves, think, "I feel that way too," weep. But Wiesel remains alone.

That is one of the awful things about history: it can debase. Solipsism for the author, sentimentality for the reader: those are unsatisfactory ways of recording what happened. But the satisfactory ways haven't been discovered yet. Perhaps that is why we find ourselves wanting to stop reading and look at the pictures.

For these are picture books: documents of Central and Eastern European Jewry's last days. Like the novels of Aharon Appelfeld, these books stop short just before the trains arrive, and that is one of the terrible things about them: the way they force us to read retrospectively, in the savagely mocking spirit of historical irony. Little do they know, these children on the page, what is approaching for them: not just death but death in despair. They will never know that we remember. And that, perhaps, is what makes these pictures even worse for us to see: their documentary proof that interpretation works both ways across the barrier of the page. We have set ourselves, as Eliot recommended, among the dead, but the dead cannot speak to us because they cannot hear our voices crying out to them.

Reduced to photographs, the history of their existence has become axiologically null. This is not because the camera is objective. To the contrary: these images document a history of two ways of seeing, a Jewish way and a Nazi way. But because the Jewish civilization recorded in these Jewish and Nazi photographs has been obliterated not just physically but conceptually, what we see in these images now is nothing but objets d'art. The ancient Egyptian religion is for us merely fabulous; so is the idea that a distinct Jewish culture once lived in the heart of Europe. We can read the chronicles, of course; we can see and believe the evidence; but the real history, the history that works through lived speech, is gone.

Consider the documents. Consider, for instance, three photographs of children in the Warsaw ghetto: one by Vishniac and a pair by the German army team of Albert Cusian and Erhard Josef Knobloch.

Vishniac's (no. 42 in *A Vanished World*) was taken in 1939, shortly before the outbreak of the war. In *A Vanished World* it faces a photograph captioned "Basement lodgings and workshop. Nine people slept in two beds." That caption is a synecdoche for extreme poverty, but the format of *A Vanished World* may encourage us not to understand its purport. Here are the photographs: grandeur of expression amid the utmost misery, printed with the richest resources of the gray scale on heavy stock with a page size of 12″ × 12″. They are to be looked at, not read. But sooner or later we may find ourselves reading an unpaginated section of moderately small print, three columns to the page, at the front of the book, and there we will find what seems to be an explanation of the scene we have been looking at. "An economic boycott of Poland's three and a half million Jews occurred in the late 1930s," Vishniac tells us in the two paragraphs devoted to photograph 20. "Fostered by the government and the Church, oppression and persecution took their ugliest forms." To synecdoche has been added personification; the photographic image has been supplemented with a verbal image. But we still do not understand.

We turn back to photograph 42. "Since the basement had no heat," the caption reads, "Sara had to stay in bed all winter. Her father painted the flowers for her, the only flowers of her childhood." And there on the wall in the background, filling the upper right quadrant of the picture, are the flowers, slightly out of focus: a stylized composition of blossoms and clouds. The flowers extend into the upper left and lower right quadrants as well, but most of these spaces are filled with blank wall and Sara's thin, patterned blanket. The lower right quadrant is Sara's. She sits up in the bed, the wall behind her and the wadded blanket in front of her, halfway back in the depth plane, lighted from the side and (by reflection) from the rear, in a modified form of what photographers call Rembrandt lighting. Her dress is dark and short-sleeved. Her hair is tangled. Her mouth is open and unsmiling. Her eyes—

Well, we can continue trying to explain. Vishniac does. He tells us that he took his photographs, all of them, with a hidden camera; the image of Sara is *wie es eigentlich gewesen*. And in his prefatory comment he provides Sara with a historical credential: "Many people have told me that they are especially moved by this image. Sara was ten, and the darling of her family. When I returned to the site of her home after the war, the home was no more, and there was no Sara." The words continue, not just about Sara but about everyone. "If I am to breathe life into the pictures that follow," Vishniac explains at the beginning of this section, "it is by providing you, the reader, with my thoughts about them. The pictures depict people and places that no longer exist, yet in my memory they do exist."

But the images into which Roman Vishniac breathes life are different from the images in his memory: they are beautiful. They have lost their fear and squalor, their presence in the domain of misery; they have become only art. They no longer exist in history. They have become members of the genre *photograph*: an array of silver halide crystals, distributed according to timeless aesthetic criteria codified in classical antiquity, in a world without Jews.

> The average German seems disinclined to talk much to the foreign visitor about this oppressed minority. However, I gathered that the general public does not approve of the violence and cruelty which Jews have suffered. But I also got the impression that, while the

> average German condemned such methods, he was not unwilling to see the Jews go and would not wish them back again. (Stoddard, *Into the Darkness* 286)

Vishniac's Sara has a name, if only a name that Vishniac provides as the caption of an image. But the children in the two other photographs (Keller nos. 143 and 144) come to us without words.

We see them at two moments in their history. On a filthy sidewalk in Warsaw lie three children, apparently asleep. Their bodies are huddled together and their clothes are wrapped around them; we can distinguish clearly only feet and the tops of heads. On the wall directly over their heads is a poster advertising the appearance of a performer named Władysław Lin at a theater called the Palladium. In the window of the shop next door is a display of women's shoes.

In the next photograph the children are awake and facing the camera. The oldest, a boy of perhaps eight, stands. He is wearing a cap, a pair of pants, socks, and shoes. The pants appear to be a grown man's, cut down; they extend to his knees. The shoes are a grown man's. A blanket is wrapped around his head, chest, and arms, leaving only his face and the bill of his cap exposed. He is looking sidelong at the photographer. The skin below his eyes is dark. Deep lines extend from the sides of his nose to the sides of his mouth. It appears that his chin may be trembling.

The second child is a boy of perhaps five. On his head is what appears to be a man's beret, trimmed with braid like a World War I German enlisted man's cap. Draped around his body is a man's coat, fastened with a safety pin. Men's socks droop around his ankles; his shoes are children's shoes; his legs are bare. Squatting, he looks up at the camera. I cannot describe the expression on his face.

Sitting on the sidewalk with her legs curled under her is the third child, a girl of perhaps two. She is wrapped in rags. She is trying to swallow a piece of bread, presumably provided by the photographer. She does not look up. She does not look at all; her eyes stare ahead and down, unfocused.

Behind the camera, watched by the two boys, is a man in a German soldier's uniform. We see the children through his eyes.

Keller tells us in his introduction that this photographer was a member of the German army's *Propaganda-Kompanie* 689. The artist filed this pair of photographs in late winter or early spring, 1941, but we do not know for what specific purpose he took them. The archive was preserved, however, throughout the war. The children may have been two brothers and a sister. They are undoubtedly dead now. We can say these things about their images, and that is all we can say. If we try to say more, we have begun to interpret, and interpretation here demands a language we cannot speak: the language of the man behind the camera, the man whose face we cannot see.

> In [Dorothea] Lange's photograph ["Okie mother and child in California, 1936"] the Okie girl nurses her son. Why doesn't she spank him or yell at him for having thrown his food on the ground? She must discipline him as well as give him suck. And she must laugh enormously too, hug her son roughly and dance him about, her face distorted with joy. No doubt she flirts, at least with her husband, and she must get mad at him, call him names, weep murderously, maybe throw things (maybe he punches her). And she yawns and scratches and giggles and cleans her nose. But these things are not shown. All her life, everything she is, gets reduced to the instrumental, to the pitiable, to a poignant helplessness and wan despair. When [Pare] Lorentz claimed that Lange's one desire was to record poor people "as they are, not as they should be, not as some doctrine insists they should be," he exaggerated. Lange's people were treated according to a doctrine, and the doctrine was documentary. (Stott 61–62)

That is, Lange is guilty of virtual history. She photographs her presuppositions; what Gertrude Stein calls nouns. But when nothing is left of a world but its nouns—names, documents signifying only that the dead had names—the only way we can read these names is virtually. Roman Vishniac does that; for him, what was is coextensive with what should or should not have been.

But in the Nazi archive the reading of history becomes an autonomous activity, free of all presupposition. This is so for two terrible reasons. First, these images are not creative. They have nothing to do with the lives they depict; they are instruments of the destruction of their subject. Second, we cannot conceive of the state of mind which made that destruction possible. We have left only the photograph in itself, mute and dumb and blind: the artifact as autonomous object, cut free by a single moral stroke from the human life of the craftsman who made it. "In an imperfect work time is an ingredient, but into a perfect work time does not enter," Thoreau tells us at the end of *Walden*, in his happy parable of the sage and his staff, and in that sense the photograph of the three children is a perfect work. It is the evidence of their exclusion from time. Because they have passed out of our time-world, they can no longer be remembered. They can only be seen: seen in the absence of any way of understanding what is seen. On the hard concrete of that sidewalk in Warsaw one morning early in 1941, a specific moment of history ceased to exist. We have the document to prove it: henceforth history is finite and mortal.

Contemporary art has worried about this. Whether or not the artists are conscious of it, contemporary painting and sculpture are a confession of despair. When we allow ourselves to realize that a painting exists only to memorialize its creator's brushstrokes, we acknowledge that there is nothing in the universe but chaos and ego. But that acknowledgment has useful consequences. If our categories of value (historical value, aesthetic value, grammatical or syntactical value) are only some of the ego's desperate contrivances of expression, we can disregard the conventional boundaries between them; they differ from one another only in the ways they give shape or voice to our selves. When Monet showed us that color and volume are interchangeable expressions, he showed us that that there can never be a picture *of*. There can only be picture and painter, and the picture is nothing but an extension of the painter.

So we paint brushstrokes. The painting becomes a projection of the ego into space: one of Monet's haystacks, say, made still under the changing light of heaven by the power of the artist's hand. But how do we read the projection of the ego into time? How can we learn to read the language of others when our own selves fill cosmos to its limit, leaving no space for the life of others or air for their words?

Claude Lanzmann, a historian of the ego, set himself that task in his film about the Holocaust, *Shoah*. Here is one of the texts he teaches us (103–05).

> Geheime Reichssache (Secret Reich Business)
> Berlin, June 5, 1942
> Changes for special vehicles now in service at Kulmhof (Chelmno) and for those now being built
>
> Since December 1941, ninety-seven thousand have been processed by the three vehicles in service, with no major incidents. In the light of observations made so far, however, the following technical changes are needed:
>
> The vans' normal load is usually nine per square yard. In Saurer vehicles, which are very spacious, maximum use of space is impossible, not because of any possible overload, but because loading to full capacity would affect the vehicle's stability. So reduction of the load space seems necessary. It must absolutely be reduced by a yard, instead of trying to solve the problem, as hitherto, by reducing the number of pieces loaded. Besides, this extends the operating time, as the empty void must be filled with carbon monoxide. On the other hand, if the load space is reduced, and the vehicle is packed solid, the operating time can be considerably shortened. The manufacturers told us during a discussion that reducing the size of the van's rear would throw it badly off balance. In fact, the balance is automatically restored, because the merchandise aboard displays during the operation a natural tendency to rush to the rear doors, and is mainly found lying there at the end of the operation. So the front axle is not overloaded.
>
> 2. The lighting must be better protected than now. The lamps must be enclosed in a steel grid to prevent their being damaged. Lights could be eliminated, since they apparently are never used. However, it has been observed that when the doors are shut, the load always presses hard against them as soon as darkness sets in. This is because the load naturally rushes toward the light when darkness sets in, which makes closing the doors difficult. Also, because of the alarming nature of darkness, screaming always occurs when the doors are closed. It would therefore be useful to light the lamp before and during the first moments of the operation.
>
> 3. For easy cleaning of the vehicle, there must be a sealed drain in the middle of the floor. The drainage hole's cover, eight to twelve inches in diameter, would be equipped with a slanting trap, so that

fluid liquids can drain off during the operation. During cleaning, the drain can be used to evacuate large pieces of dirt.

The aforementioned technical changes are to be made to vehicles in service only when they come in for repairs. As for the ten vehicles ordered from Saurer, they must be equipped with all innovations and changes shown by use and experience to be necessary.

Submitted for decision to Gruppenleiter II D, SS-Obersturmbannführer Walter Rauff.

Signed: Just

The first difficulty here is a matter of vocabulary. "The operation," "the load": these are euphemisms, doubtless employed for reasons of military and psychological security. "The key to the entire operation from the psychological standpoint was never to utter the words that would be appropriate to the action being taken," Raul Hilberg later explains to Lanzmann (139), and David Engel notes that "at one point an express order was even issued in Hitler's name forbidding public reference to the actual fate of the Jews" (174). But if we can learn from chronicle what the appropriate words were, we can translate the euphemisms into unambiguous references to an event. And the translation will be simple to read. It will say that the special vehicles were trucks whose cargo compartments could be filled with exhaust gas, the load was Jews, and the operation was mass murder. This reattachment of words to their referents is a job for a scholiast: after enough work in the archives the words will be laid out in their correct order on the page, ready at last to be read.

But will we ever be able to read them? The man who wrote in euphemisms refused to write the real words. The man who received the transmission decoded it according to a virtual grammar: a grammar of the unspoken. The textual artifact before us has escaped from its own textual history. Before we can read it, we will need to find a lexicon of its unwritten words. And that, in turn, means that the word will have to be released from its ordinary limitations in meaning. It will have to become a meaning in itself: a sound and a correlative image.

So: on a sound strip parallel to the sequence of images in his film, the voice of Claude Lanzmann speaks, in French, the words written by the man named Just on June 5, 1942. While we hear

Just's words, Lanzmann's camera shows us a terrain in motion. We are on a high-speed highway, looking out as an industrial landscape unrolls before us. It is a wet day, and clouds of steam billow out of cooling towers. We pass a road repair crew and run through a factory complex, with ductwork suspended alongside the road. Over the sound of Lanzmann's voice we hear a jet airplane. We are presumably in Germany, since all the cars in camera range are German, but a stranger sees nothing distinctive along this road; it is just one of many such places in our world, the internationalized economic geography that grew out of the ruins of the past. In any case, the past in this landscape *is* past: the Jews of Germany will never be killed again.

The past is only a short distance forward or back on the videocassette, of course. A few minutes before we arrived here, we watched while Claude Lanzmann stood on a sunny doorstep in rural Poland, asking questions of some elderly villagers who once, season after season, saw the Jews being led to their deaths. These eyewitnesses to the slaughter now live in the Jews' houses. There they remember; there they shape their memories into art. The tales subsequently brought out of the houses for Lanzmann to hear are self-serving, as could be expected, but they also partake disinterestedly of the great anonymous heritage of folk literature. Earnestly, the village narrators assure Lanzmann that the Jews were poor and disgustingly ugly, and the Jews were rich and seductively beautiful, and the Jews realized too that they deserved to die for having killed Christ. Even in a country without Jews, we learn, nothing in the literary history of Jewish-Christian relations has changed. But that is the general fact about rural Poland: nothing has changed. Lanzmann's camera shows us the hardware associated with the villagers' state of mind: steam engines, still in use; horse-drawn wagons, still in use. When we talk here, we speak in the past tense. Here, in their own literary past, the Jews might as well still be alive. And in the part of this world which impinges on the present, only a trace in the earth remains of the Chelmno death camp.

So the voice on the soundtrack now, reading a letter written in 1942, seems dissociated from its environment of chemical plants and *Autobahnen*. There are no Jews in this environment; there never were. The Jews disappeared from the land long ago, when there were still horses and trees. Now the word "Jew" is only a word lacking reference in the *Umwelt*, part of the vocabulary of dream. The industrial complex sweeps on around us: overpasses and interchanges, a building with flames shooting from its exhaust stacks. Lanzmann's voice has reached the end of the last technical recommendation: "During cleaning, the drain can be used to evacuate large pieces of dirt." Suddenly our passage through the industrial narrative is interrupted by a jump cut. We are no longer looking toward the side of the road; instead, the camera is focused out the rear window. Behind us, approaching, is a truck: medium-sized, light blue, ordinary, part of our world. Lanzmann's voice reads, "As for the ten vehicles ordered from Saurer, they must be equipped with all innovations and changes. . . ." The lens zooms in on the truck's radiator grille. There, in the grille, is an ornament bearing the manufacturer's marque: on a white field, a black tower straddling an archway.

Lanzmann has finished reading the letter. The truck draws even with us and passes. The camera looks down at its spinning rear wheel, and the scene fades out. But not before we have suddenly seen a word which tells us the history of this image: on the ornament, the picture of the tower; in the picture, on the black tower, a name: Saurer.

The camera has inserted the word into an image of motion. There it becomes a synecdoche for that uninterrupted flow of time which carries the past forever into the present with all its appurtenances intact: religion, corporate structure, notions of the human. Between the 1942 Saurer truck and the 1985 Saurer truck there is an essential continuity; the dead are gone, but that which forced them to begin their journey down roads and railroad tracks will be with us forever.

We will never be able to read the history of that journey, because it is a text that writes into itself everyone who tries to understand. But the writing has a grammar, and that, at least, we can learn to read. We can understand, for instance, that inclusion in the new grammar has changed the word *Saurer* from a proper noun to a different kind of word, something for which we need a name: a durative particle, signifying the continuity of the past tense with the continuing present. In fact, the conventional distinctions between noun and verb become vague throughout this new grammar. The subject is that which has become an image in motion, and the image is that which pictures words.

Picture words: second person, imperative mood. Roman Vishniac didn't obey that injunction. Starting with the historically determined vocabulary of European Jewish culture, he set out to illustrate it. But the words remained separate from the pictures; the images were intended only as testimony to the words' existence. When the words were rendered incomprehensible, therefore, the pictures were too. "In my memory they do exist," he protests, and we can only honor him for the fidelity of that protest—a protest directed into the void, spoken in an unhearable language. Claude Lanzmann, on the other hand, assumed when he picked up his camera that the words no longer existed and would have to be remade. Discovering then that the referents of his history still existed, he enclosed them in a grammar of images. That, probably, is the only way of making the archive comprehensible in the language of a future history.

We will have to read that history while we are in it ourselves, a part of the images we evoke from each page. That will be a hard task, but the poets have already shown us that they read history that way. From them we can learn to read unscathed. Consider, for instance, the reading habits of Emily Dickinson.

7

Emily Dickinson: Province, Ghetto, and Archive

Dickinson: because her poems are the trace of at least four different passages of history through language.

As the textual record of something that happened in the *hors-texte*, Dickinson's poems dance in a blur along the boundary between phenomenon and perception, *Innenwelt* and *Umwelt*. They are a chronicle of events, like most texts that incorporate time into narrative, but they are also events in themselves: linguistic artifacts formed along the boundary where language ceases to be a speech shared with others and becomes the secret code of a single ego. Dickinson's verse charts the abyss between language's inculcated sense of origin, sequence, and cause, on the one hand, and the ego's shocked mute perception of the unchanging *thereness* of phenomena, on the other. In Dickinson's great definitions of the term *eternity*, words and the wordless, time and no-time, touch.

And as a matter of course, much more than for most poets, so do the individual and her culture. The couch where Dickinson was born as a poet was surrounded by portents of what was to come. Emily Dickinson lived her life in her father's house, in a town whose central institution, Amherst College, ran in the Dickinson family. There on Main Street, Dickinson's culture took the form of a family life: the life of an upper-middle-class New England lady with a taste for pious ejaculations, letters of condolence, sentimental novels, the language of flowers, and snobbery. The *Atlantic Monthly*, Samuel Worcester's *Watts and Select* hymnal, a collection of small-town newspapers, and a music stand full of sentimental songs were the local grounds of her vocabulary. When she was fifteen years old, a performance by a Chinese musician reduced her to stifled giggles (L13).[1] When she attended a recital by Jenny Lind at the age of twenty, she responded most enthusiastically to her father's audible comments ("you would have *died* a laughing") and to the size of the gate ("She took 4000 $ . . . for tickets at Northampton aside from all expenses") (L46). When she was fifty, the sight of a black man brought on a panic attack (L721). We can place these reactions sociologically, and that is sufficient judgment on them. The author of "Great streets of silence led away / To neighborhoods of pause" was a provincial.

Provincialism has hurt other writers. It constricted George Crabbe's scope and made F. R. Leavis into a yokel. For Dickinson's membership in class and gender and regional history, her lifework paid a high price in affectation and sentimentality. Of course, provincialism offered Dickinson, in compensation, the useful commodities of subject matter and an agreed-upon frame of reference. Her mind explored its native ground at leisure, in detail. But that terrain was a province: offering a focused and composed view but intellectually neither broad nor populous. It offers us who read Dickinson only one advantage of location, but that is enough: the advantage of the model, the self-contained aesthetic object which extends our understanding outward from itself to our own surroundings. Dickinson heard a fly buzz when she died; taking a broader view of what could be made into art, the Nazi photographers in the Warsaw ghetto recorded the dying moments of a culture whose authenticity had been destroyed by *force majeure*. Aesthetically, the photograph and the enterprise it records partake of all the lavishness that advances in technique have made possible. But the twentieth-century image of a representative anonymous annihilation has one thing in common with the nineteenth-century image of the extinction of a protected private consciousness: each document works by depicting the

[1] Dickinson citations are keyed by item number, not page number, to Thomas H. Johnson's variorum *Poems* (P) and *Letters* (L).

progressive loss of significance which Dickinson, in her concise way, called death. Considered as documents in the history of knowledge, the photographs we have seen and the poems we are about to read have equal value. The poem makes the tiny terribly large; the photograph makes the large terribly small. Each is an episode in the history of violence directed against objective significance.

Province and ghetto have that in common: they are delimited zones in which speech and violence give birth to each other, each becoming less comprehensible as they do so.[2] In the ghetto, violence and its utterance are reciprocal effects, each tending to perpetuate the other. But in the province, speech is estranged from its origin. It is felt to enter into significance from a larger world outside, and that false consciousness is virtually the defining characteristic of the provincial. When the provincial gives voice to itself, therefore, we hear only the part of the utterance whose significance coincides with our own imposed norms. We miss out on the distinctively provincial voice: the part of the folksong which the singer knows to be not quaint but authentic. Knows but usually cannot say.

Emily Dickinson, who could say, wrote her greatest poems during the Civil War, but in the nature of things she watched that origin from a distance. Her brother Austin likewise adopted a businesslike attitude toward the conflict in which his country was being reborn: as was lawful at the time, he bought his way out of the army by hiring a substitute. Living on thereafter with his history, however, he knew, sensitive provincial, that the terms of its speech had been changed. "A lonesome Sunday gone, and tomorrow Christmas," he wrote to his mistress at the end of 1883.

> What of it! The day I was brought up to believe was a joint device of the Devil and the Romish Church for the overthrow of the true religion, and accordingly to be frowned upon by all good people. . . . True religion has changed, and it is almost as bad now not to smile upon it. (Longsworth 174–75)

[2] "The victim [in the process of scapegoating] must be the first object of noninstinctual attention, and he or she provides a good starting point for the creation of sign systems because the ritual imperative consists in a demand for substitute victims, thus introducing the practice of substitution that is the basis of all symbolization" (René Girard, "Generative Scapegoating," Hamerton-Kelly 129).

As we watch it, the sense of the phrase "true religion" changes from irony to a vaguely favorable metaphor for some undefined social good. In each case, however, the phrase is a given: originating elsewhere, accepted or modified passively ("True religion has changed"), and affecting its perceiver only in his narcissism.

Austin Dickinson's sister Emily approached the phenomenon differently. She too accepted her symbols as parts of a lexicon imposed from outside, but she redefined them actively before she put them to use, testing the words and their social contexts against one another and understanding as she did so that significances change. A Christmas wreath laid by a friend on her father's grave thus became a little index of the change death brings to our idea of the forgivable. "I am sure you must have remembered that Father had 'Become as Little Children,' or you would never have dared send him a Christmas gift," the poet wrote to her friend, in grateful complicity; "for you know how he frowned upon Santa Claus—and all such prowling gentlemen" (L425). Contemplated in memory (for Emily Dickinson never visited her father's grave), the wreath lay open to interpretation like a word: a word of the enlarged, deprovincialized body of meaning which had overtaken the poet's father tongue.

Dickinson seems usually to have read and written in that historiographic way, listening for the moments when a detail of one historical environment becomes the context of another. She understood how the imputation of temporal significance to an event changes both the event and its interpreter.

> The Past is such a curious Creature
> To look her in the Face
> A Transport may receipt us
> Or a Disgrace—
>
> Unarmed if any meet her
> I charge him fly
> Her faded ammunition
> Might yet reply. (P1203)

The manuscript offers a variant reading for the last word: "destroy."

Dickinson appears to have written those words in about 1871, just a year before the South was rejoined to the Constitution by the words of the Amnesty Act. Amnesty means forgetting: a necessary thing, but bad for poets. Because vanished words are their faded ammunition, poets may find it harder than the rest of us to forget—harder, more painful, and more dangerous, even when therefore more necessary. But if the poet's task of memory has been carried out to its end, we readers will eventually find that its embodying vocabulary has become a part of our own language. We will have assimilated memory from the page.

Something like that seems to have happened in old age to Emerson's disciple Samuel Gray Ward when he looked at Emily Dickinson's poems and recognized their memorial enterprise as a work of historiography. In them, Ward saw, there continued to live the New England culture which, thanks to the Civil War, was now only a memory under sentence of oblivion.

> She is the quintessence of that element we all have who are of Puritan descent pur sang. We came to this country to think our own thoughts with nobody to hinder. Ascetics of course, & this our Thebaid. We conversed with our own souls till we lost the art of communicating with other people. The typical family grew up strangers to each other, as in this case. It was *awfully* high, but awfully lonesome. Such prodigies of shyness do not exist elsewhere. We got it from the English, but the English were not alone in a corner of the world for a hundred & fifty years with no outside interest. I sate next to Jones Very for three years & he was an absolute enigma till he flashed on me with the Barberry Bush. . . . If the gift of articulateness was not denied, you had Channing, Emerson, Hawthorne a stupendous example, & so many others. Mostly it was denied, & became a family fate. This is where Emily Dickinson comes in. She was the articulate inarticulate. That is why it appeals so to New England women. (Letter, 1891, qtd. in Lubbers 33)

Ward's letter was sent to Emily Dickinson's chosen mentor Thomas Wentworth Higginson, who had participated in the dislocations of life and language that reduced Ward's descriptions to the past tense. Higginson had been a suffragist, an abolitionist, the commander of a black regiment during the Civil War, and the first person ever to write down the words of a black spiritual, but he was also a man who could trace his Boston and Harvard descent back through generation after generation to the early seventeenth century. Ward and Higginson, dwellers in the same province as the poet who said "I see—New Englandly" (P285), undoubtedly felt that they had a certain proprietary claim to their understanding of Dickinson's intentions. But in the nature of things, these historical associations between writer and reader are temporary. When Higginson came to edit the first collection of Dickinson's poems, for instance, his co-editor was Austin Dickinson's mistress, Mabel Loomis Todd: an equally high-minded person in her own way and equally close to the poet, but nevertheless, in the nature of things, marginal to the culture that united Dickinson with Higginson and Ward. Mabel Loomis Todd had grown up in Washington, for one thing; for another, she was only nine years old when the Civil War ended. It was she who introduced Emily Dickinson, toward the end of the poet's life, to the music of Johann Sebastian Bach. If that had happened earlier, Dickinson's meter might sound different to us today: less obviously indebted to the hymnal; less provincial.

Or perhaps only provincial in a different way, at home less in its province than in ours. Consider what happened, for instance, on May 22, 1896, when Mabel Loomis Todd delivered her set speech about Emily Dickinson in an antipodal province. The setting was a salon in the residence of the president of what was then the Republic of Hawaii; the audience was a ladies' literary club, wives and sisters of the white planter oligarchy that had overthrown Hawaii's native monarch three years earlier. One of the ladies present assumed the nom de plume "Sibyl" for the occasion and wrote down for a local newspaper, the *Pacific Commercial Advertiser*, what she had heard. The *Advertiser* misspelled the poet's name in its headline the next morning but gave the story prominent play on page 3. "Friday morning in Mrs. Dole's drawing room," the *Advertiser* told the sugar planters of Honolulu,

> Mrs. Mabel Loomis Todd gave an informal talk on Emily Dickinson. This culminated in a most delightful manner the year's discussions of the Modern Novel Club, which after this triumphant session will take a summer vacation.

> The members of this club, then, reinforced by their guests, were spellbound by the magnetic charm of the speaker. . . . She is a most faithful and sympathetic interpreter of the elusive personality of this strange poetic genius. To her the world is indebted for its whiff of the rare sweet perfume of this sweet exotic. Mrs. Todd has chosen the Indian pipe as a fitting decorative emblem for the covers of the published poems.

The Indian pipe, a white plant which grows out of dead matter, is not found in Hawaii; its home is in the cold region where Emily Dickinson took it as an emblem of herself, "the preferred flower of life. . . . an unearthly booty" (L769). On the day Mabel Loomis Todd spoke of her, far from her home, Emily Dickinson had been ten years and a week dead. Mabel Todd and her listeners in Honolulu wanted the Indian pipe to grow again, wanted what we all want, to be transported by magic words into an authenticating nature where every plant has its signature; a knowable world, a province that can be lived in entirely, occupied fully from border to border. Emily Dickinson lived in one such province, filling her room with words. Like Emily Dickinson, the ladies in Mrs. Dole's parlor would have been dressed in white. But their garb, unlike hers, was the costume of a foreign land.

Embellished with the first publication of Dickinson's poem "The reticent volcano keeps / His never slumbering plan,"[3] adventurous Mrs. Todd's account of her Hawaiian experience with the Amherst Eclipse Expedition appeared later that year in the pages of a New York Christian magazine, the *Outlook* (Todd 50). A certain conquering energy carries the prose along; reporting on the death due to exhaustion of one of the expedition's scientists, Mrs. Todd briskly concludes, "it is most unfortunate that the series of articles she was preparing could not have been finished" (51). That energy wasn't uniquely Mrs. Todd's, of course; it was a shared inheritance of her culture. It lay on the ground in Honolulu too, in the form of a new building at a Honolulu school for the children of New England missionaries. That building is the main subject of Mrs. Todd's article, and history can help us see

[3] In his variorum, Johnson credits Todd's *Poems by Emily Dickinson*, 3rd ser. (1896) with the first publication of this poem (P1748). But in her article Todd refers to the poem as "yet unpublished" (50).

why. "The fine building of native stone, with its semi-tropical style of architecture, the brilliant electric lights, the band of musicians, the polished hard-wood finish of the interior, and the paintings, etchings, casts, and books," Mrs. Todd cries out in a flash of impersonal triumph, "did not present what the average American would have imagined as a typical scene of mid-Pacific civilization" (51). That May on the island of Oahu an unearthly booty had descended: Emily Dickinson's poetry. But it fell into a little pseudo–New England, shaded from the tropical sun. Mabel Loomis Todd was not a New Englander, nor were the ladies of Honolulu. But around the corpse of the poet who saw New Englandly, covering it from sight, was unfolded a paper screen of New England words.

> Many striking incidents of her life were related by Mrs. Todd, many bits of verse were quoted, sparks of verse forged at white heat, and from her letters many epigrammatic sentences. All helped in giving us a better impression of this woman who distilled drops of the essence of things. Many eyes besides the reader's glistened as she read the letter on immortality that Miss Dickinson had written after her mother's death.
>
> Mrs. Todd finished her brilliant characterization of Emily Dickinson, this poet whose verses published after her death have lived but five years. The hush that held the company after she ceased to speak was the greatest possible tribute to her magic as a speaker, and to the absorbing interest she had aroused in her poet-friend.
>
> ---
>
> It will be remembered that Mrs. Todd and her husband, Professor David Todd, are members of the astronomical party that the yacht Coronet is bearing to Japan. They are running the risk of a great disappointment, in that the precious two minutes and forty seconds of observation may fall in cloudy time; but we will fill their sails with good wishes, however, and may our hopes give them fresh winds and brilliant, starry skies in their desired haven.
>
> SIBYL.

And the polite words come to an end. There follows an advertisement for a water filter which is alleged to prevent Bright's Disease, the nephritis that killed Emily Dickinson at the age of fifty-five. "The report of three physicians connected with the Board of Health on the condition of the water which the people of Honolulu drink is valuable," writes the sardonic advertiser, "if for no other reason, that [*sic*] it gives one time to select the right company to insure one's life with and to make necessary arrangements for cemetery lot and undertaker."

Arranged on the page by a compositor, the language laps at the edges of "Sibyl's" story and recedes. Even in 1896, the heap of words that covered the memory of Emily Dickinson was not a simple mound. The prose styles were distinctively characteristic of the era, but each had its own individual and class uniqueness: "Sibyl's," Mrs. Todd's, and the sardonic advertiser's. Congeneric in distinctly identifiable ways with other modes of writing, histories were being erected all around the poet's text. Meanwhile, within it, the sheltering walls of the province of meaning were breaking down. Keeping time with the rhythm of a private history, the text recorded the vanishing of its own internal significance.

A loss of something ever felt I—
The first that I could recollect
Bereft I was—of what I knew not
Too young that any should suspect

A mourner walked among the children
I notwithstanding went about
As one bemoaning a Dominion
Itself the only Prince cast out—

Elder, Today, a session wiser
And fainter, too, as Wiseness is—
I find myself still softly searching
For my Delinquent Palaces—

And a Suspicion, like a Finger
Touches my Forehead now and then
That I am looking oppositely
For the site of the Kingdom of Heaven— (P959)

We are far more distant than the ladies of Honolulu from Emily Dickinson's province. A phrase like "the Kingdom of Heaven" is harder now than it used to be. It has acquired a subsequent history which needs to be read according to its own conventions.

Subsequent history has shown us too that some words are readable only within the walls of their generating ghetto. Late in the century of annihilation, where are we to look for the site of the kingdom of heaven?

Dickinson, living in an era of romantic exploration, looked in herself. That is harder for us to do today, with honor; Freud and Hitler between them have reduced to an adolescent episode the Romantic quest for meaning in the individual soul. Either we know ourselves too well to play the game, or we are ashamed to go in search of our sole selves when the ghosts of murdered millions stand mutely before us. So we approach ourselves indirectly, through the elaborate stratagem of a secondary history. We read biographies; we seek *mana* in the antiquarian. R. W. Franklin's facsimile *Manuscript Books of Emily Dickinson* is meant to help us read the printed texts that sit on our own bookshelves, but when we look at its two fat brown volumes we dream first about the handwriting they contain: Emily Dickinson's handwriting. We meditate on that, or rather on the thought of it: Emily Dickinson's handwriting, Emily Dickinson's ink, paper touched by Emily Dickinson, words seen by Emily Dickinson's eyes—"eyes, like the Sherry in the Glass, that the Guest leaves" (L268). The poet becomes a fantasy figure in the *if only* game of virtual history. *I*, thinks the teenage boy or the feminist critic, *I* would have understood Emily. She wouldn't have run away from *me*. And if we are embarrassed at playing this game directly between ourselves and the poet, we play it with the data of biography and text. Whole fantasy lives are acted out in the pages of *Dickinson Studies*.

But of course those lives, *qua* transcripts of the ever-changing encounter between a self and its defining lexicon of words and phenomena, are a mirror, not a lamp. They refer only inward. Like the meeting between Mabel Loomis Todd and the Modern Novel Club, they become occasions of self-gratification. The words of the poems, the words with their history in them, remain unread.

Allen Tate, one of the authors of *I'll Take My Stand*, a southerner with a deep sense of what it meant to owe allegiance to an unread history, attempted to teach his readers what they were reading. If he had read Samuel Gray Ward's letter to Higginson, it would have mattered greatly to him that Ward (1817–1907) was reading Dickinson on one side of an abyss of time and space, while he, Allen Tate (1899–1979), stood with us and the ladies of Honolulu on the other. For Ward and Higginson, Dickinson's place in her culture was a part of the history of an event; for Tate and the ladies of Honolulu and us, it can be only a literary epiphenomenon. Having felt the New England cold before and after Emerson and Dickinson altered the climate, Ward could know what Dickinson meant, or at least could believe that he knew. But Tate in 1932, writing his way back to Dickinson through a series of aftermaths, could hope only to interpret at second hand, like a browser in an antique shop.

So the heroine of Tate's essay "New England Culture and Emily Dickinson" springs from the soil of New England culture, but she blossoms in the ground of universal history. As Tate reads her, Dickinson is a character in the text of a tale that has been told, through the ages, about every one of us, by every one of us: the story of the expulsion from Eden. Only the translation Tate uses is modern. It was originally published by T. S. Eliot, and it is called the theory of the dissociation of sensibility.

> She lacks almost radically the power to seize upon and understand abstractions for their own sake; she does not separate them from the sensuous illuminations that she is so marvelously adept at; like Donne, she *perceives abstraction* and *thinks sensation*. . . . It is impossible to imagine what she might have done with drama or fiction; for, not approaching the puritan temper and through it the puritan myth, through human action, she is able to grasp the terms of the myth directly and by a feat that amounts almost to anthropomorphism, to give them a luminous tension, a kind of drama among themselves. (Tate, "New England Culture" 159–60)

That is, Emily Dickinson's poems are an autobiography by Eve: the Eve who ate the apple and then clothed herself. They are a gloss on the horror of that second event: the emblem of a separation of outer signification from inner reality, word from meaning. Naked, Eve named the animals because she knew; clothed, she will be able only to name. Or, as Dickinson said, at the height of her power, about her words: "While my thought is undressed—I can make the distinction, but when I put them in the Gown—they look alike, and numb" (L261). Twenty-two years later, less than two years before her death, she realized that Eve's gesture of concealment had been the master trope of her own language. "In all the circumference of Expression," Dickinson wrote to Mr. and Mrs. Eben Loomis, "those guileless words of Adam and Eve never were surpassed, 'I was afraid and hid Myself'" (L946). The poet had refused to meet the parents of her brother's close friend Mabel Loomis Todd and was trying to explain why; that is this sentence's originating context. But with Tate's help we can read it in a more general way: historically, as a part of the corpus of Dickinson's language. Read from within that corpus, Dickinson's scriptural citation incorporates itself into her language at every semiotic level, in both content and form. It is an act of appropriation. Adam alone said "I was afraid" (Genesis 3:10), but Emily Dickinson had her own good reasons for claiming the words for Eve and herself. They are an ontological program for her; they tell us, when we read them in the context imposed on them by the poet of New England, that Dickinson thought of her writing as an event in the intellectual history of which dissociation is both cause and consequence: original sin. Or, as Tate put it, her poetry "comes out of an intellectual life towards which it feels no moral responsibility. Cotton Mather would have burnt her for a witch" (167).

Mather's gravamen, and Tate's, would have been something like the charm of Dickinson's refusals: a charm whose only rhetorical purpose is to conceal, while it ostensibly explains, the poet's sundering herself from the human *Umwelt*. Community alone, after all, can make language mean; only a consensus of meaning can qualify us to experience things authentically in themselves. To Tate, Dickinson's power to separate mind from moral could have occurred only in a culture whose language was socially incapable of meaning—a culture to which Tate gave the synecdochic name of "New England." Tate was able to personify and allegorize "New England" in this way because he had elaborated an apotropaic countersynecdoche two years previously: a synecdoche for wholeness of heart which Tate named "the Southern religion." "New England" is a bare noun, but "the Southern religion" has a definite article, *is* a definite article. Even before they have done any work in a sentence, the words of that phrase seem to claim for themselves an emblematic value. It is a value definitively opposed to "New England": to New England the mercurial, the alienated, the empty, that which can conceive of nothing beyond the boundaries of its estranged self. *New England* in Tate's 1930 essay was Henry Adams, "who never quite understood what he was looking for. He spent much of his youth, like Henry James, learning the manners of the English agrarians, without being by right of soil entitled to them, and thus never suspecting that the best he might hope to do was to learn them by rote" ("Southern Religion" 171). And yet there is this hopeful note: Adams suffered the harm of New England culture, but at least he was unable to communicate that harm to others. The culture limited its own evil.

In the poems of Emily Dickinson, however, Tate has discovered that the New England disease of inauthenticity possessed not only the power to blight but the power to reproduce itself and bring forth speech: to realize itself through history. New England culture, for Tate, is what enabled Emily Dickinson to teach herself and history what is very nearly an absolute language: a discourse whose substance is, because it has to be, only itself. Dickinson doesn't speak *for* anything. In the moral drama of which her poems are the record, Dickinson doesn't use language referentially, as Adams does in his third-person chronicle of his education. On the contrary; as the history of her culture passes through Emily Dickinson, it loses its acquired mass of connotation and definition and becomes language directly, without any boundary or mediation but the laws of its own grammar. Between Dickinson's perception and the word there is no *differance*. In her poems the event and the word enact forever their double origin, each arising out of the other, each becoming the other's end, each obliterating the other as it is taken into experience.

Tate's essay implies something further: that for Dickinson, word and event each articulate the unknowability of the other. In Dickinson's consciousness the event is inseparable from its past—the body of words out of which is born our consciousness of the present. The present comes into existence trailing words; the words tell of the history they have completed by uttering it; the history confronts the poet with her own inability to live free of it. This history is pure, unconcerned with mere life; the events we live and die for are only larger or smaller approximations of the idea, an idea as brilliant and distant as a star. "Momentousness is ripening," says the poet in an affectionate note. "I hope that all is firm" (L750). All is indeed firm; in this history, an absolute verbal knowability waits for us at the limit of life.

Allen Tate longs for that terminal word, yet he dreads it. In his "Ode to the Confederate Dead" he cries:

> Now that the salt of their blood
> Stiffens the saltier oblivion of the sea,
> Seals the malignant purity of the flood,
> What shall we who count our days and bow
> Our heads with a commemorial woe
> In the ribboned coats of grim felicity,
> What shall we say of the bones, unclean,
> Whose verdurous anonymity will grow?
>
> . . . . .
>
> We shall say only the leaves
> Flying, plunge and expire (627)

And Tate the critic explains: "There is nothing but death, the mere naturalism of death at that—spiritual extinction in the decay of the body. Autumn and the leaves are death; the men who exemplified in a grand style an 'active faith' are dead; there are only the leaves. . . . There is no practical solution, no solution offered for the benefit of moralists" (625 n.6). There is only consciousness, the zone between life and death where history shapes words into meaning. Tate's metaphor for consciousness in this poem is the bleak myth of Narcissus, which he interprets as a parable of "the failure of the human personality to function objectively in nature and society" (625 n.5). The self's only province is itself. To live consciously is to live suspended between knowledge and action. Consciousness, in this poem by the interpreter of Emily Dickinson, leads to—*is*—powerlessness and marginality.

The provincializing movement inward that Tate maps has been the great journey taken by poetry in the twentieth century. It has been taken under protest, and those who have mapped its path have held to the hope of counterexamples, an Eldorado of infinitely unrestricted cultural reference *là-bas*. "In its extreme self-consciousness," says Eliot of Yeats's occultism, "it approaches the mythology of D. H. Lawrence on its more decadent side. We admire Mr. Yeats for having outgrown it. . . . he has arrived at greatness against the greatest odds; if he has not arrived at a central and universal philosophy he has at least discarded, for the most part, the trifling and eccentric, the provincial in time and place" (*After Strange Gods* 50–51). Eliot was expressing a hope; Yeats never did outgrow his occultism. Like Eliot, he desired that consciousness expand from the province of the self to the imperium of the universal; only his choice of agents to effect that expansion was different. And for both poets equally, and for twentieth-century poetry in general, the very vehemence of the desire testifies to the unbreakable concentration of Narcissus's gaze. Perhaps the single most distinctive characteristic of modern art has been its power, as an artifact, to educate us about the nature of that gaze. It draws us forward to the limits of ourselves as if we were citizens of an aquarium.

The subjects of Gauguin's *Two Nudes on a Tahitian Beach*, for instance, propose to exchange a part of our sensorium for theirs. They come to us standing on a hummocky ground that is pink and metallic blue like the surface of molten steel, and what is tactile for them there has become visual for us here, on our side of the canvas: the heat, the changing temperatures and textures of what lies under our bare feet. A dog is passing behind the two women, and where they obliterate his body he ceases to exist, because in this painting of what happens under the vertical sunblaze of the tropics, perspective is only a stacking of light on light. All around the women in the canvas's flatness, the ocean erects a cobalt wall. The women can move out from themselves and into their blue space, but we cannot. For us, the sense of Gauguin's light and heat can only be nostalgia: a yearning for a shared space and time, a shared knowledge of what is, a shared history.

Gauguin's painting hangs in the Honolulu Academy of Arts. A few city blocks south of the wall on which it hangs, the Pacific Ocean really is a dark cobalt blue. You can see it there, across the street from a shopping center. But the painting is bluer. Its color is the exotic: the color of distance, dramatic irony, and a nostalgia projected from itself to us through the lightless blank of historical incommensurability. In that emptiness the ladies of the Modern

Novel Club float, forever hearing for the first time the voice of Mabel Loomis Todd as she tells them there was once a woman named Emily Dickinson. We cannot hear what they said to one another as the news engulfed them. The air we breathe holds us prisoner in our own lives. We want presence: "what [Derrida] also calls an 'ultimate referent'—a self-certifying absolute, or ground, or foundation, directly present to our awareness outside the play of language itself" (Abrams 204). But our sense of presence is always contaminated by locale: the flux of phenomena passing through us from the history of events. Locale is our sense of "the life of significant soil" (Eliot, *Four Quartets*, "The Dry Salvages"): an unarticulated and unarticulable sense that where we are is somehow a supplement to the meaning of the things we say and hear.

The provincial can be defined as a condition in which locale is felt to be at least as important to speech as is the free authenticity of the uttering self. Considered as part of an ideal topography, the provincial lies between two other historical zones: virtual history, which is nothing *but* a locale of space or time, and the ghetto. In the ghetto there is no locale; there is only a mute, latent, noumenal presence. What Dickinson called "costumeless consciousness" (P1454) is the ghetto's only mode of existence: a radical and therefore speechless authenticity that can be perceived only from the outside—"where the Meanings, are" (P258). To us looking at the bodies of Gauguin's women or to the Nazi photographer looking at the bodies of his captive Jews, there comes historical recognition through the instrumentality of dramatic irony. We who look possess the secrets of foreknowledge and retrospect; though we can never partake of presence inside its frame, we can at least know the past and the future which lie outside it. That knowledge is bleak enough, of course. In physical terms, at least, we can know, absolutely, that there is a self-certifying absolute and that that absolute is annihilation. The physicists have given it a metaphoric name: *black hole*, "supposed to be an invisible collapsed star so condensed that neither light nor matter can escape from its gravitational field" (*Webster's New World Dictionary*). Perhaps the metaphor is too cute, but the physicists had little choice: they had to name this no-thing before they could think of it, and nothingness can be represented only by virtual history's endless regress of metaphor. Nevertheless, words notwithstanding, the black hole is *there*. In its empty way, it is what the deconstructionists would jeeringly call a presence.[4] We may want to build ourselves a conceptual refuge from the annihilation that it represents to us, and reassure ourselves that the *mise en abyme* of representation has no bottom. Deconstruction at least offers us the desperate hope that there will always be something left to deconstruct. But deconstruction's consolations are counterfactual. We do possess a knowledge to the contrary. It fills us as we look.

The objects of our gaze, on the other hand, cannot know; they can only be. Their bodies remain only body. They subsist in a ghetto whose walls separate absolutely; knowledge cannot cross them in either direction.

> Die Ros'ist ohn' Warum, sie blühet, weil sie blühet,
> Sie acht't nicht ihrer selbst, fragt nicht, ob man sie siehet.
>
> —Angelus Silesius, "Ohne Warum"

It blossoms because it blossoms, says the mystical epigrammatist; the rose is without why. The inhabitants of a ghetto or a ghetto-category appear in history's record to have a similar ontological sufficiency. To the extent that they are known, they are wholly some words on a page or some pictures in a book. To the extent that they exist solely as a record compiled in a language written or read in other terms than theirs, the terms of their own

[4] At the time S. Chandrasekhar received the Nobel Prize for his efforts to visualize that invisible presence and bring our thoughts about it under the control of language, he explained what he had done this way: "Black holes are macroscopic objects with masses varying from a few solar masses to millions of solar masses. To the extent they may be considered as stationary and isolated, to that extent, they are all, every single one of them, described *exactly* [in terms of their mass and their angular momentum]. This is the only instance we have of an exact description of a macroscopic object. Macroscopic objects, as we see them all around us, are governed by a variety of forces, derived from a variety of approximations to a variety of physical theories. In contrast, the only elements in the construction of black holes are our basic concepts of space and time. They are, thus, almost by definition, the most perfect macroscopic objects there are in the universe. And since the general theory of relativity provides a single unique two-parameter family of solutions for their description, they are the simplest objects as well" (505).

language have been falsified. The truth of what they were remains unknowable, beyond words.

But of course the rose is what it is because of some inner necessity. It grows into what itself was always to be: rose. Its history is an absolute. The ghetto, on the other hand, is a garden of counternecessity. Visible in the present only as a disorder within boundaries, it becomes conceivable as a single entity only in retrospect, under the control of categories imposed on it by historical textuality. The rose, says Angelus Silesius, pays no heed to itself and does not care whether it is seen (trans. Leonard Forster 143). It exists as an idea prior to the word *rose*. But the Zulu in Johannesburg is what the statute books and the newspapers have made her. Her status as a historical subject originates in a skin-deep integument of words. The ghetto becomes a ghetto by having been entered into an archive.

Now an interesting thing about writers is that they labor to create archives around themselves. They regard this reduction of themselves to words as Thoreau does in *Walden*: "Some must work in fields if only for the sake of tropes and expression, to serve a parable-maker one day" (chap. 7, 122). But the occupation is hazardous, for sometimes the archive goes explosively to completion and becomes *écriture*: a textual mass substantially independent of any reference to the nonverbal. "I think that autumn must be the best season to journey over even the *Green* Mountains," proclaims the proud archivist in "A Yankee in Canada" (246). "You frequently exclaim to yourself, What *red* maples!" The engineer Just, who wrote about gas vans, was able to sustain such concentrated verbality for pages at a time. But Thoreau's normal expression was less pure than this. Ordinarily, Thoreau was able to keep intact a barrier of acknowledgeable reality between himself and his archive. However isolated from his townsmen's language he was, he never built himself a ghetto of his own words.

Consider, for instance, what happened separately in the summer of 1847 to Thoreau and to his fellow citizens of Concord. Somewhere out in the history of events the Mexican War was going on: a one-sided patriotic stupidity waged against the air. For the citizens of Concord, the war was an event in the only kind of history they knew: verbal history, a history to be created for its readers and hearers at a distance, passively. It was a wholly parasitic investment of language and emotion: the seizure of an idea, followed by the dissipation of its reality into words. Around Concord, words had begun forming a curtain in the air: something to separate the thought of history from its enacting deeds. From the distance Thoreau could see a ghetto taking shape around the commonwealth that gave him life and language.

We know his reaction. A writer who had gone deliberately to live in the nonverbal, Thoreau set out to create a field to work in: a palimpsest cleared out of the woods, latent with verbal meaning.

> When there were several bands of musicians, it sounded as if all the village was a vast bellows, and all the buildings expanded and collapsed alternately with a din. But sometimes it was a really noble and inspiring strain that reached these woods, and the trumpet that sings of fame, and I felt as if I could spit a Mexican with a good relish,—for why should we always stand for trifles?—and looked round for a woodchuck or a skunk to exercise my chivalry upon. These martial strains seemed as far away as Palestine, and reminded me of a march of crusaders in the horizon, with a slight tantivy and tremulous motion of the elm-tree tops which overhang the village. This was one of the *great* days; though the sky had from my clearing only the same everlastingly great look that it wears daily, and I saw no difference in it.
>
> It was a singular experience which I cultivated with beans, what with planting, and hoeing, and harvesting, and threshing, and picking over, and selling them,—the last was the hardest of all,—I might add eating, for I did taste. I was determined to know beans. (*Walden* 121)

When a slang phrase enters the archive, we know that its original impulse as slang—a random transcendence of culture's archival rules—has died. It has become merely symbolic: a signified whose signifier has been forgotten or misconstrued.[5] Unlisted

[5] "The fact that many [at Fruitlands, Bronson Alcott's Transcendentalist community] favored symbolic protests over social reform betrays the basic conservatism of a group who, no matter how alienated from their own vocations or even society in general, were still afraid of widespread popular disruptions. Samuel Larned, for example, came from Rhode Island, the most feudal state in New England with its extremely limited franchise and family system of factory labor. But Larned rebelled against the status quo by traveling through New

in the original *OED*, "He don't know beans" is traced back to 1855 (a year after the first publication of *Walden*) in the 1933 supplement, and to 1833 in the 1972 supplement. The process of archival rehabilitation has been going on for a long time. By 1847 the phrase must already have been a cliché, the kind of thing that the exasperated citizens of Concord would have said about their self-important young townsman David Henry Thoreau, who persisted in writing his Christian names backwards. Continuing to think of words as independent entities, to be shifted in and out of order in accordance with some nonverbal properties of being that he called higher laws, Thoreau tried to tell his townsmen that the word and the bean are different things, and that not to know the former is the first step toward knowing the latter. If Thoreau created an archive, it was an archive of nonverbal realities only provisionally and for the time being expressed in words.

Emily Dickinson's archive was different, different in a way that strikes everyone who has sat down and read ten pages of the *Poems* straight through. The difference is this: in Dickinson's poems and letters the archive takes on its full totalitarian shape as pure verbal power exerted only on behalf of itself. Certain words, for instance—"awe," "disc," "white" and about a dozen others—occur over and over in Dickinson's poems and letters, in contexts which imply that something of the utmost seriousness is being uncovered to our view. But that something, whatever it is, appears to have only a tenuous referential attachment to anything outside the poems. Some readers have taken that as a reason for declining to learn the poems' lexicon. For them, R. P. Blackmur's analysis—"The meanings become the conventions of meanings, the asserted agreement that meaning is there" (221)—has the oddly comforting effect of a "Wanted" notice read in the post office: it persuades them to lock up ordinary meaning with the rest of the valuables, and then to turn Emily Dickinson into a topic of ordinary conversation.

Other readers, however, have accepted the words' dominion.

England swearing at everyone he met, on the premise that profane language, uttered in a pure spirit, could be redeemed from vulgarity, even while men, women, and children clearly remained unredeemed in his native state" (Rose 129–30).

For them, the archive becomes a ghetto. From within, they have looked for coherence: some correlation, if only as a starting point, with external reference and ordinary meaning. But the inhabitants of a ghetto, virtually by definition, can never understand what is happening to them. The best they can hope to achieve is an act of faith, and of course faith is one of the most powerful terms in Dickinson's lexicon, written or read. "Dickinson's withdrawal of language was perfectly, even predictably, consistent with her life," explains David Porter in his study in Dickinsonian apologetics. "When she went into reclusion in her father's house in Amherst, she took her language with her. That is why words like 'circumference' or 'wife' have no ties to reality. They are language talking to itself, not negotiating with the outside world. In this separated state, Dickinson's idiom existed not as representation, but rather in its exclusive state only as literature" (116). So that even though we are now behind the walls of Dickinson's archive without hope of escape, we can at least be assured that our incarceration was executed in an orderly fashion, with every attention paid to the due process by which a body of fully conventionalized meanings became what Dickinsonians live with: a private symbol system—that is, an elaborated arbitrariness of reference between signified and signifier, a paranoia.

Readers over the years have attempted to reconventionalize that symbol system by attaching it to other bodies of reference. The psychiatrist John Cody, for instance, reads Dickinson's poems as a product and a description of mental illness. Approaching from the ambit of a different system, the feminist poet Adrienne Rich reads them as the rhetoric of a nonpatriarchal language, unclear only insofar as our own lives have been made unclear. And these systematizations themselves can coalesce. Cody (409) and Rich (184) agree in a general way, for instance, that poems such as P601 are about female sexuality.

> A still—Volcano—Life—
> That flickered in the night—
> When it was dark enough to do
> Without erasing sight—
>
> A quiet—Earthquake Style—
> Too subtle to suspect

By natures this side Naples—
The North cannot detect

The Solemn—Torrid—Symbol—
The lips that never lie—
Whose hissing Corals part—and shut—
And Cities—ooze away—

Insofar as we are all Freudians now, I suppose we too can agree that this poem is about (among other things) female sexuality. That interpretation may very well help us read it with greater coherence and a heightened understanding of its perceived power over us. But suppose we read *away* from the poem for a moment—say, for long enough to consider some independent connotations of the words "volcano" and "Naples."

What we may see then is this: two items of the exotic have been brought home to New England. That happened, often, in Dickinson's youth. George Frisbie Whicher reminds us that "it was not her geography alone that led Emily Dickinson to attribute to the oriole 'the splendor of a Burmah.' She had heard a returned missionary speak of the wonders of that far country, and sing 'From Greenland's icy mountains' in Burman" (20). New England was full of souvenirs: domesticated items of the exotic which, in turn, domesticated their possessors as the new names passed into the old repertoire of emotions. No American vocabulary at the time was adequate to describe the experience of this influx, because the exotic is by definition and etymology that which is always outside; that which fails to fit into the classes of any preexisting way of understanding. But then Emily Dickinson created an archive.

An archive containing, in this case, the words "Naples" and "volcano": a pair of words entered, with an arbitrarily selected array of their connotations, into a geography the reverse of the one studied by the missionary: a geography of the interior. Liberated from the boundaries of the schoolroom map, "volcano" takes on a new and universal exoticism. It is now everywhere, like the Warsaw ghetto, diffused into the air we breathe: no longer knowable in the particular but universally unknowable. If S. Chandrasekhar's black holes (505) are a perfect negativity perfectly knowable, Dickinson's volcano is something like a converse of that: a sense datum rendered unknowable by verbal representation.

Dickinson stated her theory succinctly in a love letter: "Dont you know that 'No' is the wildest word we consign to Language?" (L562). This negation—this refusal to defer to the ordinary historical conventions of syntax and association—is what makes her verse formally undecipherable. But that is the value of this verse for our sense of history. An archive of language "in its exclusive state only as literature," Dickinson's poems and letters are a counterhistory in words to the history that can be understood only in images: the history of the great annihilations. Be the locus of its power alphabetical order or a race classification committee, archive is the domain of the arbitrary. The poet of the archive gave us its theory, with examples. Historians should be grateful.

8

Sermon with Footnote

The archive is something like a library of the real: a body of words referring to what we hope or believe or desire to conceive of without words. If the "dauntingly extensible sequence [of signifieds and signifiers] end[s] 'out there,' beyond language, in the world . . . when signs are used to refer to things as they verifiably are" (Sturrock), it begins here, in the archive, where words take on whatever intelligibility they possess at the boundary between language and not-language: where the meanings are. But of course that boundary is a blurry one. Inside the turbulent zone where significance manufactures itself out of symbols and phenomena, "things as they verifiably are" lose some of their verifiable presence and take on different properties.

Consider: while I was writing this paragraph, the air was full of the sound of rifle and machine-gun fire. An armed helicopter thumped its way overhead and whirred down to a landing. Then from farther off, approaching, came the sound of a light plane in serious trouble. It flew into view, a little Cessna with army markings, veering and yawing, its wings tipping wildly up and down. It circled; almost stalled; recovered; retraced its struggling course; pushed hard into a desperate turn, churned away; returned; retreated; returned. On the ground the small-arms fire continued: a short burst, then silence, then a steady *tok tok tok* from not very far away. Meanwhile, I was sitting in front of a computer, writing a book about literary history.

The history of events was being reconstructed for purposes of instruction and entertainment. On a wooded hill across the street from my house in Honolulu, a television series was being filmed. Twenty years ago, some of you who are reading these words may have been involved in its subject: the Vietnam War. You may have memories that seem to you to possess meaning unmediated, *an sich*. But the language of your memory is now undergoing aestheticization. Like Gauguin's nudes, you are being converted by what you are—a shape and a color, or a name in a war diary—into the artifact of a history separate from yourself. You are becoming an example.

Example is that which has been taken out of our hands, then displayed to us in the vitrine of a different context. It is always alienated from its subject, because it is always separated from its subject by its speaker's purpose, a telos of discourse which the subject does not possess. If we are interested in "things as they verifiably are," example is an abuse of our faith in the comprehensibility of objects as such. Still, we seem to require that imposture. We need our experience to serve us as a body of examples. If we can't say, "For instance . . ." when we recall something that has passed from us, we have been deprived of our own role in its history. The phenomena themselves we can't know; only when we use them in the service of a personal motive do we feel we are beginning to understand, in retrospect. We can't speak the things, but we want to speak the words they are labeled with. And to speak those words we have to use them with regard to a syntax of ethical or ontological entities outside the historical grammar that governed the original transaction between us and that which has passed. Considered deconstructively, history is a language consisting of an endless regress of exemplary instances.

But consider what happens when this regress is brought up hard against the nonverbal. Consider what happens, for instance, when you attach a footnote to a sermon.

Consider the sermon especially, because the sermon is an expository genre whose examples work in a particularly pure way. Other didactic genres, such as the beast fable and the emblem picture and the narrative painting, tend to work inductively, leading their reader or viewer from the example to a conclusion based on it. But the sermon works the other way, deductively. The sermon is a machine for converting data into examples. The sermon's subject matter always becomes a body of examples *of*, and the signifying system that regulates this process is a text that originates outside the example's epistemological ambit. Orthodoxy is, after all, a reading which existed before its signifiers were discovered. It is grounded in a pre-text which has always already been read. It deciphers itself to us through examples, but it collapses every example into a single context. Under that treatment, the examples themselves cease to become the vehicle of any meaning except self-referentiality.

But sometimes an example calls our attention to the possibility that it can also exist in another context, and then something interesting happens: it stops being an example. It becomes one of the "things as they verifiably are": a datum of the preverbal material of history. Here on the page is the sermon, in all its volume; there at the bottom of the page is the quiet footnote. What happens when we drop our eyes to read that sentence is a deconstruction of the figural by the literal: an antientropic reduction of the cooked to the raw.

The text I have in mind is an American Thanksgiving sermon, "The Feast of Harvest," published in 1869. A minor problem in the exercise of historical imagination here is that we can't fully respond to this sermon as we might have in the years just after the Civil War. That first congregation of readers was a part of one interpretive community, and we are a part of another. Still, we probably do feel thankful for the good things in our lives, and we probably can still respond easily enough, *mutatis mutandis*, to the minister who reduced the idea of electricity to an example of general good this way:

> The power that at the close of the last century, by means of a pith-ball electronometer, carried signals for amusement to an adjoining room, now flashes in the real business of life, through more than a hundred thousand miles of Electric Telegraph. Verily the embryonic germ hath ripened into fruit! . . . The effects upon the breadth of commerce, and the steadfastness of trade; upon the uniformity of stock markets, and prices current, at the Bourse, on the Royal Exchange, in Third Street, and Wall Street; upon the

> perfecting of an international police, upon politics, and literature, and news, and the fashions; in a word—upon all the great physical interests of life, have been eloquently expounded. But, great as they are, they are not the greatest. They are indeed only the radiant petals of a seed-infolding flower, whose ripened fruit is in the *moral.*
>
> A great transformation in the conditions of national life—a breaking down of the barriers of national prejudice—a virtual union of all races by the ties of amity and common interest—these, and such as these, are to be the nobler results of this achievement! These magic wires, stretching over all lands, through all waters, are *earth's strong hearth-cords!*—making the dead planet a living creature, sensitive, through every fibre of its gigantic frame, to a rude touch anywhere—along whose quivering nerves and throbbing pulses, the great human HEART shall beat, and the great human MIND think! (294–95)

It goes on, but you can see what this minister is doing: turning a historical fact into an example by reducing it to the vehicle of a metaphor. There's nothing unusual about that—about either the procedure itself or the use to which it is put here. Americanists will probably have noticed a family resemblance, for instance, between these two paragraphs and Clifford's "ascending spiral curve" speech in chapter 17 of *The House of the Seven Gables*. Part of the intention behind that speech is satiric: Hawthorne distrusted the Transcendentalists' habit of spiritualizing everything they saw into an intimation from the Oversoul.

> "Then there is electricity;—the demon, the angel, the mighty physical power, the all-pervading intelligence!" exclaimed Clifford. . . . "Is it a fact—or have I dreamed it—that, by means of electricity, the world of matter has become a great nerve, vibrating thousands of miles in a breathless point of time? Rather, the round globe is a vast head, a brain, instinct with intelligence! Or, shall we say, it is itself a thought, nothing but thought, and no longer the substance which we deemed it!"
>
> "If you mean the telegraph," said the old gentleman, glancing his eye toward its wire, alongside the rail-track, "it is an excellent thing;—that is, of course, if the speculators in cotton and politics don't get possession of it. A great thing indeed, sir; particularly as regards the detection of bank-robbers and murderers."

And though he sounds Platonic enough in the excerpt we have just read, the author of the Thanksgiving sermon would probably have agreed with the old gentleman. Generally speaking, after all, preachers are practical critics. Their concern is to discover the nature of "things as they verifiably are," and their hermeneutic of sacred history is prior to any text. Because scripture is the record of that which has always already been, the sermon is always an interpretation a priori. Its archive is a fully deconstructed lexicon, an endless regress of examples.

Here is the preacher, therefore, intent on plucking a thing out of the universe and reducing it to an example of *doxa*; here, sullenly facing him, squats the thing in all its fractious, irreducible substantiality. Lewis Carroll's Humpty Dumpty got his stubbornest words to mean what he wanted them to mean by paying them overtime, but the preacher has no such resources at his disposal. All he can do with his example is to point it out and then move on to the next one. The preacher's examples aren't susceptible to anatomy; they can only be alluded to.

So this preacher alludes. But what his analysis lacks in depth it makes up for in sweep. He chooses for his examples of spiritual progress not just science and politics—what the Victorians called the march of intellect—but also some contemporary manifestations of what we would now call pop culture: spiritualism, for instance, and the productions of the loud and fuzzy late-Romantic poets who were known then as the Spasmodic School. He doesn't approve of such things, of course. But they have a use: they provide him with the ultimate example of them all. Their name is legion; they are an emblem of ubiquity. And as such, they can testify. That is their purpose for existing: to serve as the example that they are. "All these things," the preacher says,

> ludicrous and lamentable as they are, self-considered, nevertheless, as indications of the movement of the popular mind, are, to a thoughtful man, full of moment. They are like refuse-wood on the waters, indicating the great tide-currents of thought toward a higher spirituality,—like sere leaves, falling in a forest, signifying with their sad voices that the autumn-time is near, with its grand gathering of harvest.

> Nor are these signs false. For, in the midst of these manifestations, *the true Church of God hath been wonderfully roused to a new life of spirituality!* . . .
>
> Since Christ came, there have been but three revival seasons comparable with the present; the old Pentecost, in the first century, the Reformation in the sixteenth, and the great Awakening in the eighteenth; and each of these was an epoch of change in the Church, not only general, but permanent. Each lifted the Church to, and left her in, a higher spiritual condition.
>
> Now, if this be the law of the present, then we seem to be drawing nigh to the great millennial day-spring. (298)

And the preacher goes on adducing examples for another full page, drawing the conclusion that these examples demonstrate "a new law of Christian progress." The existence and working of this law are incontrovertible, for they too can be demonstrated by example.

> Let a man walk through the husbandry of a land, and find, here and there, a small field, wherein are a few ripened and scattered ears, and he regards them as the premature fruits of a shallow soil, or an untempered sun, and reads therein no sure sign of the golden autumn. But if, on the contrary, as he walks abroad, he finds the whole land roused by a common impulse—if every hamlet is noisy with men who sharpen the sickle and drive the wain afield—if all the sunny mountain slopes are vocal with the song of the grape-gatherers, and the mower's scythe gleams in every valley, and reapers bind the yellow sheaves in all the great corn-fields—then he feels sure that no inconsiderable and untimely growth is being gathered, but that truly the latter rains have fallen, and autumnal suns have warmed the broad earth, and that this song of girded men is the great hymn of harvest. (299)

And here we have it, example in its ideal state: a single metaphor, two huge sentences long, elaborated into a statement which enjoys equal epistemological status with the preacher's citation of the fact of the telegraph. Example has brought us almost to the brink of pure poetry, a body of statements whose only truth-value is in their having been uttered.

Almost, but not quite. Because at the end of his second sentence ("autumnal suns have warmed the broad earth, and . . . this song of girded men is the great hymn of harvest") the preacher has placed an extra little punctuation mark: an asterisk. And when you look down at the foot of the page, you see a strange little three-word footnote appending itself to the preacher's example. It reads: "Preached in 1858."

You see what that does: it sends us outside the text, back into the domain where the preacher's example once ran wild and free. If we follow it there, it will lead us to a history book—say, Perry Miller's *Life of the Mind in America from the Revolution to the Civil War*. And in that book we will find that the Great Revival of 1857–58 was indeed a major event in the history of American Protestantism. It was indeed spontaneous; it did indeed sweep the country; what Miller calls its calm delirium (92) did indeed presage the millennium to thousands of serious, well-meaning men and women. But it also fared as other revivals have done: it came to an end. And then there came something else to occupy the minds of the preacher's congregation. As Miller says, "1858 lifted the populace to its most grandiose conception of unity just before slavery sundered the country" (94).

So that the preacher's footnote tells us this: the example was misleading; the prophecy was false; the sermon was untrue. But four years after the end of the Civil War, the preacher went ahead and published it anyway. His footnote is an appended scrupulosity, I suppose, but it isn't meant to retract any of its antecedent. And it needn't and shouldn't, because the preacher's example is still valid. It is still valid because it is an example. In the rhetoric of example, the distinction between use and abuse vanishes. We can see that in the preacher's sermon. What is an example? It is the vehicle of a metaphor that can be continually redefined as circumstances change around it. Outside the text our apprehension of fact is subject to verification and falsification, but once something has been subsumed into example it becomes true a priori. That power makes example into an instrument of deconstruction, perhaps *the* instrument of deconstruction.

But it does more. Those machine guns across the street from my house were firing blanks, of course: I mean bullets which could just as well have been labeled "you see what I mean" or perhaps "*exempli gratia*." And I wasn't hurt at all by them: such is the power of example. But twenty years ago the bullets were real. We fired them, and things happened, but we couldn't make ourselves understand what or why. One reason was that the intellectuals in their think tanks were used to thinking of such things in exemplary terms. I don't suppose we'll ever be able to do otherwise. History tells us we won't, and history speaks to us in the first instance through examples.

Consider this, for example: the name of the preacher was Charles Wadsworth.

Readers of Emily Dickinson will understand the significance of the identification, for Wadsworth played a major though now unclear part in the poet's life. Although she was a recluse, Dickinson received Wadsworth in her home at least twice (*Letters* III: 957). She corresponded with him for many years, and in 1882, after his death, she entered with two of Wadsworth's friends, the brothers James and Charles Clark, into a prolonged exchange of elegiac letters, which ended only with the poet's own death four years later. "He was my Shepherd from 'Little Girl'hood," she mourned to James Clark in her first of these, "and I cannot conjecture a world without him, so noble was he always—so fathomless—so gentle" (L766). The emotion only deepened after that. In April 1886, with James Clark dead, Emily Dickinson wrote to Charles Clark from her own deathbed: "With the exception of my Sister who never saw Mr Wadsworth, your Name alone remains" (L1040).

More: after Dickinson's death, her sister found among her papers the rough drafts of three long, anguished, searingly passionate love letters (L187, 233, 248). No one knows whether these letters were eventually recopied and dispatched. No one knows even for whose eyes they were intended, because the beloved is addressed throughout only as "Master." We look without historical comprehension at the words in R. W. Franklin's facsimile. They may signify some state of "things as they verifiably are"; on the other hand, they may be something like an experiment in fiction or a symptom of mental illness. From within the text we cannot tell. But it has been conjectured on independent biographical grounds that there was an actual "Master" outside the text, a man of flesh and blood, with a voice that could have spoken to us of its own intentionality as the letters cannot. And though no one in the present state of the record can be certain, it appears possible that this "Master," Emily Dickinson's beloved, "a Dusk Gem, born of troubled Waters, astray in any Crest below" (L776), may have been Charles Wadsworth of Philadelphia and San Francisco, the artist of the inane platitude.

Who was Charles Wadsworth in relation to Emily Dickinson? What does Charles Wadsworth mean in relation to our experience of reading Dickinson's poetry? Realizing both that we should know and that we can't know, we find ourselves trying to read around, or past, or through a lacuna in the archive. The Dickinson-Wadsworth relationship appears to presage something of great significance to our understanding of Dickinson's poetry. It comes to us bearing the appearance of an example. But whenever we read it, it is not yet—never quite yet—an example *of* anything we can name. Its words plead their own incomprehensibility. They remain an archive.

We can't simply ignore them either; now that we know about the archive, we realize that it has always been present under the primary texts, a catacomb of significance. Dickinson and Wadsworth visited it themselves. As Emily Dickinson told James Clark: "Once when [Wadsworth] seemed almost overpowered by a spasm of gloom, I said 'You are troubled.' Shivering as he spoke, 'My Life is full of dark secrets,' he said. He never spoke of himself, and encroachment I know would have slain him" (L776).

And Charles Wadsworth wrote to Emily Dickinson, in the only item of the Dickinson-Wadsworth correspondence which is known to survive (L248a), "My Dear Miss Dickenson [*sic*] I am distressed beyond measure at your note, received this moment—I can only imagine the affliction which has befallen, or is now befalling you." *That*, at least, is a sentence we do understand. It is exemplary: a paradigm of our own bewilderment when we read.

Dickinson has always been considered a bewildering writer, of course. But a part of our bewilderment doesn't originate with her; it is generic. It grows out of language itself, from the gap between the signifier and what it signifies. It has a history of its own, too, a history that manifests itself in grammar.

Consider this sentence from a work of unplayful nonfiction: a history of the Cold War in the United States.

> White-haired, pale-faced, dressed in dark, expensive suits, Budenz was received back into the faith on October 10, 1945, by Monsignor Fulton J. Sheen, in St. Patrick's Cathedral, New York. (Caute 123)

From this sentence and the sentences that precede and follow it, I can learn what David Caute intended me to learn: the interesting story of Louis Budenz, an editor of the *Daily Worker* during the high Stalin era who became a professional anti-Communist during the Truman-McCarthy era. But of course the stream of knowledge coursing from this text is not undivided. As I read I am learning about Louis Budenz, but the words that surround his story are making themselves into other contexts as well. I may discover that I have begun to think about St. Patrick's: its architecture, its location, its significance in the history of Irish-American New York. If I am old enough and in a nostalgic mood, a green double-decker bus may materialize on a Fifth Avenue of my mind, filling me with the tender happiness of memory reborn as it rolls past the gray Gothic stonework behind which Louis Budenz is repeating childhood vows. Or I may recall, with a faint stirring of unfocused irony, that the handsome, charming, slightly vulgar Monsignor Sheen was to become a major television star during the ascendancy of Milton Berle, Howdy Doody, and Joseph McCarthy.

It goes on. If I have been teaching freshman English lately, my reaction to the text will be directly physical. I will reach by reflex for my red pen, and a sentence of comment will spring ready-made into my mind: Yes, Mr. Caute, but *how many* dark, expensive suits was Louis Budenz wearing on October 10, 1945? Eventually I will come back from my daydreams to the sentence I have been reading, and then it will become apparent that it and I have written ourselves into semiotic inextricability. Louis Budenz and I are now joined like Siamese twins in the text, along with a bus, a bishop, a pedagogical response conditioned by the grammatical history of several thousand pages of freshman writing, and a pedagogical memory of those eighteen-year-olds, fresh out of high school, students who have never heard of Budenz or Sheen or World War II or Emily Dickinson. Now it will be harder to think about Louis Budenz as he might have existed outside his documentation. I will have to read this historical figure as if he were a poem.

And of course the story of changeable Louis Budenz continues to change both itself and me as I read. "I quote another man's saying," says Emerson in "Experience"; "unluckily, that other withdraws himself in the same way, and quotes me." To read historically, it appears, is to exchange one alienation for another. Having heard in my class about subject-verb agreement, the freshman can now read poetry, but his parents now seem to speak with a foreign accent. What I misunderstood when I began to read the sentence, I now misunderstand differently.

Still, some things don't change.

Consider the image that comes to mind when we say "worker." Consider, for instance, the faces that stare into the camera from a photograph captioned "Workers during Chrysler plant strike, 1937" (Salzman 107). There they are, held still for us by the camera: the men whose blurred voices we have heard shouting in the background of black-and-white newsreels. One holds a crudely lettered sign that reads "WE ARE HERE TO STAY DEPT. 82." A second sign in the background, this one professionally lettered, reads "82 IS SITTIN' TOO." Up front, another homemade sign proclaims "SPIRIT OF 1937." To anyone who has lived in Detroit, the faces in this tableau from the Roosevelt years will be startling: all of them are white. But that isn't the only thing that seems uncanny half a century later. Look at the finger-waved hair; look at the worker in the right foreground, the one with the little snare drum and the seven union buttons arranged on his jacket in the form of Christ's Latin cross. They no longer exist, but these are the faces that Norman Rockwell drew. It no longer exists, but this is an America that once really was.

And now look at the two effigies the men are carrying. One is a shapeless scarecrow thing wearing a worker's cap; the only way you can tell what it is supposed to represent is by reading the sign around its neck: "FENCE JUMPER." The other one, though, reads more easily. For one thing, it isn't labeled at all; it carries its own word into the assembly. Its carefully constructed arms are folded across its chest, and from them dangles a scroll marked "INJUNCTION." Above the arms the torso is hunched, so that the top of the figure's hat barely rises above the plane of the shoulders. The hat covers the eyes, but we can see that the figure has a big hooked nose and a goatee. And on the jacket, just over the heart, is something we are used to seeing in European photographs taken a few years after this one: a star of David.

In the last fifty years the metaphor hasn't changed. We can still recognize it without a label. The workers in Chrysler's Department 82 are, as people say, history. Their lived reality exists now only as documentation. Not having read that documentation, I don't know who they were, or how they lived, or exactly why they were on strike. But I do understand the significance of their effigy of the Jew. It is an image, after all, which has a lived reality in the present. We don't know it mediately, through its documentation; we know it in the part of memory which doesn't speak words.

In their precise delineation of emotional states whose sources remain secret and unutterable, Emily Dickinson's poems provide us with the language of this historical situation. They frolic in definition and abstraction, but at their heart is an incommunicability, communicated to us as such. Reading, we are brought up exactly to the edge of the abyss between knowledge and speech, and stopped exactly there. The confusion we feel when we read those poems is a model in language of memory's problem: the inability ever to say through time, in changing words, what we have seen and, having seen, know as such, forever. As we speak, our words only footnote other words, deferring meaning margin by margin. But Emily Dickinson's words work differently. They bring the process to a stop.

Here is one of the poems we have all read.

There's a certain Slant of light,
Winter Afternoons—
That oppresses, like the Heft
Of Cathedral Tunes—

Heavenly Hurt, it gives us—
We can find no scar,
But internal difference,
Where the Meanings, are—

None may teach it Any—
'Tis the Seal Despair—
An imperial affliction
Sent us of the Air—

When it comes, the Landscape listens—
Shadows—hold their breath—
When it goes, 'tis like the Distance
On the look of Death— (P258)[1]

We have been reading this report on the mind's climate since Mabel Loomis Todd and Thomas Wentworth Higginson printed it in 1890, in their first selection of Dickinson's verse. Joseph Duchac's annotated bibliography summarizes fifty-two separate commentaries on the poem's seventy-two words, and Duchac is now more than a decade behind the tickertape. In this poem's presence, we keep on talking, nervously. As if we were waiting for a funeral to begin, we try at all costs to fill the silence. There is always something else to say; anything to put off the reading for one more minute. We react to the poem with the emotion that the poem describes, as if it were writing our feelings in the course of being read. "I never was with any one who drained my nerve power so much," wrote Thomas Wentworth Higginson to his wife after he had spent his first afternoon with Emily Dickinson. "Without touching her, she drew from me. I am glad not to live near her" (L342b). This isn't necessarily a permanent or general phenomenon; I suspect the Nazi photographer's reaction would be different.[2] Nevertheless, here we are now in the archive with the

[1] Johnson prints a dash between "it" and "Any" in line 9. This does not appear, however, in Franklin's facsimile of the manuscript.

[2] My colleague Mark Wilson regularly asks his sophomores at the end of the semester which of Dickinson's poems they have liked best. During the 1970s, he tells me, their favorite was P919: "If I can stop one Heart from breaking / I shall not live in vain." During the Reagan years, on the other hand, and for the first time, several students chose P540: "I took my Power in my Hand— / And went against the World." As to the professional scholars: if Duchac's chronology is correct, not one of them was moved to speak about "There's a certain slant of light" until 1936, forty-six years after its first publication. Then the poem began to explain to them, though they didn't yet understand its words, that the chiaroscuro of the clouds over Auschwitz and Hiroshima needed recording.

poem, in our present state of history. And what is disturbing is this: in our present state of history, the poem we read seems to be directing our perception toward a state of existence that our words can't speak of. To us as we are here and now, "There's a certain Slant of light" comes as a footnote appended to the wordless. In an age of words, of radio and television and advertising, the poem's words tell us that words are never enough, that something in us is too dreadful to say.

We read Wadsworth's sermon first, and then his footnote. Sun-warm in our hands with the earth of lived history clinging to it, the footnote did to us what the weather did to Emerson while he was composing his Divinity School Address: it convinced us that "the snow-storm was real; the preacher merely spectral; and the eye felt the sad contrast in looking at him, and then out of the window behind him, into the beautiful meteor of the snow." It was history appended to but still separate from its embodying words. The footnote we append to Dickinson's poem works differently. It doesn't simplify, as Wadsworth's footnote does; it complicates. And of course it isn't a word in a margin; it is a silence. It enters into us as we read the poem's words and shows us that they too have the silence in them. A footnote such as that is the proper annotation to any history read in the twentieth century. It makes us know what we can and cannot say about our passage into the quiet.

9

Archive, Body, and Possibility

For its victims, there is only the quiet. For the artist of history, the quiet is an aesthetic effect, one technical possibility among many, a *donnée*. When we read history, therefore, we are forced to choose in every sentence between the claims of the dead to the silence that is their due and palm, and the claims of the living on behalf of the words which alone can remind us that the silence exists.

And we pass through history every day. Walking down the street, carrying a volume of Emily Dickinson's letters—say, the one containing L296, with its icy dismissal from the poet's consciousness of most of the rest of the human race ("Anna Norcross lives here, since Saturday, and two new people more, a person and his wife, so I do little but fly")—we see someone who, like Emily Dickinson, is perhaps more than normally sensitive to the voices he hears in his head ("my own Words so chill and burn me, that the temperature of other Minds is too new an Awe"; L798). He on honeydew hath fed, but only his silence can speak, and that only of a social-engineering program given the name (at the time of its inauguration during the Kennedy administration, that reign of words) of Community Release: the dumping of mental patients onto the streets of the United States of America, where the men of words had created for them, unfortunately only out of words, a community, waiting in love.

Things don't work out as planned. The poor silent dead still lie under our feet; the wretched insane wander the streets of our Republic; Emily Dickinson was taken care of all her life by a houseful of servants ("most women and men don't have the privilege of being crazy in that way"; Lentricchia 782)—and we are reading lyric poetry: pure words of an ideal language, or so we fear. Out of fear we may joke, as the Bollingen jury did when it honored Ezra Pound, that "to permit other considerations than that of poetic achievement to sway the decision would . . . in principle deny the validity of that objective perception of value on which civilized society must rest" (Casillo 9). Or we may discover that we love the movies: a dark room, music from an orchestra we don't have to listen to, the roaring lion of the phenomenal world safely caged in a frame inscribed *Ars gratia artis*. That keeps us feeling good: happy in the clean dark where the big people play without seeing us; unblamed; as we once were. But the punch line of the joke is *mauvaise foi*.

> He must send a telegram from the Ice Palace,
> although he knows the muzhiks don't read:
> "If I am ever to find these trees meaningful
> I must have you by the hand. As it is, they
> stretch dusty fingers into an obscure sky,
> and the snow looks like a face dirtied
> with tears. Should I cry out and see what happens?
> There could only be a stranger wandering
> in this landscape, cold, unfortunate, himself
> frozen fast in wintry eyes." Explicit Rex.
> (O'Hara, "On Looking at *La Grande Jatte*, the
> Czar Wept Anew," sec. 3)

And then there are those who went into the dark bearing words.

Robert Frost was one of those: a man who suffered and caused others to suffer. He came to maturity as a poet in England, just as the great carnage of World War I was about to begin, and it is enlightening to consider our own historical reactions when we think of his life against the background of a group of parallel biographies—say, the lives of Frost's slightly younger contemporaries, the minor British poets of the war. Raging into terrible life in the pages of Lawrance Thompson or William Pritchard, Frost springs from the text a devouring monster of egotism, the artist who used to decline joint invitations with a little poem which ran, "I only go / When I'm the show" (Pritchard 129). We will remember that, just as we have remembered "Stopping by Woods on a Snowy Evening." But here to reproach us from the pages of a forgotten history are the touching, unread documents of self-sacrifice which once lent other words to our language.

> JEFFERY DAY. Born at St. Ives, Hunts., 1896, and educated at Repton. An admirer of Rupert Brooke, he joined the Royal Naval Air Service, and became a sub-lieutenant at eighteen. He soon became one of the most famous pilots, credited with legendary exploits. He was shot down by German planes; was awarded the D.S.C. ("for great skill and bravery as a pilot"). He wrote a number of his war poems actually in the air. Aged twenty-one he was promoted to flight-commander. On February 27, 1918, he engaged six enemy aircraft single-handed, and was shot down and killed.
>
> PATRICK SHAW-STEWART. Born 1888, the son of a major-general, and educated at Eton and Balliol College, Oxford, with Julian Grenfell. One of Edward Marsh's most favoured young friends. Rupert Brooke described him as "the most brilliant man they've had in Oxford for ten years." Hertford and Ireland Scholarships; Double First. Lieutenant-commander, Naval Div. With Brooke at his death. Fought at Gallipoli, where he wrote in a letter home: "I continue to believe that the luck of my generation must change . . . nowadays we who are alive have the sense of being old, old survivors." Killed in action in France, 1917, having refused to go back after his ear had been torn off by shrapnel a few minutes before. (Gardner 163, 177)

Some of these men died gladly, some with resignation, some in fear. Their lives are a tragic footnote to history's words, and probably a better guide to conduct in history than the life of Robert Frost. But I think their poems are going to remain unread. At Repton and Eton, Day and Shaw-Stewart did the wrong kind of homework. Their poems are full of an authenticity purchased at the price of life itself, but they are verbally uninteresting. You hear in them echoes of G. K. Chesterton, William Ernest Henley, A. A. Milne, a whole museum of Edwardian prosody, but inside the stanzas there is little but a diffused and generalized earnestness. That earnestness had a cause which was once terribly real, but history has blurred its outlines and faded its colors. As I read, I feel embarrassed and ashamed. I want the poets' language to suffice for the making of a poem, but as I read, I know I am hearing a language which I cannot make myself pretend means anything to me. The binding of the volume of war poems is frayed; the pages have softened with age. I return to the library, replace the book on its dark shelf, and start hoping that I will find a historical excuse for my failure of sympathy, my callousness.

These poets died young, of course. But part of the pathos of their deaths is that their classical education failed to teach them the vocabulary of what killed them. Instead, it gave them an analogy. Before the summer of 1914, Sir Henry Newbolt was being nothing but a good teacher when he spoke of war as a game—a brutal Darwinian game, to be sure, but nevertheless a game, played according to coherent rules decided beforehand in some transcendent *hors-jeu*. In "Clifton Chapel" (Munro 296), a poem frequently quoted to schoolboys for purposes of inspiration and explanation, Newbolt expanded the analogy into a metaphysical proposition based in equal parts on the scriptures and on Herbert Spencer.

> To set the Cause above renown,
> To love the game beyond the prize,
> To honour while you strike him down
> The foe that comes with fearless eyes:
> To count the life of battle good,
> And dear the land that gave you birth,
> And dearer yet the brotherhood
> That binds the brave of all the earth,—
>
> My son, the oath is yours: the end
> Is His, Who built the world of strife,
> Who gave His children Pain for friend,
> And Death the surest hope of life.

But at some time shortly after the first charge of infantry against machine guns, it became apparent that the terms of the soldier-athlete analogy had left some reality unaccounted for. The Boer War had been fought for England by Australian and Canadian troops, but the implications of that fact remained blanketed under the metaphor until the summer of 1914. Then the concealment vanished, and what the naked words revealed was devastating. As Rudyard Kipling chided his countrymen in "The Islanders" (Munro 243),

> ye vaunted your fathomless power, and ye flaunted your iron pride,
> Ere—ye fawned on the Younger Nations for the men who could shoot and ride!
> Then ye returned to your trinkets; then ye contented your souls
> With the flannelled fools at the wicket or the muddied oafs at the goals.

The metaphor was seen to be sufficient no more. The historical crisis had to be recognized and understood immediately, without the misleading interventions of rhetoric. Suddenly the imperialist appropriations of the classical tropes, all undertaken in the service of an analogy between Victorian England and Augustan Rome, had to be seen as falsifications; suddenly a whole language had been discredited. And the Days and Shaw-Stewarts, writing in that language as if its words were sterling yet, died mute.

To the extent that history is narrative, every historical crisis is a crisis of language, and the linguistic crisis tends to take the same form as the crisis in the historical *hors-texte*. World War I is ordinarily thought of as one of the culminations of a century of technological progress; similarly, the prosodic experiments of a century of Romantic and Victorian poets can be thought of as issuing in the Petrarchan sonnets of Rupert Brooke and the pulpit rhetoric of Woodrow Wilson. Such language, freighted with the connotations of a dead era, was of little use to the poets whose aim was to describe the phenomena of the new. Let us pay Siegfried Sassoon all the honor that his extraverbal morality is due, but let us also recognize that a poem like his "'Blighters'" (Gardner 115) shows us little more than the inability of old language to take on new meanings.

"Blighters"

The House is crammed: tier beyond tier they grin
  And cackle at the Show, while prancing ranks
Of harlots shrill the chorus, drunk with din;
  "We're sure the Kaiser loves our dear old Tanks!"

I'd like to see a Tank come down the stalls,
  Lurching to rag-time tunes, or "Home, sweet Home,"
And there'd be no more jokes in Music-halls
  To mock the riddled corpses round Bapaume.

A century before this poem was published, William Blake was writing, "The harlot's cry from street to street / Shall weave old England's winding sheet." The word "harlot" meant approximately the same thing for Sassoon that it meant for Blake, but Sassoon's England was no longer Blake's. Between the two poems there had supervened a calling into question of the veracity of the Bible, the first successful chemotherapeutic treatment of a bacterial infection (the disease was syphilis; the curative agent was named Salvarsan, after the Latin verb *salvare*, to save), and a concomitant change in the semantics of the word "harlot." Now that we think differently about the Authorized Version, a harlot can be anyone who literally or figuratively perverts the act of creation by turning it into a commodity, making the live act a dead thing. Singing their song about the tanks, the blighters—noncombatants at home in "Blighty"—are all of them, female or male, harlots of meaning, translating significance into meaningless noise. Reality—the sound and smell and feel of a real tank—deserves to mean in its own context, under its own sky. But here there is no light. That is the pathos of the poem's situation. The pathos of the poem itself, however, is that Sassoon's harlots are verbally coextensive only with King James's. They are just women.

Meanwhile, Sassoon's technical problem was that the tank had to be thought about on its own terms. Restoring mobility to the front lines of World War I, it made the nightmare of the trenches historically meaningless. No one henceforth would be able to remember the mud and gas of the trenches for what they meant when they were real in the present—nobody except, if they could find words to describe it, the poets. "Tank" was one of the words Sassoon found, so fire-warm still that he wrote it with a capital letter. He probably wanted to work on the word while it was still unformed, before it could be removed from its forge in the wordless domain of experience and given into the care of harlots and historians. His desire was to make it tragic. But "tank" and "harlot" are words from different languages. In the historical language in which the word "tank" has a meaning, the word "harlot" is only an etymology signifying "a two-syllable word required by the meter." It should have been appended to a word of English. Because it wasn't, because the words of "'Blighters'" can therefore give us only a Cliffs Notes summary of the emotional experience that the poem's entire eight-lines-plus-title-in-quotation-marks purport to recreate, we have to go back to the original. And when we take "'Blighters'" along to the library for that purpose, we find that the library's history books and dictionaries of slang are more significant, bear a more comprehensive vocabulary of feeling, than the poem. We find that the poem itself has become little more than an index to a glossary. That doesn't happen when we read Homer.

But as Yeats said, thinking of himself in the portentous month of April 1916, "When heroism returned to our age it bore with it as its first gift technical sincerity" (162). Consider, in contrast to "'Blighters,'" this small poem by Edward Thomas about a peasant vegetable which in American English is called the rutabaga.

Swedes

They have taken the gable from the roof of clay
On the long swede pile. They have let in the sun
To the white and gold and purple of curled fronds
Unsunned. It is a sight more tender-gorgeous
At the wood-corner where Winter moans and drips
Than when, in the Valley of the Tombs of Kings,
A boy crawls down into a Pharaoh's tomb
And, first of Christian men, beholds the mummy,
God and monkey, chariot and throne and vase,
Blue pottery, alabaster, and gold.

But dreamless long-dead Amen-hotep lies.
This is the dream of Winter, sweet as Spring.

This is a poem of metonymies. Working from the yellow turnips in their clay-walled pile to the image of a gold-encrusted mummy in its tomb, from the mummy to winter, and from winter to an idea of death without resurrection, it moves us incrementally from one idea to the next, and not only the ideas but the increments themselves are conventional, accepted, traditional. Only at the end does a link of the metonymic chain become the linking signifier—half inside the poem, half outside—of a larger referent. But that is enough. Historical change has occurred: the referent has been shown to be more obscure than could have been conceived through Sassoon's positivist clarity. In another domain of space or time, something about the plant world remains undiscovered: the allegory of something we don't yet understand. "Swedes" tells us that the history of our relation with the earth hasn't yet begun; that we still have to undergo the happy work of finding truthful names for the things around us in the garden. We have to realize. For the time it takes to utter one verb ("lurching"), "'Blighters'" brought us close to realizing one thing: how a tank would move through the mind, over the barbed wire or the rows of plush seats. But then the poem dropped back into its archive. "Swedes," by contrast, is heroically impure throughout. Its vocabulary contaminates itself with a range of history, ancient and modern. Edward Thomas would have been able to sing the missile base: if not his feelings of triumph or indignation, at least the important work being done on it by the weather and the passage of time.

Meanwhile, the moral significance of ahistorical vocabularies like Sassoon's and ours has changed, because history is swirling around the walls of our archive. Emily Dickinson, Klaus Lubbers tells us, was read one way before World War I, another way after. After the war Herman Melville became what he is today; in 1900 he had been worth exactly one sentence of posterity's notice (with his name misspelled) in Barrett Wendell's 574-page *Literary History of America*.[1] "The trouble with posterity," K. K. Ruthven reminds

[1] "Hermann [*sic*] Melville, with his books about the South Seas, which Robert Louis Stevenson is said to have declared the best ever written, and with his novels of maritime adventure, began a career of literary promise, which never came to fruition" (Wendell 229).

his students and ours, "is that we do not know who they will be" (193). Men and women made out of words, we are not in a position to say anything more about what changes us and our perceptions than can Stevens's Men Made out of Words: "Life consists / Of propositions about life." How exactly those propositions are made, in what ideal Paris, we cannot know. Propositions are made out of history, and all we have to know them with is their husk of words.

Still, something in us demands to consider Siegfried Sassoon a poet in some large sense of the term: one who can keep up with the propositions. If Sassoon's words mean nothing in themselves, they at least do signify, deeply, by reference to external history and an external sense of the moral. We seem to be capable of reading "'Blighters'" for something that isn't in the text: a potential meaning. We are partially the authors of that meaning ourselves; our lived and read experience gives a syntax to the isolated signifiers of the text, making them intelligible by historicizing them. As to the words actually printed on the page, we tolerantly allow that poems are "a corrupt version of some text in nature" (Emerson, "The Poet"). We know words mean more than words can say; we know lines are there for us to read between. Between the lines, Sassoon is still alive.

When we read, therefore, our ambition is only to dwell in possibility: "A fairer House than Prose," as Emily Dickinson says in P657. Consider, for instance, the interesting fact that there is such a thing as literary biography, useless though mere life must be to the text it has brought forth. Consider only, for a start, how we crave it; consider its effect as a read text on our own extratextual values. If we cannot read the poet's work unambiguously, we turn for help to the life, confidently hoping that that body of para- or metaverbal footnotes will tell us what the words cannot. We revel notoriously in the life of the quiet recluse Emily Dickinson, but not in hers alone. While Robert Frost still had a year to live, for example, M. L. Rosenthal found it necessary to refer to some of his poems in the past tense as legacies of a personality, the personality made out of words of "the 'true' Frost" (257). To do that, he had to construct an opposing false Frost, a critical personification made equally of words and of their creator's history. Insofar as the creator is a mercenary clown, in this formulation, his words are false; insofar as his words are a fiction—a noble betrayal of the sordid spirit in which their creator wrote them on the page we read—they are true. Criticism works against biography here, but the point is, it requires it. "He is the handsomely craggy-faced sage and official bard. . . . For two decades now he has frequently donned this sage's mask and costume, as of a good gray Walt Whitman without beard or other taint, and treated us to verse-sermons on sundry topics: science, religion, socialism, capitalism, his own brand of twinkling-eyed pragmatic idealism right out of the cracker barrel, and almost anything else" (256).

Frank O'Hara's "Personism," conversely, makes language into a direct extension of the poet's life, a projection of desire into a continuum of words extending impersonally from person to person, with no possibility of determining where the human ends and the vocabulary begins. If Eliot's theory of impersonality concentrates on the medium, O'Hara's pre-AIDS calculus of orifices concerns itself with the act of mediation. The poem ("This poem drooping shy and unseen that I carry, and that all men carry", Whitman, "Spontaneous Me" line 10) becomes figuratively (or literally—in this optimistic theory the terms are interchangeable) an extra, independent penis. The men made out of words also have a sex life made out of words. Words are the carriers of genetic significance between them, latent in the telephone line.

> As for measure and other technical apparatus, that's just common sense: if you're going to buy a pair of pants you want them to be tight enough so everyone will want to go to bed with you. . . .
>
> One of [Personism's] minimal aspects is to address itself to one person (other than the poet himself), thus . . . sustaining the poet's feelings about the poem while preventing love from distracting him into feeling about the person. . . . It was founded by me after lunch with LeRoi Jones on August 27, 1959, a day in which I was in love with someone (not Roi, by the way, a blond). I went back to work and wrote a poem for this person. While I was writing it I was realizing that if I wanted to I could use the telephone instead of writing the poem, and so Personism was born. . . . It puts the poem squarely between the poet and the person, Lucky Pierre style, and the poem is correspondingly gratified. The poem is at last

between two persons instead of two pages. (O'Hara, "Personism: A Manifesto," *Selected Poems* xiii–xiv)

Fantasy and the poem: the two things become one, mediated by the idea of possible meaning.

That idea is fundamental to poetry, as it is, I suppose, to every effort to communicate. We have to believe that there remains something to say that we haven't yet said, something to understand that we haven't yet understood. A poet like Frank O'Hara, searching desperately through nostalgia and promiscuity for a clue to what went wrong, must at times have felt an overwhelming need to know that this impending moment, the experience that is just about to happen or the memory that is just about to occur, will show us itself in all its wholeness, comprehended at last, unbounded in its significance.

There I could never be a boy,
though I rode like a god when the horse reared.
At a cry from mother I fell to my knees!
there I fell, clumsy and sick and good,
though I bloomed on the back of a frightened black mare
who had leaped windily at the start of a leaf
and she never threw me.

I had a quick heart
and my thighs clutched her back.
I loved her fright, which was against me
into the air! and the diamond white of her forelock
which seemed to smart with thoughts as my heart smarted with life!
and she'd toss her head with the pain
and paw the air and champ the bit, as if I were Endymion
and she, moonlike, hated to love me.

All things are tragic
when a mother watches!
and she wishes upon herself
the random fears of a scarlet soul, as it breathes in and out
and nothing chokes, or breaks from triumph to triumph!

> I knew her but I could not be a boy,
> for in the billowing air I was fleet and green
> riding blackly through the ethereal night
> towards men's words which I gracefully understood,
>
> and it was given to me
> as the soul is given the hands
> to hold the ribbons of life!
> as miles streak by beneath the moon's sharp hooves
> and I have mastered the speed and strength which is the armor of
> the world.
>
> (O'Hara, "Poem, To James Schuyler")

The idiom of this yearning for transcendence has traditionally been Romantic, and O'Hara, punctilious about his origins as a poet, duly alludes to Keats. Both men died young, while they could still hope to run as fast as the westward-speeding sun.

> Gatsby believed in the green light, the orgastic future that year by year recedes before us. It eluded us then, but that's no matter—tomorrow we will run faster, stretch out our arms farther. . . .

Forever panting, and forever young: only thus can we live on in virtual history. A virtual history of our century is inevitable and necessary, because so much of what there was to love in our time has died young. But the history of the old must be of a different order. And as Wallace Stevens said in "Mozart, 1935" of the classic artist, "that lucid souvenir of the past," in a Romantic age, "He was young, and we, we are old."

James Schuyler tells us that Frank O'Hara "had a Yankee way of speaking, nasal, yet not unmusical" (44). On the cover of O'Hara's *Selected Poems* the voice acquires a body in Larry Rivers's multiple drawing. The poet's hands rest on top of his head as it rises, slightly out of register in collage, above the black-socked feet, the legs throwing the hips to one side, and the genitals. The picture is, I suppose, O'Hara at work: the poet presiding over a language working its own way through the body, a language containing only the big letters of Rivers's comforting ego-words, FRANK O'HARA. It is a language which embodies the state of realized desire; which wants not to speak but, silent itself, to hear.

Robert Frost's poetics had that in common with Frank O'Hara's: it was, as his letters from England in 1913 and 1914 stated explicitly, a poetics of sound, the creation of a body of poems balanced as carefully as the poet could make them on voice, voice held in the mouth almost disembodiedly, as a lexicon of sense. But when Amy Lowell, the author of a book of verse bearing the Shelleyan title *A Dome of Many-Coloured Glass*, wrote in 1917 that Frost's poems had grown out of New England's soil, the craftsman of sound had to repudiate Lowell's Romantic historicism on the biographical grounds she had chosen. The result was a document that shows us the relation between possibility and the archive: between the polymorphous limitlessness of the desire that leads us to conceive of poetry and the historical order of language through which it is realized.

Frost first undertook to refute Lowell with the factual detail of a life objectively conceived. "For twenty-five of the first forty years of my life," he carefully explained in a long letter to his literary-political ally Louis Untermeyer, "I lived in San Francisco, Lawrence, Mass., Boston, Cambridge, Mass., New York, and Beaconsfield, a suburb of London. . . . I was among the first men at Amy's brother's old college during my two years there, winning a Detur and a considerable scholarship. . . . It is not fair to farmers to make me out a very good or laborious farmer." Only when the data were firmly in place did Frost attempt to find in them a significance—and that significance, when he found it, took the form of an equally firm insistence on the poet's impersonal occupation as a manipulator of signifiers. Frost wished to read his biography as an installment of the history of language. "I wish for a joke I could do myself," he mused, "shifting the trees entirely from the Yankee realist to the Scotch symbolist" (*Selected Letters* no. 172). "Amy's brother's old college" was Harvard, where in 1917 A. Lawrence Lowell held the office of president. Frost's condescending phrase gets the priorities straight: the people who belong in universities are the poets. The schoolmen's universals come out of books that poets write, not out of the ground. There, in the books, are the possibilities and the means to realize them. And there, in the letter to Untermeyer, is a poetics of possibility: a poetry that takes up the things of this world—say, the trees—and shifts them, making them more real with every word by changing them into the counters of a symbolic game.

But the possible comes to ground in time. That is the tragedy associated with Frost's New England landscape of abandoned things, hopes lost—the landscape of "The Wood-Pile" or "Directive." The archive of our desires has an end. So the subject of Frost's emblem-poem "The Oven Bird" sings *memento mori* to the idea of possibility, and his text is the maxim of Job's young adversary Elihu: "All flesh shall perish together, and man shall turn again unto dust" (Job 34:15).

> He says the early petal-fall is past,
> When pear and cherry bloom went down in showers
> On sunny days a moment overcast;
> And comes that other fall we name the fall.
> He says the highway dust is over all.

This is not a song of the death of the year; it is a song of the death of its aesthetic form. Shelley's skylark soars above words into a transcendent language of endless possibility:

> Better than all measures
> Of delightful sound,
> Better than all treasures,
> That in books are found,
> Thy skill to poet were, thou scorner of the ground!

But Frost's bird came too late to Eden for spontaneous meaning. His is the voice of a discourse which has been named by Adam after the fall, when all the letters became scarlet. Stevens's singer of the idea of order sings her song, word by word, in Key West, the only place in the continental United States where frost has never been recorded, and the enchantment of her song spreads outward beyond limit, unconstrained by the force that freezes the ripple. But Frost's bird, who lives everywhere else, sings a song that is less free. In his throat, song stops short just before it might have realized the power of words to call memory back from its descent into silence.

> The bird would cease and be as other birds
> But that he knows in singing not to sing.
> The question that he frames in all but words
> Is what to make of a diminished thing.

The bird may be a New England Stoic, too honest to sing a song of comfort in the zone where truth must be hacked from a frozen ground. He is not incapable, at any rate, of asking aloud what time has done to him, and what it will do to all of us who hear his song. But he is Frost's creature, and Frost refuses to anthropomorphize. In "The Need of Being Versed in Country Things" a nest of birds adds poignancy to the sight of an abandoned farm, but the verse stops firmly at the threshold of symbolic interpretation. For Frost, verse is made in the domain of natural law; we human beings move our perceptions into it at our own risk, and never for long. There is something vainglorious about the desire to remain in contact with the phenomenon beyond our first immediate perception; it signifies that we dare to interpret what we think we have experienced. Those who follow their interpretations through into action—like the confused liberal in "To a Thinker,"[2]—would do best simply to accept the verbal as passively as Frost accepts the phenomenal: "Don't use your mind too hard, / But trust my instinct—I'm a bard." Wisdom's heart beats silently, but only the poet can tell us that in words. And what makes a poet is something in the life that can't be expressed in words. Living his life where words come into being, the poet alone is entitled to decide for us which things have been privileged to mean.

> One had to be versed in country things
> Not to believe the phoebes wept.

[2] For the political history of this poem and its reception, see Frost, *Selected Letters* no. 329, and Thompson's headnote.

Whatever sadness we hear in the song of the oven bird is all ours. We listen to the bird's call; we recall with sad irony Wordsworth's assurance that Nature, personified, never did betray the heart that loved her; and what we think we hear is tragedy. But the bird is not tragic. He exists before ideas. He has refrained from words; he knows in singing not to sing.

The poet's task is to punctuate the line differently: singing-not, to sing. Preserving the silence which his life as a man shares with the rest of us, he touches it with words. He lives the double life of the archive and the possibility in a lexical Key West, where meaning comes up to the shore of consciousness word by word. There, history must be achieved one signifier at a time, far from nature. Perhaps the strongest criticism we can make of Siegfried Sassoon as an artist is that too many of his signifiers are merely flotsam on the shore of the poet's history, givens from Stepmother Nature. In "'Blighters,'" Bapaume and the music hall have their only significant existence outside the poem, as objects of a constricted range of allusion. They aren't historical in the poem; they haven't been translated by the poem's machinery into its own language of sound and reference.

By contrast, in a passage from another British poem of World War I, Isaac Rosenberg's "Louse Hunting"—

Then we all sprang up and stript
To hunt the verminous brood.
Soon like a devil's pantomime
The place was raging.
See the silhouettes agape,
See the gibbering shadows
Mixed with the battled arms on the wall

—the antiquarian effect of the participial *-t* in "stript" acquires, from its very oddity in the context of this poem, the power to call into question the reality of the natural world that Rosenberg is struggling to describe. Rosenberg forces us to pay attention to his words *as* words. This isn't, or isn't just, the *Verfremdungseffekt* in subversive action, deconstructing the unquestioning faith in words which led England from *Idylls of the King* to the battle of Ypres. It is more; it is the reflection of an attitude toward history in language which the self-consciously modernistic Rosenberg shared with the self-consciously conservative Frost.

That is: we could say in terms of aesthetic history that Rosenberg, who was a painter as well as a poet, learned from his contemporaries in the postphotographic era to reconstruct his poems out of grammar and syntax and as little else as possible, just as they were reassembling their pictures from paint and light, without finding it necessary that they be pictures *of*. Like Picasso's bottles and guitars or Rosenberg's lice and dead man's dump, Frost's abandoned houses and Yankees maimed by loneliness have one overriding value for the artist's purpose: they are raw material. But they are raw material that is first given a worth as such by being taken in at present value, disinterestedly, without concern at the moment for what it is about to become. In a poem such as Frost's "A Servant to Servants," a mentally ill woman is seen first for what she is. Or, as Frost said:

> A little of anything goes a long way in art. Im never so desperate for material that I have to trench on the confidential for one thing, nor on the private for another nor on the personal, nor in general on the sacred. A little in the fist to manipulate is all I ask. My object is true form—is was and always will be—form true to any chance bit of true life. . . . I fight to be allowed to sit cross-legged on the old flint pile and flake a lump into an artifact. (*Selected Letters* no. 278)

In the twentieth century, political history has tended to develop in parallel with aesthetic history, but with one critical difference. Craving the *donnée* as intensely as the artists, craving the data of experience to shape to their own ends, statesmen have gone beyond art and created their own raw materials. America's street people are what they are because a statesman visualized them without provocation as a tableau by Norman Rockwell. Stopped for a moment in freeze-frame, history shows us the mountain of toothbrushes at Auschwitz. Because it insists that words grow out of an archive, that there must be a grammatical domain in which the possible gives way to aesthetic order, a language like Rosenberg's or Frost's offers us our only hope of depicting that feature of nature's new landscape—a feature which grew out of the earth when some experimentalist had conceived it as a disinterested possibility.

But at the turn of the century, Patrick Shaw-Stewart grew up reading what he was assured was such a language: a language directed toward what seemed at the time to be only the actual. He himself had always been immersed in what school and speech, Homer and Sir Henry Newbolt, told him was reality. At Oxford, D. A. N. Jones tells us, Shaw-Stewart had "a shameless appetite for success in competitions" and was "ludicrously snobbish." The general's son thought in class terms; he must have believed he had a logical right to expect the cosmos to mean significantly in the language he inherited with his name. His untitled poem in Brian Gardner's anthology *Up the Line to Death: The War Poets* 1914–1918 (59–60)[3] therefore ends with an appeal from the trenches at Gallipoli to someone else's name: a luminous word he had been brought up to believe was real and comprehensible, an emblem of the human in war.

Was it so hard, Achilles,
  So very hard to die?
Thou knowest and I know not—
  So much the happier I.

I will go back this morning
  From Imbros over the sea;
Stand in the trench, Achilles,
  Flame-capped, and shout for me.

There followed only silence. Some poems written in this century are a chronicle of the coming of that silence, and we have learned from them not to expect the shout. Reading them is therefore a part of our education in history. These texts have one chief thing to show us, and that is this: how much of what is unsaid remains possible to history when it works through the human to reach the places in the soul where words are not

[3] The fourth of the lines I quote appears in Gardner as "So much the happier am I." For reasons of meter and idiom, this seems to me to be a misprint.

understood. If their language marks the silence well, these poems belong to a new genre: a paratragedy in which recognition, the dawning of consciousness, has been replaced by a curtain rising on emptiness.

10

The Waste Land: History in the Eliot Era

But before we can recognize the new genre for what it is, our knowledge of the way we read will have to undergo a change. We will need to learn to answer, in words, the questions that the history of our time has asked us in all but words. "What to make of a diminished thing": that is Robert Frost's translation into words of the oven bird's lyric. When James Agee tried to translate a similar question on behalf of God's poor in *Let Us Now Praise Famous Men* (76), he found that he could carry out only an educational simulation of what would have to be said. Marked off in parentheses and held down on the page for us to see, the word made of silence presses at its black temporary bounds.

> (But *I* am young; and I am young, and strong, and in good health; and I am young, and pretty to look at; and I am too young to worry; and so am I, for my mother is kind to me; and we run in the bright air like animals, and our bare feet like plants in the wholesome earth: the natural world is around us like a lake and a wide smile and we are growing: one by one we are becoming stronger, and one by one in the terrible emptiness and the leisure we shall burn and tremble and shake with lust, and one by one we shall loosen ourselves from this place, and shall be married, and it will be different from what we see, for we will be happy and love each other, and keep the house clean, and a good garden, and buy a

> cultivator, and use a high grade of fertilizer, and we will know how to do things right; it will be very different:) (? :)
>
> ((?)) :)
>
> How were we caught?

Near the end of his book (398–99), Agee seeks an answer beside a little girl's grave in rural Alabama. The grave has been decorated with all that can be lavished on memory by a relatively wealthy family in rural Alabama, at such-and-such a moment in American history and with the dollar worth such-and-such in the international bourses:

> not only a tea set, and a coca-cola bottle, and a milk bottle, ranged on her short grave, but a stone at the head and a stone at the foot, and in the headstone her six month image as she lies sleeping dead in her white dress, the head sunken delicately forward, deeply and delicately gone, the eyes seamed, as that of a dead bird, and on the rear face of the stone the words:
>
> We can't have all things to please us,
> Our little Daughter, Joe An, has gone to Jesus.

It is a terrible passage. And what is most terrible about it is this: the grave speaks our language. That is why we respond to its poor desperate attempt to mean through a symbol system, and that is why, from Agee's point of view, the symbol system must be changed. Because Agee's words can be read disinterestedly, as literature, the language that has swallowed up the grave in Alabama is guilty of a historical crime. Distant from the scene, beneficiaries of the alienation that language imposes on the dead, we can contemplate the grave in Alabama aesthetically. Over the course of centuries of culture, various artists have placed at our disposal a wide range of symbol-reading techniques that enable us to do this. Agee too knew the techniques. He was aware of their names—names like "genre" and "sociology"—and the political sections of *Let Us Now Praise Famous Men* testify to his knowledge of their power over him. That is why he desired so passionately to escape from them. Writing through the hot nights in Alabama,

James Agee tried to help himself understand a-symbolically, with the help of something that nevertheless, fatally, had to be named: something named something like love.

That is, Agee was possessed of the ancient dream of undissociated, immediate knowledge. The man of words wanted there to be no words between the grave and him. A Romantic, with the Romantic's blind need to rediscover everything for himself, Agee had rediscovered that words are not knowledge but only "anglosaxon monosyllables [such as] god, love, loyalty, honor, beauty . . . marx, freud, semantic . . . woman, man, Woman, Man, humanity . . . Jesus, Jesus Christ, Jesus Christ, Jesus H. Christ, Jeez, jeez fellas, The Nazarene, The Nazarene Carpenter, The Galilean, Our Lord, Our Savior, Christ, christ, kee-rist, crissake, gawd" (415–17). He didn't want to *say* love; he wanted to love.

We are entitled to say that that ambition, so many years after the expulsion from the Garden, was sad and silly. A user of symbols can't, shouldn't try to, construct the nonsymbolic out of symbols. The only concrete result of Agee's illogic, we can say if we want to, was sprawl: a book that goes on too long because its author thought that writing the words The End would be an admission of failure. We can say, if we want to, that Agee was a victim of the Romantic fallacy of transcendence. Agee seems to have tried to believe that we readers can and should strive to bring about a new history through new language. But what he seems really to have desired was not history at all but something indescribable, a politics of the human taking place timelessly and forever, in silence. And the last mystic who thought in political terms was Adolf Hitler.

It does seem foolish: just what we might have expected from a man like Agee, an alcoholic who lived in an obsessed contemplation of his shattered childhood. But that foolishness, perhaps, is the value of *Let Us Now Praise Famous Men*. Pleading in language for silence, Agee articulates a virtual history: the first, the only history his poor subject-victims can ever have had. So that when he stands by the grave, addressing—whom?—what reader, what Listener?—Agee is only attempting to reclaim for history some old words. The words are in need of a new reading, and Agee offers us one: a reading humbled by the knowledge of meaninglessness in the world. So he prays: "Let us know, let us *know* there is cure, there is to be an end to it, whose beginnings are long begun . . . and in the teeth of all hope of cure which shall pretend its denial . . . let us most quietly and in most reverent fierceness say, not by its captive but by its utmost meanings:

"Our father, who art in heaven, hallowed be thy name. . . ."

But we will never be able to speak his words as he or we would want. As words, they bear a history. As history, they change us from wordless angels to something other.

(you mustn't be puzzled by this, I'm writing in a continuum)

—James Agee, *Let Us Now Praise Famous Men*

When he came to write the *Four Quartets*, T. S. Eliot brought himself as close as he could to a problem like Agee's: the problem of representation without symbols. Before he could do that, however, he had to understand what symbols are in time, while they are still subject to history. That necessitated the asking of some historical questions. What, for instance, happens to our words, and why, when we begin to read in a new way?

This is what happens, says Eliot in a famous sentence: "The existing order is complete before the new work arrives; for order to persist after the supervention of novelty, the *whole* existing order must be, if ever so slightly, altered" ("Tradition and the Individual Talent," *Selected Essays* 5). As we read, it turns out, we have been taking part both passively and actively in literary history. We are intermediary devices for the conversion of poems and prayers into the histories of poems and prayers. At the time we start reading a poem's sequence of words, we know our repertoire of language in one way; by the time we finish, we know it in another. The existing order of things experienced in the world is complete before the new word arrives; for order to persist after the supervention of novelty, the whole existing order of words must be, if ever so slightly, altered. History is the record of what we have read into existence. The present—that which we haven't yet read into the record—is incomprehensible. That is both the effect and the cause of our bewilderment before the passage of time over us. The pathos of the child's tomb is that it attempts to extend into the future the record of a moment which has only a present tense.

Literary language too speaks only in the present tense, both although and because the great literary modernists' theories of simultaneity have become our paradigms of history. But this doesn't imply that we literary readers misread every history into existence in the same way. We can get to the bottom of the newspaper's language because the journalist's who-what-where-when-how five dimensions of chronicle are positive data, independent of words. Similarly, because our formal education has told us that we should consider feminine rhymes funny (please us / Jesus), we possess something that the parents of Agee's dead girl don't: an alphabet of irony with which we can fill the blank distance between life and death, and then read what we have written as pathos. We can read the words in the newspaper or on the tombstone historically, shaping their sense around our own sense of change in reference. But T. S. Eliot, because he gave us a model of history in language, has been read not at all.

Our vocabulary is Eliot's, of course. Most of us probably grew up in the shadow of that green mountain range, his *Complete Poems and Plays*. But there's an odd thing about that shadow: it hasn't changed as our sun has sunk in the sky. Always the same, it has followed us wherever we have gone since the day we first read "April is the cruellest month." Eliot doesn't seem to exist for us as a historical presence as, say, Shakespeare does. We don't read Eliot in history at all; we read him in an eternal present. When we read Harold Bloom on Wallace Stevens or Hugh Kenner on Ezra Pound, we are helping to inter the poets in the institutional structure of literary history. But it is harder to read about Eliot. As Marjorie Perloff says:

> Read synchronically, against the backdrop of the avant-garde arts of Europe in the period *entre deux guerres*, Pound's structures seem quintessentially modern. Read diachronically, against the paradigm of the Anglo-American lyric from Blake to Emerson to Emily Dickinson, Pound will seem, as he did to Stevens, "an eccentric person." A "Last Romantic" and a "First Modern"—William Carlos Williams, who was able to appreciate Stevens's "discipline" even as he admired Pound's experimentation and invention, bridged the gap between the two by finding a third party to vilify. That party was,

> of course, T. S. Eliot, a bloke whose work both Pound and Stevens had been reading since its inception.[1] But then no one today, whether we look to critics like Bloom or Kenner or Vendler or to poets like John Ashbery or James Merrill or Adrienne Rich or Allen Ginsberg, seems eager to call the first half of the twentieth century the Eliot Era. And thereby hangs another tale—a tale whose telling will help us to work out the puzzle which is Modernism. (506)

Of course Perloff may be exaggerating here for rhetorical effect. There does, for instance, exist a book by Russell Kirk, published in 1972, called *Eliot and His Age*. For that matter, Bloom himself has urged readers to "thrust aside utterly, once and for all, the critical absurdities of the Age of Eliot" ("Central Man," 37). And of course William Carlos Williams gave a name to the power that *The Waste Land* came to wield over American poetry: "the great catastrophe" (*Autobiography* 146). Still, Williams's rage can be read only synchronically, as an attitude originating in and defined by a specific historical circumstance with its own *termini a quo* and *ad quem*. It wasn't just poetry that Williams wanted to spring from "a primary impetus, the elementary principles of all art, in the local conditions": it was emotion in general. Williams saw that his younger contemporary was making the American dialect readable in a new way—perhaps readable *only* in a new way, at a distance from its origins in a particular space and time. Henceforth Williams, the celebrant of perception unmediated, would be writing to readers whose language and whose ways of feeling Eliot had contaminated with history. We readers will have to understand Williams's hatred and fear of the consequence. That we have been educated not to share them is evidence enough that it was justified.

For diachronically, with regard to the passage of time between his time and ours, the fact remains that when we read Eliot, we are afflicted with historical dyslexia. "Whatever we know in *The*

[1] Perloff is echoing Pound's dismissal of Stevens, in a letter to William Carlos Williams, as "yr/ pal/ Wally S/ . . . a bloke I haven't read
and DOUBT like all
hell that yu will be able to PURR-suade me to venture on
with such a
hellUVAlot I don't know and WANT to find out." Stevens was equally brusque with Williams about Pound (Perloff 485).

Waste Land," says Andrew Ross, "it is not enough" (63). There does seem to be something in Eliot's language which resists the comparative reading across time and space and social conditions that we call culture. The poem appears to have consigned itself to a history all its own. Overlooking the history that includes books written outside a particular critical domain, Perloff demonstrates that she is a reader educated to Eliot's way of reading Eliot's history. But the question that follows from Perloff's demonstration is this: how else can that history be read? Can a history sui generis be a history at all?

Let us consider a single line by way of making the problem specific. "April is the cruellest month" is a part of the speech of the middle class now. It may, for all we know, remain in the English language as long as Chaucer's April. It may well survive there anonymously, an artifact separated from its poem and its poet, as has happened to many texts. But if "April is the cruelest month" survives in that way, as a conversational cliché or a line in Bartlett, it will have been taken out of context in a way that wasn't possible until Eliot showed us how. Other poems have quotable lines in them, and the quotable lines can be taken out of the poems without violating the larger cultural context in which those poems are imbedded. When people say "at one fell swoop" without realizing they are quoting from *Macbeth* (Act 4, sc. 3) they miss out, of course, on the precise, vividly accurate significance that this line creates in its dramatic context. But Shakespeare's phrase also inhabits a general context of meaning. We will be able to read it more fully once we have discovered Macduff's full metaphor of his children as chickens and Macbeth as a bird of prey, but the dictionary can tell us about *swoop* and *fell*, and that really will give us a close approximation of a significance communicated to us by the poet of nature. "At one fell swoop" has a general meaning deducible from the grammar and vocabulary of the English language. It is a part of the culture associated with the English language; it has become a part of what Eliot called the mind of Europe.

But "April is the cruellest month" comes to the mind of Europe from *The Waste Land*, and *The Waste Land* resists definition. We can't analyze that poem into coherent areas of knowledge called grammar and vocabulary, because *The Waste Land* is a text whose authenticity depends precisely on its being read as it was read by its first readers: as a midden of fragments, the shattered mirror of an incoherent consciousness in an incoherent age. How is the swoop fell? The dictionary can tell us. It will trace *fell* and *swoop* back through an unbroken, sufficiently coherent, sufficiently undeconstructible sequence of lexical association until we can believe that we know. But how is April cruel? Well, the rest of the poem establishes a context for us to read in. It will help us understand that a mood is articulating itself through the agency of a symbol. But that mood and that symbol have meaning only within the context of the poem itself. The swooping hell-kite that is Macbeth has meaning across the whole associational lexicon of English, but April is cruel only within the bounds of its one embodying poem. Off the page where *The Waste Land* has its only comprehensible existence, words fail.

So *The Waste Land* is a cryptic, private poem. But that aspect of it hasn't been what's responsible for our problem. There are other cryptic, private poems in the canon, and we're reasonably confident that we have learned how to read them. No, our continuing bafflement by Eliot has nothing to do with the power of our critical technology. Our confusion comes to us self-generated. It's a matter of institutional sociology, and it can be expressed this way: we academics have read *The Waste Land* too accurately. We have been exclusively faithful to its spirit, and that has led us into anachronism. We have preserved *The Waste Land*'s ruins *as* ruins, in the entirety of their disconnectedness. We have wanted our entropy in toto or not at all. As a condition of reading, we concede that this poem's intimation of an impending extinction of consciousness is permanently true. When we read *The Waste Land*, we happily accept it as a history of the end of history—and we have been doing that continuously for the last two-thirds of a century. We live our lives in history, but the locus of our reading is a poem written in a language that precludes the possibility of further historical change. At a time when we feel ourselves to be living intensely through a tragic period of history, *The Waste Land* comes to tell us that both history and tragedy are now dead. And yet it also tells us that that deadness has a historical context, and that that context is rooted in language, and that we therefore have to try to understand it with words, futile though our attempt must be.

All this is by way of saying two things about *The Waste Land* and the history of its reading: first, *The Waste Land* is a poem in the Romantic tradition; and second, in the wake of the modernist reaction against the nineteenth century, we have read it as if it weren't. We haven't been able to slot Eliot comfortably into our conventional literary-historical categories because we've been working with the wrong categories. And our taxonomic error has had two interesting consequences: first for the way we have read Eliot, and second for the way we have written the history of modernism.

I mean, first: it is probably time for us to consider that *The Waste Land* has something in common with the orphic preoccupations of a Romantic poem such as *Ode to the West Wind*. Certainly there is a continuity between Eliot and Shelley, and it runs backward in an unbroken line through the works of two poets who troubled Eliot throughout his career as modernist; I mean those icons of nineteenth-century culture whom Eliot patronized (in "Cousin Nancy") as "Matthew and Waldo, guardians of the faith": Arnold and Emerson, chief claimants during Eliot's youth to the poet's unique ability to see life steadily and see it whole.

I don't mean just that there may be something in common between Eliot's theory of the dissociation of sensibility, say, and Arnold's baffled yearning for the life of the Scholar-Gipsy who had "*one* aim, *one* business, *one* desire. . . . O life unlike to ours!" That thematic continuity has a good deal to tell us about the nature of Eliot's thought, but it says little to our immediate experience of reading Eliot's verse. But there is one Romantic preoccupation that directly affects Eliot's poetic utterance, and that is the striving to express passion immediately, transcending the limits imposed on signification by words. Every persona in Eliot's oeuvre cries out to us from the hither boundary of that limitation. The voice of J. Alfred Prufrock protests, "It is impossible to say just what I mean!"; the voice of Sweeney snarls in stoical despair, "I gotta use words when I talk to you"; and at the end, the disembodied voice of the *Quartets* whispers to itself in "Burnt Norton," that

Words strain,
Crack and sometimes break, under the burden,
Under the tension, slip, slide, perish,
Decay with imprecision, will not stay in place,
Will not stay still.

That is the voice of a Shelley grown old, and it has something to say to us about the ways we have read Eliot in history.

For the wind which turned the poet into the trumpet of a prophecy came forth in words, and words (we all discover this as we grow old, but Shelley died young) lie. They lie especially when they tell us, as Eliot's Sweeney tells us, that they are the only reality accessible to the human, and that rebirth and transcendence are not for us.

SWEENEY: You see this egg
You see this egg
Well that's life on a crocodile isle.
There's no telephones
There's no gramophones
There's no motor cars
No two-seaters, no six-seaters,
No Citroën, no Rolls-Royce.
Nothing to eat but the fruit as it grows.
Nothing to see but the palmtrees one way
And the sea the other way,
Nothing to hear but the sound of the surf.
Nothing at all but three things.
DORIS: What things?
SWEENEY: Birth, and copulation, and death.
That's all, that's all, that's all, that's all,
Birth, and copulation, and death.
DORIS: I'd be bored.
SWEENEY: You'd be bored.
Birth, and copulation, and death.
That's all the facts when you come to brass tacks:
Birth, and copulation, and death.
I've been born, and once is enough.
You dont remember, but I remember,
Once is enough.
(*Sweeney Agonistes*, "Fragment of an Agon")

Eliot's character Sweeney speaks against Shelley, but it is clear whose side Eliot takes. Eliot feared his characters, and Agee loved his, but in one thing the two poets would have been agreed: birth and copulation and death are not all; they are symbols of something other. The author of "Tradition and the Individual Talent" thought historically, and to think historically is to know two things, at least: first, that if we perceive something (birth, or copulation, or death) to have some meaning, it *does*, ipso facto, have some meaning, if only a meaning as a signifier of perception; second, that in time, as language changes and we change, the regress of signifiers must pass out of language itself to—at the least—a larger range of signifiers in the world. To think historically is to look through the world for what Agee called the general pattern.

In "Tradition and the Individual Talent" Eliot called the general pattern the mind of Europe; in "Burnt Norton" he called it the dance. "There is only the dance," said Eliot the historian, and Agee the film critic desired to agree instrumentally.

> That is the general pattern, its motions within itself lithe-unfolded, slow, gradual, grand, tremendously and quietly weighted, as a heroic dance: and the bodies in this dance, and the spirits, undergoing their slow, miraculous, and dreadful changes; such a thing indeed should be constructed of these persons: the great, somber, blooddroned, beansprout helmed fetus unfurling within Woods's wife; the infants of three families, staggering happily, their hats held full of freshly picked cotton . . . Mrs. Ricketts, in that time of morning when from the corn she reels into the green roaring glooms of her home, falls into a chair with gaspings which are almost groaning sobs, and dries in her lifted skirt her delicate and reeking head . . . : I see these among others on the clay in the grave mutations of a dance whose business is the genius of a moving camera, and which it is not my hope ever to record. (*Let Us Now Praise Famous Men* 293–94)

"East Coker" begins with this dance of life and death: "The association of man and woman / In daunsinge, signifying matrimonie— / . . . / Feet rising and falling. / Eating and drinking. Dung and death." "The Dry Salvages" ends, the dance ended, with words growing out of our graves into the word-bearing soil of history: "We, content at the last / If our temporal reversion nourish / (Not too far from the yew-tree) / The life of significant soil." From them, from the words—"every word . . . / The complete consort dancing together"—we are born again into significance: "born with the dead" ("Little Gidding"). Robert Frost, not a particularly romantic man, is reported to have said of Eliot, "I play euchre and he plays Eucharist." But the hidden ambition of every Romantic poet, I suppose, was to be an angel, or at least to speak with the tongue of one. It is an ambition that Eliot shared.

But the era of *The Waste Land*—the Eliot era in its classic phase—wasn't the time to talk about such things. Aside from the fact that it went to school to a bleak passage from F. H. Bradley that Eliot made notorious as a footnote to *The Waste Land* ("my experience falls within my circle, a circle closed on the outside"), the generation that discovered memory with Freud was simultaneously carrying out a massive repression of its own past. For reasons equally aesthetic, historical, political, and Oedipal, the artists of the Eliot era scoured the ground that gave them birth, frantically seeking to expunge every trace of the nineteenth century's quest for the sublime. And to the extent that they succeeded, those artists have dictated the subsequent terms of their own history.

That, perhaps, explains the astonishing durability of the modernist aesthetic. To the extent that modernism represents a break with earlier ways of thinking about the self in time, it has rendered the vocabulary of earlier poetic histories incomprehensible. Emily Dickinson could speak the words *eternity* and *immortality*, but we can't. Our vocabulary has been strategically impoverished: we can think about the modernist poets only in the words the modernist poets themselves have chosen for us. For the modernist enterprise this has been a fortuitous triumph. Because we lack the words to conceive of an alternative aesthetic, modernism remains dominant. It has given us a vocabulary to think in and another vocabulary to explain what we have thought. Criticism has blossomed under modernism. Even in the grip of deconstructionist paranoia, it has achieved something like an undissociated sensibility: it can't feel anything that it hasn't expressed. But literary history comes to tell us that the correct name for this condition is aphasia. It is a pathological condition, and it needs the therapy of a new way of reading.

This brings me to my second point about *The Waste Land*, which is that our error in reading it has been an error of historiography. During the 1920s, when the artists were demolishing the temple of the nineteenth century, we readers of history picked up our own hammers and started reducing a way of thinking to rubble. Arguably, we succeeded. We don't look at Sir Edwin Landseer's paintings any more. We no longer think of oratory as one of the fine arts, or of the sermon as a literary genre. A whole culture has vanished. But while we were destroying the nineteenth century we felt the need to create something in its place, and so we and the artists collaborated on the invention of an antihistory we called modernism. It was an astonishingly successful collaboration: modernism has been the dominant mode of high-cultural expression in the West for three quarters of a century. But when we think of that phenomenon historically, we keep coming up against the Eliot problem. And that problem turns out to call the very existence of modernism into question.

Consider: here, on the one hand, is an aesthetic movement, apparently as clearly defined as any aesthetic movement in history. Here, on the other hand, is T. S. Eliot, one of that movement's clearly central figures. And yet there seems to be no way of reconciling any conventional history of modernism with the existence of Eliot's central achievement, a poem directed against history. Around Eliot is a dead zone into which history hasn't been able to enter. That phenomenon must make anyone wonder: was what we call modernism simply a fortuitous aggregation of talents? Was the term "modernism" simply a temporary taxonomic convenience, like the term "Lake School"? Was there ever really such a thing as modernism?

I think, myself, that there was. I think it can be defined with some degree of rigor, and I think the definition will be useful. And I think too that part of our Eliot problem results from a simple confusion between two pairs of different things: poetic power and poetic influence; the power of Eliot the man of letters and the power of Eliot the poet. As a poet, Ezra Pound, like Alexander Pope, had both power and influence; T. E. Hulme, like Sir John Denham, had influence but not much power; T. S. Eliot, like William Blake or Emily Dickinson, had power but not much influence. Sooner or later we will figure out that Eliot's reputation rests precisely on the uniqueness of his achievement in verse, and then we will be able to define that reputation in nice clear historical terms, with respect to other reputations. I'm not worried about that; I think the future can be trusted to sort out the confusions we are now struggling through. Still, I think we ought to give the future as much help as we can. And to that end I ask again: was there such a thing as modernism?

The answer in terms of poetic power is a literary answer and, as such, no more useful than literature can be. But suppose we try to answer the question historically and say: There was such a thing as modernism because there had to be, as effect or cause. If we then take *The Waste Land* as the paradigm text of modernism, defining modernism according to the textbook criteria we have inherited from the modernist era's own efforts to understand what it was doing ("It employs a distinctive kind of imagination, one that insists on having its general frame of reference within itself. . . . *Modern* implies a historical discontinuity. . . . It not only rejects history, but also rejects the society of whose fabrication history is a record"; Holman, s.v. "Modern"), we may be able to see ourselves as citizens of a sort of Colonus of reading, waiting for the stranger whose coming we can understand for what it was only after he has arrived and then departed.

The Waste Land will then matter as a read text, that which both exemplified and caused a way of reading which has caused us, in turn, to think differently about ourselves. Eliot's Old Possum disclaimer of the poem as "only the relief of a personal and wholly insignificant grouse against life" (*Waste Land Facsimile* 2) will matter then, but not necessarily as a biographical datum (say, that the great man was the first Romantic poet since Byron to have a sense of humor) or a literary-political maneuver (say, that he wanted us to stop reading Jessie Weston and start rereading the poem). We have to read the joke in one of those ways now, but a historical reading will allow us to think of it in a third way: as the poet's own recognition of his text as a historical artifact, linked inextricably but in an ever changing way with himself, on the one hand, and its (his) readers, on the other.

Considered in that way, as the testimony of its own interaction with a historically constituted readership, *The Waste Land* won't be able to show us in itself what modernism was or whether it existed. But it will be able to show us how we have read ourselves into a state of receptivity to modernism. As to whether modernism can be considered to exist in itself, as a *mentalité*, Eliot's example in itself can tell us little. Eliot's example may show us that there was a modernism, or maybe on the other hand that there wasn't. Hugh Kenner's reading of the record may be right: posterity may think of us all as subjects of the Pound Era. On the other hand, Harold Bloom may be right when he proclaims that "Modernism in literature has not passed; rather it has been exposed as never having been there" (*Map* 28). Modernism may be mirror or lamp. Either way, however, Eliot's reputation and the history of modernism are reciprocally illuminating problems. Thinking of either one will probably change our attitudes toward the other. For a start, I wonder what will happen to our perception of Eliot if we try to situate him in a continuum that originates late in the eighteenth century, with the origins of Romanticism. If we can do that, I think I would like to wonder then how modernism managed to take into its history this poet who was rooted in the very past against which modernism claimed to be reacting. The counterhistory of modernism may turn out after all to be directly continuous with the traditional canon of literary history. But that doesn't need to concern us now, practically speaking. If modernism turns out to be an isolated, unassimilable fragment of history, that too will be worth knowing. The main issue before us at the end of the twentieth century is only this: we children of modernism, we who knew *The Waste Land* before we knew Tennyson, have grown up with Eliot. We are old enough now to find out for ourselves who he is. Like the citizens of Colonus, we need to know the history of the man who will have made ours.

11

History in the Waste Land: "Tradition and the Individual Talent"

We already possess an idealized model of such a history. Even in its title, "Tradition and the Individual Talent" marks out a zone for the living of life historically. Read in that zone, literature takes on the only moral value it can have: its value as a testimony of the place of its subject in time, with respect to the life of its reader.

> vurry hard for an ang-sax to deal with swaddling clothes
> —Ezra Pound, *Selected Letters*, no. 344

Consider how we might read an explicitly autobiographical novel in the zone of history: *The Way of All Flesh*, say, or *Look Homeward, Angel*. Within the layer of ink on each page, a protagonist lives out two simultaneous lives: one depicted in the dimensions of space, the other depicted in the dimensions of time. Here, coextensive with the words that reconstitute it, is the vicarage or the North Carolina town, in more or less circumstantial detail, physically evocable, the counterfeit history that we call literature. Here also, however, not exactly in the words but somehow associated with them, is a coextensive implicit underlay of what we uneasily come to feel must be memory. This—this feeling, this thing we can't exactly locate in the words on the page—is what makes us nervous about what we have been reading. We are afraid that it may be real: the unassimilated, unmediated thing, that which James Agee tried so desperately to extract from the lives of the Rickettses and the Gudgers and the Woods. We sense this thing somewhere between the page and us; we register it as something describable in literary terms (say, an atmosphere or an extra dimension of detail), and we give it a name (say, Religion or Adolescence), but we still fail to understand it. The first level of depiction, the matter of space depicted in time, belongs to the history of events. Its historical authenticity is determined by such things as accuracy of detail in clothing styles, and its readability is characterized by the possibility of closure. We can know when to exit from its domain and resume our course through wordless life. But there is no "The End" after the last word of the second level of depiction. Its extension in space and time includes our lives as both site and origin, and its historical presence there is to be understood in terms of a problem in the ontology of reception: which came first, our emotion or the author's word?

For the *Erziehungsroman* the elaborated perception of this affective history is a matter of life and death, for it alone determines whether or not the protagonist can live on in the lives of successive generations of readers. Because religion among literate people in the Western world doesn't affect child-rearing practices in the ways that it did before Freud, *The Way of All Flesh* has moved from the student's coat pocket to the professor's seminar room. Because adolescence continues to be experienced in the Western world as a separate stage of human development, *Look Homeward, Angel* remains available to the experience of being sixteen years old. It doesn't matter that Samuel Butler's mind and style are more interesting than Thomas Wolfe's; the formal properties available to a disinterested aesthetic reading turn out to matter less than some matters of internal history.

The New Criticism, which in practice if not in theory was generally ahistorical, had trouble with that fact; that is why it concerned itself so intensively with lyric poetry. Ideally, the lyric is a moment of separated, analyzed perception, set off on the page by a large blank margin, isolated from the world, wholly itself: an experience in and of words. Its mode of development is by revelation, a sudden discovery that an end has now come, has been here always already, without regard to time: "Forever wilt thou love, and she be fair!" But insofar as this revelation must be granted to us word by word, in sequence, the lyric is always contaminated by time. That is its poignancy: its desperate attempt to convey its truth to us in words which, insofar as they *are* words, embody a lie. The novel is less scrupulous about its own stuff. It takes the poem's lie of the absolute and remanufactures it into a second-order relational truth, deploying its words on the field of meaning as if they were stolid, immortal machines for the conversion of nonverbal sense into verbal ideation. Insofar as the novel's language is purely referential, its words are, in Eliot's famous metaphor, catalysts: reagents unchanged by the reaction they provoke.

But consider what happens to the words in a novel about language.

David Schearl, the little boy who is the protagonist of Henry Roth's *Call It Sleep*, is locked in an Oedipal struggle with four implacable antagonists: his seductive mother, his terrifying father, the incomprehensible menace of the universe outside his parents' door, and the words of his life, which hold out to him an ever receding promise of understanding. To "provide a mediation between social phenomena and private facts" (Jameson, "Imaginary and Symbolic" 338),[1] David has only those words, reaching out from themselves toward other words but always eluding him. The words are Yiddish, spoken at home but incomprehensible outside and incapable of rendering the outside comprehensible; Polish, the incomprehensible secret tongue of the parents; Hebrew, the language whose hints of the ineffable the cheder boy David is expected to speak without comprehension; and the English of the streets, a maimed creole through which David makes his bewildered contact with the world at large. David speaks and hears, but every language is foreign to him because he

[1] This is my translation, slightly abridged. The original Jamesonian reads: "The attempt to coordinate a Marxist and a Freudian criticism confronts—but as it were explicitly, thematically articulated in the form of a problem—a dilemma that is in reality inherent in all psychoanalytic criticism as such: that of the insertion of the subject, or, in a different terminology, the difficulty of providing mediations between social phenomena and what must be called private, rather than even merely individual, facts."

has come belatedly onto the stage of the family drama. From the beginning, its words have proceeded without him. David has no mother tongue.

Roth's plot, the engine of this estrangement, brings David at the end of the book to seek in the physical world for a way to understand. His native language, Yiddish, is a father tongue: a speech forbidden to him. But the words of another language offer to guide him through images to a wordless light. Earlier in the book (227, 366–67), preparing for his bar mitzvah, David has been moved to uncomprehending tears by an infantile memory brought to consciousness in Isaiah's image of words rendered by the destructive element worthy of understanding: "Then said I, Woe is me! for I am undone; because I am a man of unclean lips, and I dwell in the midst of a people of unclean lips: for mine eyes have seen the King, the Lord of hosts. Then flew one of the seraphims unto me, having a live coal in his hand, which he had taken with the tongs from off the altar: And he laid it upon my mouth, and said, Lo, this hath touched thy lips; and thine iniquity is taken away, and thy sin purged" (Isaiah 6: 5–7). David knows the coal: earlier (253), he has dropped a sheet of steel down the third-rail slot of a streetcar line and been dazzled by a blaze of electric flame. Now, at the end of the book, fleeing in terror, guilt, and uncomprehended shame from his father, David rushes through a babel of voices in the hot, pullulant street. Around him is the human, talking. An elderly night watchman, toiling through the dark on his rounds, tells himself over and over again the story of how he accidentally killed his wife. A laborer shouts about sex to a bartender, and a prositute tells a story of revenge on a former lover. A British sailor wonders to himself whether it would be feasible to open a fish-and-chips shopt in New York; boys play a call-and-run game in the street; a streetcar's motorman rings his bell furiously at the crowd; some poker players make obscene jokes at a ground-floor window; and somewhere at the center of the mass a Communist agitator's voice tries to organize the words into a language. But his voice is only one more sound, uncomprehended. David understands nothing. He can hope only that Isaiah's words describe him: a man of unclean lips, undone by having seen the King, the Lord of hosts.

Kneeling over the streetcar track, David takes hold of his

father's milk dipper. He reaches it down into the slot in the earth (418–19).

> "Dere's a star fer yeh! Watch it! T'ree Kings I god. Dey came on huzzbeck! Yee! Hee Hee! Mary! Nawthin' to do but wait fer day light and go home. To a red cock crowin'. Over a statue of. A jerkin'. Cod. Clang! Clang! Oy! Machine! Liberty! Revolt! Redeem!"
>
> *Power*
> *Power! Power like a paw, titanic power*
> *ripped through the earth and slammed*
> *against his body and shackled him*
> *where he stood. Power! Incredible,*
> *barbaric power! A blast, a siren of light*
> *within him, rending, quaking, fusing his*
> *brain and blood to a fountain of flame,*
> *vast rockets in a searing spray! Power!*
> *The hawk of radiance raking him with*
> *talons of fire, battering his skull with*
> *a beak of fire, braying his body with*
> *pinions of intolerable light. And he*
> *writhed without motion in the clutch of*
> *a fatal glory, and his brain swelled*
> *and dilated till it dwarfed the galaxies*
> *in a bubble of refulgence—Recoiled, the*
> *last screaming nerve clawing for survival.*
> *He kicked—once. Terrific rams of dark-*
> *ness collided; out of their shock space*
> *toppled into havoc. A thin scream wobbled*
> *through the spirals of oblivion, fell like*
> *a brand on water, his-s-s-s-s-ed—*
>
> "W'at?
> "W'ut?
> "Va-at?
> "Gaw blimey!
> "W'atsa da ma'?"

David lives. He is rescued and brought back home. His father sits shaken at his wife's kitchen table. Throughout the book, except for a single tiny passage necessitated by the plot, this brooding, violent man has spoken only in a Yiddish which Roth's translation renders in the cadences of the King James Bible. Now, broken, he speaks the broken English of the comic Jew, contemptuously interrupted by the policeman who has saved his son's life (437). Standing in his doorway, a large crowd witnesses the son's Oedipal victory, and comments on it. But "the psychobiolgraphical form remains shackled to the categories of individual experience, and is thus unable to reach a level of cultural or social generalization without passing through the individual case history" (Jameson, "Imaginary and symbolic" 344). No one in the crowd can understand what has happened. And the comic triumph of *Call It Sleep* is that David doesn't understand either. He has passed into silence and returned without words.

> "Sleepy, beloved?"
>
> "Yes, mama."
>
> He might as well call it sleep. It was only toward sleep that every wink of the eyelids could strike a spark into the cloudy tinder of the dark, kindle out of shadowy corners of the bedroom such myriad and such vivid jets of images.... It was only toward sleep that ears had power to cull again and reassemble the shrill cry, the hoarse voice, the scream of fear.... It was only toward sleep one knew himself still lying on the cobbles... and [could] feel... not pain, not terror, but strangest triumph, strangest acquiescence. One might as well call it sleep. He shut his eyes. (441)

The book ends there, in sleep and silence. Roth's novel has proclaimed its hero the victor over words. He has gone down to death and left his words there, a ransom to the darkness. An Orpheus of silence, the protagonist of this novel of our times can be happy because he has surrendered the history that might tell him who he is. Knowing the history we know, we can only envy him.

The Communist speech that extends, phrase by interrupted phrase, over several pages in the last section of *Call It Sleep* is an arbitrary and *voulu* afterthought to the story of David and his words. Roth, a dutiful Communist who has since, in *Shifting Landscape*, blamed the Party for the half-century of artistic impotence that beset him after *Call It Sleep*, thought it necessary to create the outline of a political context for David and his words.

But of course all that happens is that David's history creates a verbal context for the politician. Within that context the politician is only an absence: his words pass through the air in David's spatial and temporal vicinity, but only the author of the book seems to hear them. Heard but not seen in this highly visual novel, the revolutionist is an organ separated from its body: nothing but voice. He is virtual history. His words are static on the page. They are written but not read.

But though the Communist never succeeds in becoming more than a voice, there is a fully realized politics in this book: a politics made of language. *Call It Sleep* is a history of the making and shaping of what Eliot called "*significant* emotion" ("Tradition" 11):[2] sign-bearing emotion, emotion bearing the insignia of its own meaning into the time-structure of speech. In *Ulysses*, Eliot thought, the medium of significant emotion is the myth of the Odyssey: a narrative which, far from being "an amusing dodge,or scaffolding erected by the author for the purpose of disposing his realistic tale, of no interest in the completed structure," is in fact a means of shaping into a realized whole "material which [the creative artist] must simply accept" ("*Ulysses*, Order, and Myth," *Selected Prose* 175, 177). The myth served Joyce as the Black Mass served Baudelaire: "It is redeemed by *meaning something else*. He...cannot limit its symbolism even to all that of which he is conscious" ("Baudelaire," *Selected Essays* 378). The myth is a syntax of meaning, a pattern to be imposed on the data of consciousness, erecting them into that which can *mean something else*. Inserting itself into the progress of our lives from birth to death, it breaks the wordless flow of things into words, words ordered by syntax in time. The myth is a history always becoming.

"Tradition and the Individual Talent" is a history of this history. for my purposes, it can be read as a history of language.

By overlooking its provenance in the structure of language, Terry Eagleton has gotten some jolly Vishinskian fun out of Eliot's historiography. "The grounding of [Eliot's] thought in polite opinion of the [18]80s and '90s is always worth noting," Warner Berthoff comments (10 n. 2), and Eagleton makes the note

[2] Original emphasis. All citations to "Tradition and the Individual Talent" are keyed to the text in Eliot's *Selected Essays*.

at length. He does so by drawing our attention to Tradition's large household of embarrassing relatives. "The existing classics within the cramped space of the Tradition politely reshuffle their positions to make room for a newcomer, and look different in the light of it," he explains in his sophomore version of "Tradition and the Individual Talent,"

> but since this newcomer must somehow have been in principle included in the Tradition all along to have gained admission at all, its entry serves to confirm that Tradition's central values. The Tradition, in other words, can never be caught napping: it has somehow mysteriously foreseen the major works still unwritten. . . . Membership of the club is by invitation only: some writers, such as T. S. Eliot, just do discover that the Tradition . . . is spontaneously welling up within them, but as with the recipients of divine grace this is not a question of personal merit, and there is nothing much you can do about it one way or the other. Membership of the Tradition thus permits you to be at once authoritarian and self-abnegatingly humble, a combination which Eliot was later to find even more possible through membership of the Christian Church. (39–40)

Like William F. Buckley, Jr., Terry Eagleton likes the ad hominem argument. It allows metaphor to accumulate more metaphors at interest, creating author-value out of the capital of an author's words. As the account swells, author and word and all become vehicles of a single grand metaphor whose tenor is what Fredric Jameson approvingly calls "the political perspective . . . [conceived] as the absolute horizon of all reading and all interpretation" (*Political Unconscious* 9). This horizon is finally the only literary form there can be; within it, all else is content, and only content can bear meaning from word to word. So Eagleton can find Julia Kristeva's quest for the disruptive, pre-Oedipal, "revolutionary" dimension of literary language "dangerously formalistic" on the grounds that Kristeva "pays too little attention to the political *content* of a text" (190). But on the other hand, content can be read from within the controlling metaphor where others have read only form. All that is required is that the reading be pragmatic. Language must be seen to be nothing but a container for actual or potential action. The resistance to thinking of literary theory in political terms

> is not only . . . a matter of . . . biases being covert or unconscious. Sometimes, as with Matthew Arnold, they are neither, and at other times, as with T. S. Eliot, they are certainly covert but not in the least unconscious. It is not the fact that literary theory is political which is objectionable, nor just the fact that its frequent obliviousness of this tends to mislead; what is really objectionable is the nature of its politics. (195)

So Eagleton conceives of thought dynamically, as an inert mental state energized by contact with a properly arranged sequence of historical events. In retrospect, that arrangement will be seen to have been an absolute, a universal, bearing some such name as Science or the Laws of History—anything but Tradition.

Meanwhile, before those angels descend, Fredric Jameson finds the word "properly" to be a good succedaneum. It is one of his favorite words, as in (the first instance of many in *The Political Unconscious*) "the yield and density of a properly Marxist interpretive act" (10). Apparently a literal translation of the French *proprement* (*à proprement parler*: strictly speaking), Jameson's "properly" also carries the connotations we hear in a phrase like "properly dressed": connotations of propriety, of doing the nice thing, of being good and obedient, of conforming. "Properly" is a word from a book of etiquette for the conduct of the universe.

If it were ever written down, such a book would be interesting: a text communicated in the language of a para-reality (Jameson's word is "Utopia"); the dialect of a future history. And Jameson is concerned with writing that language. When he says in one of his earthly approximations of the ideal rhetoric that, for instance, a certain effort at criticism "confronts—but as it were explicitly. . .—a dilemma" (above, 197 n.1), he is taking the first step toward creating a signification apparatus that digests content into words *an sich*, words radically separated from content by their own figural elaborations. That absolute language will of course be fully readable only in the future, under the interpretive conditions of "those new forms of collective thinking and collective culture which lie beyond the boundaries of our own world" (11). Here and now, meanwhile, in the preliminary absence of that Utopia, Jameson's language looks as self-contained and self-referential as, say, Kenneth Burke's. But here is a puzzle in reading: if we try to reconstitute Jameson's language on our own terms

> ["as it were explicitly" means "figuratively explicitly" so its alright to talk about confronting the dilemma cause language is you know *metaphoric* and metaphors always you know like *sublate* their subjects like okay when you say its raining cats n dogs you mean it like *isnt* raining cats n dogs i mean its you know the dialectic]

> [but what does "but" mean?]

we will suddenly realize that Jameson's thick murk of mixed metaphors and *franglais* has something in common with T. S. Eliot's epigrammatic clarity. This thing is something like an attitude, but it isn't—or isn't directly—a result of the two critics' shared political mandarinism. On the contrary, it is a rhetoric. Specifically, it is a prepolitical, almost presocial rhetoric whose ground is in the linguistics of time. In "Tradition and the Individual Talent" Eliot does something from within language that Jameson tries to do, belatedly, from without: he shows us the content at the heart of language's form and teaches us its significance.

Look: here, again, is Jameson's parenthetical string of qualifiers, with its vanishingly abstract subject:

> The attempt to coordinate a Marxist and a Freudian criticism confronts—but as it were explicitly, thematically articulated in the form of a problem—a dilemma.

During the first half of this century, for many reasons, many novelists of sensibility made use of this rhetoric of the regress of perception, each nuance leading to another nuance. Henry James, Marcel Proust, and Virginia Woolf come immediately to mind, but the general technique can also be found in writers as thematically compromised as Willa Cather, as crude as Theodore Dreiser, and as dilute as Katherine Mansfield. In fact, the morphology of this technique can help us draw part of a distinction between major and minor writers, authentic and inauthentic. For James, Proust, and Woolf, the regress of significance is a fundamental way of seeing the world. A way of analyzing reality into its fundamental components, it pervades the work of these writers under every novelistic circumstance. For Cather or Mansfield, on the other hand, it is only a stylistic expedient, useful on occasion for evoking reactions to the decor (Cather) or the schmerz of Chekhov in translation (Mansfield). Dreiser, who uses the technique in a deep but unconscious and not wholly coherent way, occupies a complicated middle position between the minor writers and the major ones. For the major writers and for them alone, however, the technique is fully historicized. It is a way of building into the language of narrative a deep structure for the depiction of time.

Jameson, operating under different sociological conditions, has seized on a similar technique. His counters of significance are not emotions but abstractions, and he is afflicted with a tin ear, but he has experienced the same time-nostalgia as the major novelists. And he has this in common with them, as he does not with such other utopians of time as H. G. Wells: his time-nostalgia is translated into the rhythm and vocabulary of his prose style. Whether the nostalgia is for the past, as it is for Proust and Woolf, or for the future, as it is for Jameson, is beside the point. The point is the nostalgia itself and its significance as articulated for our time by T. S. Eliot in "Tradition and the Individual Talent." The controlling sentence there is this one: "Very few know when there is an expression of *significant* emotion, emotion which has its life in the poem and not in the history of the poet" (11).

We can notice first that this sentence displays itself as a piece of adversary connoisseurship. Clearly, reading in search of *significant* emotion is a heroic, a Dantesque task. It involves journeying step by step through the text and through the self, listening and testing. This journey must always be slow and painful; only in that way can it accumulate time around itself. Time, says Eliot about his own experience, offers the poet "tradition and . . . accumulated wisdom" ("The Function of Criticism," *Selected Essays* 18). That is the familiar rhetoric of Eliot's political conservatism, here communicating a merely relational, merely metaphoric idea of time as a neutral medium, a sort of ether through which signs are transmitted unchanged from dead mouths to living ears. The view of time in "Tradition and the Individual Talent," however, is more radical. For Eliot's famous formula that "the historical sense involves a perception, not only of the pastness of the past, but of its presence" (4) applies not just as a principle of criticism but as a linguistic principle beyond the individual writer's or reader's critical control, perceptible after the fact only in its residual effect on language, "in the poem and not in the history of the poet."

That is, Eliot asks us to understand that some critical principles are inherent in language, in what we can call its historical syntax. Jameson and Eagleton are concerned with language as narrative: an external history constrained to the rhythms of extraverbal time, imposing its own time-constraints on language. Theirs is a dynamic view of history, one in which, for instance, impressionism and Joseph Conrad's descriptions are the results of specific concatenations in the history of events.

> The very activity of sense perception has nowhere to go in a world in which science deals with ideal quantities, and comes to have little exchange value in a money economy dominated by considerations of calculation, measurement, profit, and the like. This unused surplus capacity of sense perception can only reorganize itself into a new and semi-autonomous activity, one which produces its own specific objects, new objects that are themselves the result of a process of abstraction and reification, such that older concrete unities are now sundered into measurable dimensions on one side, say, and pure color (or the experience of purely abstract color) on the other. . . . [The description of the impending storm in Conrad's *Typhoon* is a product of an] unfamiliar sensorium which, like some new planet in the night sky, suggests senses and forms of libidinal gratification as unimaginable to us as the possession of additional senses, or the presence of nonearthly colors in the spectrum. (Jameson, *Political Unconscious* 229, 231)

"Surplus capacity of sense," "measurable dimensions on one side," "unfamiliar sensorium . . . like some new planet in the night sky": these are metaphors, and Jameson's conclusion—for all its length and aside from any rhetorical persuasiveness—is finally nothing but an asserted metaphor. But of course that is exactly the point. In a dynamic view of history's discourse, anything utterable in the language of record is possible in fact. Ipso facto, what is spoken shows itself to be the trace of its having been conceived in a prior nonverbal history. Having said a thing, we know we have conceived it; having conceived it, we know that in some sense it exists. Speech as color, scientific observation as empowerment of the body, all the hopeful reconstructions of ourselves that the young Marxist Auden called (when he prayed for them in "Sir, no man's enemy") "new styles of architecture, a change of heart"—to speak of these things in Utopia, where the world is coextensive at last with the speaker and all his *mana*, is to achieve them.

But the central metaphor of "Tradition and the Individual Talent" calls the materialist dynamic into question. "When [oxygen and sulphur dioxide] are mixed in the presence of a filament of platinum," says Eliot, "they form sulphurous acid. This combination takes place only if the platinum is present; nevertheless the newly formed acid contains no trace of platinum, and the platinum itself is apparently unaffected; has remained inert, neutral, and unchanged" (7). With respect to the transmutation of experience into poetry, Eliot concludes, "The mind of the poet is the shred of platinum." It is passive; more important, it is static. Language passes over it, being changed; it remains still. The agent of the change only lurks in the background of Eliot's formulation; it is given the category-names of "tradition" and "the mind of Europe," but the nature of its agency—what it does and how it does it—remains unspoken of. All we can do is to search in the archive for its trace.

That trace will be written in history's ultimate genre, the epitaph. "No poet, no artist of any art, has his complete meaning alone," writes Eliot. "His significance, his appreciation is the appreciation of his relation to the dead poets and artists. You cannot value him alone; you must set him, for contrast and comparison, among the dead." And Eliot adds, in a too frequently overlooked coda to the famous apothegm, "I mean this as a principle of aesthetic, not merely historical, criticism" (4–5). Biography can help us understand the distinction. It will help us notice, for instance, that in Eliot's disclaimer of large meaning —"a personal and wholly insignificant grouse against life" (*Waste Land Facsimile* 2)—the words "personal" and "wholly insignificant" are synonymous. In general, we can come to realize, Eliot's theory of the effacement of personality realized itself through his own life, as cause or effect or symptom or cure, in an attitude toward action, the living, and time.

Here are the data. At the beginning of 1919, with *The Waste Land* three years in the future, Henry Ware Eliot died, bitterly certain at the end that in giving up an academic career his son had chosen to make himself a failure. On the eve of his fame, the poet's words were unheard in the house that had given him himself and his language. Time and mortality had conspired to cheat him of reconciliation. He had tried to know and say, and his work had come to nothing. Then he wrote: "Only those who have personality and emotions know what it means to want to escape from these things" ("Tradition" 10–11).

Eliot knew: if we ever do escape from these things, it will be toward what the poet of the *Quartets* was to call the still point of the turning world: that which absorbs change and its words into silence, instant by instant. "My father has died," Eliot wrote to his patron John Quinn on January 26, 1919, "but this does not weaken the need for a book at all—it really reinforces it—my mother is still alive" (*Waste Land* xvi). Reading that interestingly punctuated sentence in their own dynamic way, the psychobiographers (has he had any other kind of biographer?) have placed Eliot among the dead who inhabit case history. But case history, as Eliot might have said, is a genre of merely historical criticism. In its emphasis on the merely personal, it fails to take into account the universal of *significant* emotion. On the other hand, Eliot's epistemology of the past in "Tradition and the Individual Talent" is, among other things, a statement in aesthetics, because it allows for a continuing mutual alteration of consciousness among entities in time, the past and the present continuing to affect each other. "The difference between the present and the past is an awareness of the past in a way and to an extent which the past's awareness of itself cannot show" (6): this personification of the past, making it into a conscious entity, allows significance to subsist in the blur where time and the human meet each other. In Eliot's formulation each of these entities, the human and her chronicle, possesses with respect to the other what Walter Benjamin called aura: "its presence in time and space, its unique existence at the place where it happens to be" ("Work of Art" sec. 2). To think of history in this way is to understand why dynamic theories of action in time must be oversimplifications. Psychobiography and psychohistory, for example, originate in the dynamic oversimplification of pragmatism. Thinking of phenomena in the present only as results of the past and not as causes of the past, the psychobiographers read only backward: from the art to the inferred life; from *The Waste Land* to its inferred origins in a particular man, at a particular time, under the influence of this or that particular mood or meal or memory. They can see only unitary origins, and those origins they can see only as incomprehensible. Like the aged narrator of L. P. Hartley's *The Go-Between*, who looks back in wonder at his innocently tragic childhood, they can only say in the opening sentences of their every narrative, "The past is a foreign country. They do things differently there." Such readers cannot speak the language of that country because they do not understand that it speaks theirs. Mother is there, in the dynamic reading; that's all; Mother is there, Mother is there.

The aesthetic reading that Eliot commended is more compassionate. Read without its aura, the history-word "Mother" is only an item in the bill of particulars that we call the poet's personality. But the word as T. S. Eliot spoke it—in history, at the place where it happened to be—can be thought of aesthetically as part of a willed historical act. What guided that act was a sense of the place of feeling in time. Eliot called it "the historical sense . . . a perception, not only of the pastness of the past, but of its presence" ("Tradition" 4). My mother is still alive, says the individual; but the artist's historical will is what makes that fact into an aesthetic truth—say, the general aesthetic truth that we call happiness. "Mother" is a word of Eliot's monitorily italicized phrase, *significant* emotion.

Out of significant emotion, Eliot's will to write the language of history was about to make *The Waste Land* retroactively into the emotional dossier of each of thousands of individuals. And that, perhaps, is why the Eliot Era can't be said to exist. At the time *The Waste Land* was shaping language and sense around itself, it nevetheless didn't exist—not in the ordinary way in which we regard a human creation. *The Waste Land* didn't stand, as other works of art do, between us and entropy and death, and its power didn't extend the power of the human to live in time. Instead, it was a construction downward: from a single text down through successive dissociations of quotation and fragmentation and excision to the rubble foundation of a single mental collectivity, in language but below coherent thought. *The Waste Land* doesn't have an ordinary history, because it isn't an ordinary text. It is the grammar of an antihistory: a principle for reading against sense, erected on the ruins of its readers' annihilated personalities.

And it is a static principle. Perhaps that is what has made "Tradition and the Individual Talent" the central literary-historical document of the twentieth century: its idea of history as the wholly passive, ever changed center of language. "Some can absorb knowledge, the more tardy must sweat for it," Eliot reminds us. "Shakespeare acquired more essential history from Plutarch than most men could from the whole British Museum" (6). Essential history, I take it, is that which has preceded the names and dates and battles that we call history, and preceded too the words that we call the historical record. It is what Eliot calls a principle or what a Kuhnian might call a paradigm: a way of organizing thought around the fundamental things in our lives. Essential history is that which is human: the consciousness that one is living in time, with all that that implies of grief and joy. The living itself changes, but the knowledge of time does not. Amid the annihilations we have needed to know that in our time.

Eliot's "tradition," that notorious word, can be thought of as something like a latent form of this knowledge. Whatever we call it, it is a time-experience that we experience aesthetically. Reaching into the earth to touch power at the end of *Call It Sleep*, little David also touches the ruins of words that once were, the significant emotion that now lies mutely buried in the parents' cold bed. Fredric Jameson might call David's gesture an aesthetic experience within a social horizon; Eliot might have called it an experience of tradition. The two might have agreed that it is comprehensible only from within a continuity of time in language—that is, from what our time has brought close to an end.

Henry James once had a glimpse of tradition from without that continuity. "That excess of lurid meaning, in some of the old men's and old women's faces in particular," he mused when he visited New York's Jewish ghetto in 1906, "would have been absurd, in the conditions, as a really directed attention—it could only be the gathered past of Israel mechanically pushing through" (132). James couldn't understand the language of that gathered past; he could only hear it. Eliot heard it in himself and tried to write a language in which he could speak of its loss and its regaining. "Tradition and the Individual Talent" is a rhetoric of time. History is its grammar.

12

History and Text: A Theory

The ladies of Honolulu understood Emily Dickinson according to the social codes prevailing in their own community of interpretation, which is not ours. Somebody keeps teaching America's high school seniors that the quantifier "a lot" is a single word. Franz Suchomel, in charge of the gas chambers at Treblinka, now refers to his victims as "those poor people" (Lanzmann 110). It is hard to write a grammar of the language in which we mean, because that would necessitate understanding the syntax of change. How can we know, for instance, what the simple adjective "poor" means now, in relation to what it once meant, for a single speaker, a small functionary in a large history? How can we continue to know the changing instant in which any word was present to our understanding?

If we ask that question in the vocabulary of semantics, we will be frustrated. Language's questions can't be answered from within language. But language can at least show us what was meaning at the moment the question's words were uttered.[1] It can help us see

[1] "What was meaning" is awkward, but I can't think of a shorter periphrasis. I mean by it something analogous to "what was happening": a clause signifying the context in which predication occurs. This act of predication in a context must always be historical. Consider, for instance, the historical grammar of the sentence "She saw what was happening." Onto the scene of an action strides a subject, and proceeds to reduce it to a noun—"She saw <what-was-happening>" — thus freezing the action in time. The action's unbroken internal continuity

the remnants of context which words bear with them as traces of the moment when signifiers enter into the domain of what has been significant and the whole existing order is, if ever so slightly, altered.

I suspect that Emily Dickinson's verse continues to fascinate readers because its central emotion is a profound nostalgia for the moment before this alteration. Certainly the poet's biographers have sought hard enough in the life for a source of the words, as if they have intuited that "the 'mythogram,' a writing that spells its symbols pluridimensionally; [where] the meaning is not subjected to successivity, to the order of a logical time, or to the irreversible temporality of sound" (Derrida, *Of Grammatology*, qtd. in Scholes 292), is to be found, if anywhere, at the origin of its speaker. Cynthia Griffin Wolff, for example, has hypothesized that the rhetorical secret at the heart of Dickinson's verse is withheld meaning, and that this negative language in turn grows out of the primal fault of her mother's absence from the infant's wordless gaze (52–54). The poems, explains the biographer, are a pathetic effort to achieve in words what should have been communicated without words. Analytic theory teaches us to think that in the absence of mirror phase and love, the poet shaped words into a doll-substitute for her mother. Such a reading appeals to us because it is only an extreme case of the general history of lack. The silent plenitude of our prehistory, when our desires were made wholly known without words, has been replaced by a devouring incomprehension that we don't know how to fill. Derrida's mythogram is Chandrasekhar's black hole.

There is something to be said for that silence where we once rested, "Enamored—impotent—content—" (P505), in an entirely synchronic domain of desire and simultaneous fulfillment, wholly comprehended. But Dickinson could never finally say that thing,

---

with its own past has been separated from it and routed through grammar into a prenarrative. What is left of the action in the present can now be perceived only under the terms of the subject's nominalizing grammar. And what is to come after its transformation has become dependent on the existence of a further series of perceptions. Unless it includes a perceiver, any future that follows on the construction of the noun will be grammatically meaningless. The sentence "She saw what was happening" therefore documents a redistribution of power across time.

and neither can we, because we have to speak in words. We cannot comprehend in our speech; we can only utter segmentally, moment by dissociated moment, word by word.

Sometimes, therefore, we have tried to reclaim history from words. T. S. Eliot, for instance, with a political agenda in mind, suggested in "The Metaphysical Poets" that words might have possessed absolute meaning when England was an absolute monarchy. Frank Kermode, having gone back and looked at the historical record, has demonstrated that Eliot's theory is just one more installment of the myth of the golden age: a very old story that we aren't likely ever to bring to a conclusion. In truth, the Fall occurred when Adam first gave a thing a name. But we still want to retell the myth. It reminds us of our delinquent palaces.

And it tells us that the distress calls that are the texts of our life stories will sooner or later be heard, understood, and acted upon. So, for instance, recognizing that no two people since 1819 have agreed on the meaning of the eighteen-word sentence "Beauty is truth, truth beauty,—that is all / Ye know on earth, and all ye need to know," E. D. Hirsch has asked us to wonder what would happen if "there [should appear] on the scene a scholar-critic of great authority . . . with the following sensational announcement: he has discovered a new Keats letter explaining exactly what Keats meant to convey" (47–50) To ask the question that way, begging the question of the word "exactly," is to anticipate a hopeful answer, and that is what Hirsch supplies us. Given proof of intentionality, Hirsch assures us, Keats's lines will "have now been placed in a different cultural category than they occupied before, and they will find themselves alongside that great army of verses that everybody understands."

Well, it sounds good. It's always cheering to see intentionality vindicated. Robert Scholes has gotten some good low comedy out of Jacques Derrida's enraged protestations that his critics haven't understood what he meant to say. But of course, as we realize when we think it through, Hirsch's "everybody understands" is true only within a specific cultural category, and this category is smaller than Hirsch seems to think. It isn't the class of everyone culturally literate enough to have heard of Keats, for instance, because it doesn't include, for instance, the subclass of folk deconstructionists who say, "Everybody's got a right to their own opinion, ain't they?" In fact, it appears to include only that small class of readers to whom the phrase "a scholar-critic of great authority" means something—a class that doesn't extend to (for instance) the leadership of the Great Proletarian Cultural Revolution in China, or the Reagan White House in the United States. And practically speaking, we have many letters from Wallace Stevens explaining exactly what he meant to convey, but Canadian forests still die for the Stevens industry.

Nevertheless, there is such a thing as great authority. In Cambodia a few years ago, it was great authority that decreed the death penalty for women who sat with their legs crossed. Be they proletarian etiquette or poetic diction, symbol systems are not after all the lingua franca of the universe; they are delimited within boundaries, and within those boundaries they obey control. Those odd adverbial sentences from the Cultural Revolution, in the imperative mood but with no indication of who was giving the order—"Warmly welcome foreign visitors! Closely follow the teachings of Comrade Enver Hoxha!"—speak, once they have been translated, of language imprisoned by its grammar. The interpretive community too is in that prison, and the prison is escapeproof. We have an anecdote to confirm it, an anecdote involving a poet's ghost hovering disconsolate around the scene of a lost vade mecum.

Once upon a time, we learn, W. H. Auden, turning Dag Hammarskjöld's *Markings* into English with the help of a Swedish translator, ran into this quotation from Hölderlin:

> Die Mauern stehen
> sprachlos und kalt, die Fahnen
> klirren im Winde.

The German words puzzled the Englishman and the Swede. "The trouble was," the Swede recalls, "that 'klirren' (rattle) seemed to us an odd verb to apply to 'Fahnen' (flag, banner)" (Sjöberg 188–89). So Auden found a more onomatopoetically cogent word ("*Obs.* or *dial.*") in the *OED*, and Hammarskjöld's Hölderlin has been read in English ever since as

The walls stand
speechless and cold, the banners
faffle in the wind.

Unfortunately, as the Swedish translator realized after some years had passed, what was agitated by the wind was not banners but weathervanes: *Wetterfahnen*. The conclusion is inescapable and not subject to vote by the interpretive community: "rattle" was indeed the right verb. Meanwhile, Auden had died, and so long as his translation survives, it will be embellished by an editorial footnote pointing out the error that the poet is now past correcting. His collaborator is filled with remorse, for history is not going to deal lightly with "faffle." If *it* survives, it will be as a marker of the poet's idiosyncrasy, like Byron's "There let it lay." It has acquired an absolute meaning, albeit a meaning associated with the poet, not the poem. It signifies, forever now, W. H. Auden in his moral aspect: a man violating the laws of a language.

Which means, among other things, this: under some circumstances, texts have meaning.

But the circumstances have not always been propitious for meaning. Establishing the textual archaeology of a notional Grecian urn, E. D. Hirsch tried to demonstrate the existence of an absolute meaning, established once and for all by the author and readable as a recovery of the author's intention. That project failed because, in his oversimple metaphor of literary history as a linear series of priorities, Hirsch neglected to take into account the reciprocity of every relation between author and reader: each reading the other; each, with respect to the other, acting as "a functional principle by which . . . one limits, excludes, and chooses" (Foucault 159); and both changing through time. Other modes of criticism than Hirsch's, of course, have been able to take into account these reciprocal or differential relationships. One such mode is deconstruction, with its Saussurean base; another is the type of feminist historicism that Frank Lentricchia calls "manichean" (775). But in practice these criticisms have been able to grant the text at best an exemplary status: that which exists only to evoke and confirm the existence, or always-already preexistence, of "an uneasy joy of interpretation, beyond nihilism" (J.

Hillis Miller 253). At each critical extreme the reader has priority over the text: on the left, with Miller, as a Barthesian rapist, extracting his *jouissance* and then abandoning the broken body of the text to his own readers; on the right, with Hirsch, as a Nurse Ratched of intentionality, regressing the text to its historical infancy and keeping it there.

Suppose, however, we try to keep ourselves out of the reading; or rather, suppose we consider what happens if we think of the text and ourselves as entrained, in its and our own way, in history.

The entrainment certainly exists. As I suggested in the introduction to this book, our essential linearity with respect to language, the fact that we must hear one word after another, ensures that language must have a time dimension. Keats's Grecian urn has a complex relation to history, existing simultaneously as a testament of the past to the present, an object for contemplation in and of the present, and an idea *sub specie aeternitatis*; but Keats's poem about that relation is constrained by a single historical dimension. Commemorating time in all its intricate richnesses, the poem must proceed only forward, as read, left to right down the page, word by word. That limitation in turn requires of the writer, more than of other artists, "an ambition . . . to deliver his text as an object whose interpretation—by virtue of the exactness of its situation in the world—*has already commenced* and is therefore already constrained in, and constraining, its interpretation" (Said 171). The task for the reader, then, is to separate her own perceptions from those constrained on her by the text. Her own past has been changed by what she has just read. Newly at home in the delinquent palace, she finds that its language has been in her mouth all her life. All she has to tell her who she was a moment ago, before reading, is circumstantial evidence: the evidence of the world around her which has not yet been touched by words.

Over the years, of course, we have become adept at reading the circumstantial evidence. Looking around him at a new culture, Emerson tried to define it with reference to primal origins. "Words are signs of natural facts," he proclaimed in *Nature*, adapting the Christian tradition of typology and the Greek doctrine of signatures to a political purpose, and he proceeded to read history as a chronicle of the coming into existence of natural facts. To understand historically, according to this model, is to read facts as words.

> On my way a moment I pause,
> Here for you! and here for America!
> Still the present I raise aloft, still the future of the
> States I harbinge glad and sublime,
> And for the past I pronounce what the air holds of the red
> aborigines.
>
> The red aborigines,
> Leaving natural breaths, sounds of rain and winds, calls as
> of birds and animals in the woods, syllabled to us for
> names,
> Okonee, Koosa, Ottawa, Monongahela, Sauk, Natchez,
> Chattahoochee, Kaqueta, Oronoco,
> Wabash, Miami, Saginaw, Chippewa, Oshkosh, Walla-Walla,
> Leaving such to the States they melt, they depart, charging
> the water and the land with names.
>
> (Whitman, "Starting from Paumanok," sec. 16)

"I pronounce what the air holds": history's imperium speaks through the poet's body, one *pneuma* of word and event. And the grammar of history's language is to be found in the self. "We, as we read," declared John Dewey's predecessor Emerson in "History," "must become Greeks, Romans, Turks, priest and king, martyr and executioner; must fasten these images to some reality in our secret experience, or we shall learn nothing rightly." And he summed up the curriculum of his school of history in an epigram: "All history becomes subjective; in other words there is properly no history, only biography." Humming the song of himself to himself as he read this conflation of event with actor, Whitman determined to write an American history in body language. The red aborigines lived and died in order to furnish that language with a bibliographic resource.

Not every water or land, however, is charged with the names of the peoples that have melted. We breathe their ashes in our air, but breath and ash are nameless in themselves—and nameless in our selves too. If we try to name them in ourselves, where the meanings are, we will find nothing with which to speak of them but what has been retained unspoken in our own breath: the words that haven't risen to consciousness, the shameful reserve of dirty words. All exploration is a looking inward, and our silence on the peak in Darien has in it some fear of what we may say when we speak at last. "I did not do a translation of 'Jabberwocky,'" Antonin Artaud explained from his mental-hospital bed. "When one digs into the shit of the individual being and his language, the poem must necessarily smell bad; 'Jabberwocky' is a poem that its author has taken special pains to keep outside the uterine being of suffering into which all great poets have dipped, and from which, delivering themselves into the world, they smell bad. In 'Jabberwocky' there are passages of fecality, but it is like the fecality of an English snob who curls the obscene in himself like ringlets around a hot curling iron." So Artaud's nontranslation of "Jabberwocky"—"L'Arve et l'aume, tentative anti-grammaticale contre Lewis Carroll"—gropes beneath Carroll's grammar in order to touch the dirt where the death-screams of (among others) the red aborigines lie smothered. The English lyric beginning "'Twas brillig, and the slithy toves" is a poem made of changed words in unchanged social structures, but Artaud's translation (qtd. in Deleuze 279) is an exchange of tongue-sounds and hot breath in the foul rag-and-bone shop of the heart.

Il était roparant, et les vliqueux tarands
Allaient en gibroyant et en brimbulkdriquant
Jusque là où la rourghe est à rouarghe à rangmbde et rangmbde à
    rouarghambde:
Tous les falomitards étaient les chats-huants
Et les Ghoré Uk'hatis dans le grabugeument.

Rein ist fein, explained the poster in the antechamber where the victims of Auschwitz made themselves naked: we who cleanse the world of you want to write poems in pure language.[2]

Such a language, if the vicissitudes of military history had allowed it in the fullness of time to be written, might have been

[2] The translation in Lanzmann 124 reads, "Clean is good." In the film the rhyme is spoken in German.

conceivable as the tongue of a universal virtual history: the history of a world whose terms have established full contact with the wordless earth and become as final once again as they were in Eden. Wholly exterior to the human, the world defined by this history would be Eden's full epistemological complement: a garden of unnaming, a museum of death. There, at last, the "semiotic circularity" that Michael Riffaterre sees as the distinctive characteristic of poetry could become a universal principle. Under its control, history would write no past; it would be an endless present, having only one comprehensive desire, aiming finally at a single gratification: the abolition of time. It would be a history written by Heraclitus or, let us say in political terms, by Jay Gatsby, or by Adolf Hitler: an endless party or a collective orgasm lasting a thousand years. "In the reader's mind [the poem's semiotic circularity] means a continual recommencing, an indecisiveness resolved one moment and lost the next with each reliving of revealed significance, and this it is that makes the poem endlessly rereadable and fascinating," says Riffaterre (166), cheerfully assuming that what has happened to us over the years will be comprehensible forever after on its own terms, however we and the terms that make us may change. It is true, of course, that for dwellers in the world of real life and real death, the foul rag-and-bone shop is always open for business. But the history of some experiments in chemical engineering, chiefly carried out in Poland between 1941 and 1945, indicates that in some jurisdictions the boutique has been zoned into a ghetto whose language can no longer be understood.

Let us try to understand the language of one such ghetto. Here is its lexicon.

Late in 1987, an archivist discovered some 170 items of cultural journalism that America's most influential deconstructionist critic, the late Paul de Man, had published between 1940 and 1942 in his native Belgium, which was then occupied by the German army. Some of those essays and reviews, nationalist in theme, could be read as favoring the occupation. Of these, one article about literature was an explicitly anti-Semitic piece contributed to a special anti-Semitic number of a Nazi-controlled newspaper. Made public in the course of a conference at the University of

Alabama, this finding soon reached the *Chronicle of Higher Education* and the *New York Times.* At about the same time, the documentary evidence in Victor Farias's newly published *Heidegger et le nazisme* was destroying the accepted classroom alibi for Martin Heidegger's political past. The progenitor of modern literary theory had not, as it turned out, been an *engagé* Nazi only briefly, out of tactical necessity, and in order to bore from within. On the contrary, he was a vindictive and unrepentant Hitlerian from the beginning to the bitter end and beyond, a denouncer of his anti-Nazi colleagues and students during the Third Reich, a falsifier of his political curriculum vitae afterward.

These were revelations. And the literary theoreticians reacted accordingly, but perhaps not as we might have predicted. The followers of Heidegger and de Man didn't, for instance, by and large, ask new political questions about hermeneutics or deconstruction, or wonder in new ways how their own words ought to be read as part of the literary histories called "Heidegger" and "de Man." Instead, over the pages of journals ranging in their degree of theoretical rigor from *Boundary 2* and *Critical Inquiry* to he *TLS* and the *New Republic*, there poured a flood of exculpatory rhetoric: denying, minimizing, extenuating by deconstructing, in a demonstration of sympathy for evil perhaps unmatched since the Ezra Pound controversy thirty-nine years earlier.[3]

Professional *amour-propre* had something to do with this, of course, and ordinary human reluctance to change one's mind. Cultural history was also a guest at the table, no doubt. Tzvetan Todorov was only confirming some of Matthew Arnold's more depressing predictions when he surveyed the battle for the soul of literary criticism and concluded that "for want of external criteria accepted by all, the aesthetic model has acquired an increasing importance" (684). For many among us, Heidegger and de Man

[3] I am speaking primarily of the American reaction. As to the European reaction: "Response to the French publication of [Farias's] book was lively. In Germany, professional philosophers held back from taking positions. With some justification, it was pointed out that the topic of 'Heidegger and Nazism' has been treated often in the Federal Republic . . . while in France Heidegger was instantly denazified and even given the status of a resister. But in Germany also, the effect of the critique was minor" (Habermas 456).

have represented a beauty too precious to sacrifice—too precious to sacrifice, indeed, because beauty is all there is.

I would stipulate only this additional datum by way of trying to understand the philosophers' desire: the beauty it conceives is a beauty of language. Its ideal in this century, expressed over and over again in works of art and philosophy, has been something like a pentecostal experience of immediate comprehension, knowledge flowing so cleanly through its mediating words that it leaves no trace of itself hanging on letter or syllable. Such a language must be too intimately a part of its perceiver ever to be disinterested. It would come out of the perceiver's life and his sense of mortality, and its promise would be the promise of control over that sense. That would be the perfect performative: a language that grants its speaker the power to understand each moment as it comes, without words. But the poets and the philosophers, those creatures of words, have known that they are self-excluded from the domain of ecstatic mortality. Like Emily Dickinson's loaded gun caressed by its owner (P754), they have sensed their lack of what Heidegger called the essence of death.

> Though I than He—may longer live
> He longer must—than I—
> For I have but the power to kill,
> Without—the power to die—

Which perhaps is why they have been attracted to the men with the real guns.

In political terms, we can state the issue this way: poets (*sensu lato*) in the twentieth century have desired to colonize a tract of history for their own. This tract may be broad, as in *The Cantos*, or circumscribed, as in *Paterson*, or (at least in ambition) both, as in *Maximus*. Sometimes the territorial desire expresses itself negatively, as a yearning for an inviolable inward timelessness, no matter how small. At other times it becomes a candid desire for aggrandizement, as in the territorial metaphor with which Fredric Jameson, in his "Digression on Maoism," stakes a claim for the absolute value of "Maoism and the experience of the Chinese cultural revolution" and exhorts the middle-aged "not . . . to abandon rapidly and without thoughtful reconsideration any of this terrain to the 'other side'" ("Periodizing the 60s" 188–89). But regardless of the form this desire takes, it is one desire only: a desire for history. History, controlling the sense of time through its words, is to be the poets' way to power.

And so the poets have brought Paul de Man and Martin Heidegger into their ghetto and covered them with words to shut out the silence of the dead. In the case of de Man, the men of words have built a barrier of history-words between the mature scholar and the twenty-two-year-old journalist, who in turn has been differentiated by history-words from his more unquestionably fascist contemporaries. In the case of Heidegger, for whom no such discontinuities in life or thought can plausibly be worded into the record, the strategy has been to discriminate the man from his work. That, as it turns out, has been largely a matter of literary criticism: *nouvelle critique* in the service of historical and moral partitioning. Anthony Trollope invented the mailbox, but that datum has little to do with *Barchester Towers*, as cause or effect or correlative phenomenon. A part of our education has consisted in accepting such distinctions. "The intellect of man is forced to choose / Perfection of the life, or of the work," wrote William Butler Yeats, whose work demands moral compromise of its readers across a whole range of social and ethical concerns. And William Carlos Williams wrote to Ezra Pound in 1946: "No one forgives you for what you did, everyone forgives you for what you are" (qtd. in Torrey 221).

On such a reading of a life and what it produced, *Sein und Zeit* too is discriminable. It is a text. An authorial product with an accurately delimitable place in history, it *has been* written. It is now separate from its author; its ideas are no longer his. Any connection between the actions in an author's life and the words in his book is merely historical, an artifact of the isolated and textually unimportant moment when the former were being absorbed into the latter. To deconstruct all is to forgive all—or, rather, in a maneuver taught to us by Martin Heidegger, it is to place the word "forgive" *sous rature*. At the present instant, for us who are alive and reading, *il n'y a pas de hors-texte*. And some may feel themselves strong and free enough to step beyond good and evil and add:

We live in a time-ghetto, and the past is outside its walls.

Within, there is neither remembering nor forgetting; there is only *écriture*. There is no past—or if there is, it is ours to admit or not admit to significance, ours to control. There is only language: *our* language.

In their ghetto, the poets are probably exaggerating. There is language outside the walls, and there it does matter that Heidegger's side lost the war and our side now dictates the terms. Still, our control is limited. Outside or inside the ghetto, we can never deconstruct language enough to reshape it into a template for what Austin calls happiness. Insofar as it originates in ourselves, insofar as the metaphysical entity *mind* is implicated in the physical entity *brain*, language will have an independent power of its own, and we will be subject to its rules for as long as we exist. Nature does not freeplay. Flipping a coin, tossing the ball onto a spinning roulette wheel, rolling a pair of dice, shuffling a deck of cards: these ludic things are implicated with physical laws, and, as the statistician Persi Diaconis said after studying all of them, "Each is its own long story and for each the results are roughly similar. If you look hard, things aren't as random as everyone assumes" (qtd. in Kolata 1069). Mallarmé has been superseded by current research; we now know that *Un coup de dés abolira le hasard*. Original sin is a grammar.

Eliot called our fall into this grammar "dissociation of sensibility" and our inability to extricate ourselves from it "tradition." Thought of in that way, tradition can help us understand how history, embodied in texts, affects us as we read. But the word "tradition" itself has become politically unusable since Eliot's time. It connotes too much, now, of the anti-intellectual, the bigoted, the hypocritical: of the arbitrageur buying his ancestral flatware. It can't be used without rehabilitation. Let us rehabilitate it with a disguise—say, with the disguise of a narrower, more technical, but vaguer term: "sequence." Take it that sequence is the intrinsicality of history in a text. And then notice this about it:

Part of the intrinsicality of sequence is fixed. Determined by the syntactical structure of the language in which the text is written, it is beyond the author's control or even his consciousness. In English I am more or less rigidly constrained to think of subjects before objects, and my thinking is more or less constrained accordingly. But there is another part of sequentiality which is more malleable, more susceptible to control by an author's will. Arbiters of style have affected my repertoire. At the present time I can write "says J. Hillis Miller" without affectation, but etiquette no longer permits me to write "says he." This etiquette is part of the dynamic of a living language, and it affects the history of future readers as well as present writers. For since in the rules of our engagement with language there is always a tension between the fixed and the variable, since the variable part of language sometimes expands and becomes relatively more important for a while, historical conditions sometimes permit us to say something perceptibly original: something that isn't yet ready for its historical context.

If we think about it in this historical way, we can see that origination is always a relative thing, original only in relation to previously existing contexts. Since the days of Eden there has been no spontaneous generation, in life or literature. Instead, there has been a progression of themes and genres, each changing, stabilizing, and then passing into a successor form as time passes through it. As this happens, one historical context is replaced by another, and then our relation to the original changes. Time either obliterates it or rubs its edges off. In time, if it is given time, the original becomes friendly; it perseveres in being itself until it and we have come to terms with each other, changing each other in the process. *Finnegans Wake* passed through the avant-garde into the academy, and the avant-garde and the academy and *Finnegans Wake* have all been undergoing a sea change ever since. As we have read the book, we and it have imparted to each other the terms in which we understand. Being read, the book accretes significance around itself like a pearl in an oyster.

Sequence is the matrix of time in which this accretion takes place. It is a complex of many historical things: linguistic, political, physical. We cannot detect its presence directly, either in what we read or in ourselves, but we can know it is there. By attaching terminal dates to the record of an event, by saying "Once upon a time" and "The end," history has called time to our attention and required us to notice our entrainment in itself. That call is an aesthetic imperative. It requires us to help history look at itself in the mirror of its own structure. And a criticism which allows us to speak of that narcissistic task while we take part in it would be a highly desirable addition to the repertoire of knowing. It would help us see history with its clothes on, as it exists externally to ourselves: as aestheticized sequence. Seeing history that way, we will be able to follow its steps in and out of the boutiques of idea.

Consider, for a practical instance, a change in George Orwell's language with regard to a theme in the politics of literature.

The theme was enunciated for Orwell by the autobiography of Salvador Dali, which is a detailed record of its author's adventures in coprophilia, necrophilia, and sadism. "It is a book that stinks," Orwell tells us in his 1944 essay "Benefit of Clergy: Some Notes on Salvador Dali" (3: 159). "If it were possible for a book to give a physical stink off its pages, this one would—a thought that might please Dali, who before wooing his future wife for the first time rubbed himself all over with an ointment made of goat's dung boiled up in fish glue." But amid the stink of the wound stands the archer with his bow. Look at his power, says Orwell, and keep this in mind: "Dali is a draughtsman of very exceptional gifts. . . . He is an exhibitionist and a careerist, but he is not a fraud. He has fifty times more talent than most of the people who would denounce his morals and jeer at his paintings." He is both vile and great, and that creates a dilemma which most of us have chosen not to resolve. "People are too frightened," Orwell condemningly says, "either of seeming to be shocked or of seeming not to be shocked, to be able to define the relationship between art and morals" (3: 160). Our era should know not "seems." What we need is the intellectual prophylaxis of reality.

> In an age like our own, when the artist is an altogether exceptional person, he must be allowed a certain amount of irresponsibility, just as a pregnant woman is. Still, no one would say that a pregnant woman should be allowed to commit murder, nor would anyone make such a claim for the artist, however gifted. If Shakespeare returned to the earth tomorrow, and if it were found that his favourite recreation was raping little girls in railway carriages, we should not tell him to go ahead with it on the grounds that he might write another *King Lear*. And, after all, the worst crimes are not always the punishable ones. By encouraging necrophilic reveries one

> probably does quite as much harm as by, say, picking pockets at the races. One ought to be able to hold in one's head simultaneously the two facts that Dali is a good draughtsman and a disgusting human being. The one does not invalidate or, in a sense, affect the other. The first thing that we demand of a wall is that it shall stand up. If it stands up, it is a good wall, and the question of what purpose it serves is separable from that. And yet even the best wall in the world deserves to be torn down if it surrounds a concentration camp. In the same way it should be possible to say, "This is a good book or a good picture, and it ought to be burned by the public hangman". Unless one can say that, at least in imagination, one is shirking the implications of the fact that an artist is also a citizen and a human being. (3: 161)

For Orwell, therefore, the relation between art and morals is permanently knowable, stationed as it is on an absolute moral standard. But of course Orwell's grammar has ideas of its own. The historicizing prefix "In an age like our own," for example, effectively undercuts everything that follows it. Once upon a time, in some happy undissociated world, the artist was not an altogether exceptional person, but now . . . well, now, things are different. At the moment, therefore—and of course, as it turns out, at any other moment as well—our appeal to the absolute can base its claim only on nostalgia.

Orwell wrote "Benefit of Clergy" in 1944, when things were indeed becoming different fast. By 1949, when he came to write the three paragraphs of "The Question of the Pound Award," such words as "deserves," "ought to be," "no one would say," and "we should not tell him" must have come much less confidently to Orwell's mind. Several years before the structuralists stated the idea in formal terms, history must already have been constraining him to think of subjects as mortal things, in play only up to the threshold of the gas chamber or the memory hole. So, at the end of the next-to-last essay he would complete, George Orwell retreated from his consensus terms "no one" and "we" to a few positive data: the words *I*, *they*, and *he*. *He* becomes the occasion of a long paragraph: a history of Pound's politics since the 1920s, with conclusions expressed in moral terms. "[Pound's] broadcasts were disgusting," Orwell tells us to believe, and palliative revisions of their history have all been "plain falsehood" (4: 490). But finally we must stay close to the data—those data which posit that there is no more *we*.

> None of this is a reason against giving Pound the Bollingen Prize. There are times when such a thing might be undesirable—it would have been undesirable when the Jews were actually being killed in the gas vans, for instance—but I do not think this is one of them. But since the judges have taken what amounts to the "art for art's sake" position, that is, the position that aesthetic integrity and common decency are two separate things, then at least let us keep them separate and not excuse Pound's career on the ground that he is a good writer. He *may* be a good writer . . . but the opinions that he has tried to disseminate by means of his works are evil ones, and I think that the judges should have said so more firmly when awarding him the prize. (4: 491)

That is, a phase in the history of events has passed. The Jews are not now being killed, the words "common decency" and "evil" may still be assumed to exist, and readers may still be assumed to know what they mean. But such words can no longer be thought of as universally meaningful. They have passed into the specialized vocabulary of obsolescent sensations, and there they have been attached as identifying historical tags to certain obsolescent constructions of reality: class conventions, counters in a social game. That is why they stand alone in Orwell's sentences, as subjects in themselves rather than as the grammatical objects of any human action. Decency and evil no longer act or are acted upon; they merely are. Having entered human history, the words now make their exit. They retire into the plenum of undifferentiated language: language without achieved meaning.

Orwell's two essays are a record of that entrance and exit. Changing over time, their grammatical structures echo a historical change. The disappearance of verbs indicating moral consensus parallels a disappearance of that consensus from the history of which Orwell's language was a part. So that if "to be inside history's meaning is to be inside its form, and this form's most elusive meaning (its strange contact with writing) may simply be itself" (Sollers 203), we can say that Orwell's words "decency" and "evil" have been lost to form, at least for now, and consequently lost to sequence. But though we cannot decode them in sequence, sense by sense, they remain in the archive. A part of our repertoire of understanding is conditioned on the readability of words referring beyond ourselves, and though these words may no longer have meaning, we still desire the significance they once promised to give us. When we discover the absence of that significance, we may go in search of new ways to read. And that is cause for hope.

I take it that one such new reading would work like the second of Sergei Eisenstein's "two basic tendencies struggling within the cinema of today."

> One—the expiring method of artificial spatial organization in front of the lens. From the "direction" of a sequence, to the erection of a Tower of Babel in front of the lens. The other—a "picking-out" by the camera: organization by means of the camera. Hewing out a piece of actuality with the ax of the lens. ("Cinematographic Principle" 41)

As it is available to such a reading, language is the archive of history. It exists—it has preexisted—to be read. Reading it with an eye to its construction in time, recovering it from time word by word, we make meaning in our selves, hewing achieved significance out of the virtual. Wallace Stevens's singer walking by the shore offers us both a paradigm of the technique and a premonition of hope. Significance may yet be, she tells us; memory may be true; we may one day learn our history. Its words are before us now, in sequence, waiting.

Conclusion: Rereading

> The defect of all written texts is not the fault of speech, but the condition of time. Everything that is decisive may be known (in fact has probably been known since the ancient world) but unfortunately what the mind knows in simultaneity it must ploddingly unfold in speech. Words, alas, must follow each other, one after another, for pages on end, holding hands like a line of blind men. What we receive, however, when we read is not the sequence of the words, but the undulance of time. We come to the word requiring not sense, but time. Surely it is the presence of time that prevents us from anticipating, that requires that we await each revelation of the word patiently, that compels our recognition that everything upon which we depend for life and truth must be wrested by one understanding from another.
>
> —Arthur A. Cohen, "Myths and Riddles"

Plot, situation, incident, and character development arise from the passage of time through language. They incorporate time into theme, and of course time is the fundamental subject of all narrative. Once upon a time, we say, invoking the idea of continuity. "Not in imparting what they have thought, which indeed were often a very small matter, but in exhibiting what they have undergone or seen, do talkers dilate," says Carlyle. But of course time isn't the subject just of narrative in its ordinary genres: the novel, say, or the essay. Insofar as language has sequence, it incorporates time; insofar as time is in language, it is there to be read, in any genre. As we read, we continually, consciously or unconsciously, locate history in the text, and locate ourselves with respect to history. Entering language from time, history makes words mean by entraining them in grammar and syntax. As it is read, therefore, history is not just a vocabulary; it is a bridge of language that extends from the ego, across time, to the world.

I have read three groups of writers in this book: some southerners marked for myth and memory by an irruption of history that occurred before they were born, and a midwesterner, the son of a southern father, who codified the language of nostalgia; three New England poets and a British poet of the First World War, all feeling themselves to be speaking alone amid the silent dead; and a group of Jewish writers marked by the knowledge that they have been hated to the death a priori. I could have chosen other writers to think about, in other groups. My concern was with the traces of history in language, and I thought that writers who had lived through an extreme history might know history's language more intimately than the rest of us.

Such writers do stand in an exemplary way, after all, for the possibility of a language filled with history. When they speak of time, it is in the optative mood. Hope, trust, expectation: positively or negatively, Appelfeld and Fitzgerald, Dos Passos and Dickinson all deal in such terms: the terms of a complicated double semiotics of the future and the past. In their tragic language is history's optimistic gift to language: the possibility of wishing that things might previously have been better.

The gift is a reciprocal one. Because they incorporate syntax, words give desire a history. Watching her father light the evening's first marijuana cigarette and open the evening's first can of beer, the child grows sad, wishing that things an hour from now could be otherwise. As that hour passes, she looks back wistfully, each minute, to what was, one minute before. She remembers the words that were spoken when she last smiled. That moment has gone, but she can make an image of it in words. Her hope is a historical construction made of words contemplated in time. Such words are what make chronicle into history. Because as terms of feeling they come into being only under extreme conditions, they account for the felt extraordinariness of even the dullest historical record. If the event was recorded, it was memorable; if it was remembered, it partook of feeling, and may again.

The time available to the majority of our feelings is not distinguished in this way, of course. It lacks the vocabulary of event.

Meaning in this state exists perpetually at the instant of its annihilation, when each word has been neutralized by a desire wholly fulfilled or wholly defeated. Amnesia has struck at it. Struck silent by a blow, the beaten child clings to her father because he has withheld from her the vocabulary of tense. She cannot imagine a past or a future in which things might be different. She and her father form an interpretive community of just two, and the terms of interpretation are not shared on an equal basis. And we who read her story in the newspaper the next day can contribute nothing in retrospect but dramatic irony: the vocabulary of language uncomprehended, of *if only* and *little did he know*. In retrospect, we luxuriate in that guilty history. We suddenly realize that we are native speakers of its language. But we cannot comprehend innocence. Innocence, after all, comes before the word. It is the state of immediacy, of the last instant before the propositus surrenders to history and accepts its terms.

Here, in the chronicle, is one record of innocence before history. In the Chelmno extermination camp the child Simon Srebnik was given the job of accepting gassed corpses and semi-corpses (for not all of the bodies were quite dead) and throwing them into ovens to be burned. "When I saw all that," he now recalls (only two human beings survived Chelmno: Srebnik, shot and left for dead, and one other),

> it didn't affect me. Neither did the second or third shipment. I was only thirteen, and all I'd ever seen until then were dead bodies. Maybe if I'd been older, I'd have understood, but the fact is, I didn't. I'd never seen anything else. In the ghetto in Lodz I saw that as soon as anyone took a step, he fell dead. I thought that's the way things had to be, that it was normal. I'd walk the streets of Lodz, maybe one hundred yards, and there'd be two hundred bodies. People were hungry. They went into the street and they fell, they fell. Sons took their fathers' bread, fathers took their sons', everyone wanted to stay alive. (Lanzmann 102–03)

From such an interpretive community, history has been driven away. Its inhabitants remain in a ghetto of unmemory. Theirs is a terrible innocence: not the animal innocence of wholeheartedly unconscious life and death that Whitman celebrated in section 32 of *Song of Myself* but a radical simplification of desire. Like angels, they want only one thing. Thoreau appears to have failed to anticipate the form simplicity would take in our time: a chastity arriving in tanks and speaking the language of geopolitics. That simplicity abolished much, including the words in which someone might remember its epiphany. But Simon Srebnik has been granted the reparation of memory after the fact.

Now that he remembers, however, the history implicit in his words has separated him from his deeds. A spectator of what he once did, he has been deprived of complicity. In the film *Shoah* we see Simon Srebnik stop at the edge of the field where he once burned the bodies, pick up a piece of something, look at it, and let it go again. If hope were possible, he could hope now. Since the time when he finished working here, a language has been taught to him. He speaks it, here and now, to the camera on Claude Lanzmann's shoulder. But the bodies are all gone, of course. Here and now nothing remains but words: instruments of the language he could not speak at the moment when it should have been comprehended. "The gas vans came in here . . . ," he tries to explain.

> There were two huge ovens, and afterward the bodies were thrown into these ovens, and the flames reached to the sky. It was terrible. No one can describe it. No one can recreate what happened here. Impossible? And no one can understand it. Even I, here, now. . . . I can't believe I'm here. No, I just can't believe it. It was always this peaceful here. Always. When they burned two thousand people—Jews—every day, it was just as peaceful. No one shouted. Everyone went about his work. It was silent. Peaceful. Just as it is now. (Lanzmann 6; original ellipses)

The peace is wordless, as—most terrible of all—it always was. While Simon Srebnik worked silently on their bodies, men, women, and children with names were reduced to metaphors. We cannot remember metaphors; we can think of words only in other words. Simon Srebnik has only a virtual memory of what once lay beyond those words. All he can do now, therefore, is to sing the song that preserved his life in Chelmno until the end: the song his guards liked him to sing for them, a sentimental Polish ballad about nostalgia for the *biały domek*, the white little house. Here, in the present, at the source of memory, the song flows once more through Simon's mouth. But nothing remains for him and the bodies he touched except the song's words and its melody in time: two historical fictions.

Virtual history is the history we write when nothing remains but words. It is the trope in which we figure alienation from our own time by translating perception into metaphor, and metaphor into metaphor. Everything in virtual history is *like* something else that *was*; nothing *is*. Read word by word, virtual history leads only to a regress of other words—"to narrative," as a theorist of literary history says, speaking of Fredric Jameson's historical system, "to a principle posited in literature and indicative of a totality that is at best literary, and as such likely to raise precisely the hermeneutic questions that it had been designed to foreclose" (Simpson 740–41). And narrative itself achieves nothing historical. Samuel Larned, who tried to purify discourse by swearing at people, matters less to the United States of America than John Brown.

Suppose, however, we think about the other half of Simon Srebnik's song: its melody, its sounds which have taken on meaning from their distribution across a tract of time.

The words of the song recall happy memories of a little white house. But the Jews of the Lodz ghetto where Simon Srebnik was born were dying of starvation and overcrowding long before the Nazis arrived. We can read their history in David Engel's book, and see their faces in Roman Vishniac's. The words of Simon's song—the metaphors—we have a moral duty to disregard. They are only art. But they are sung in order, in time, and that changes them. They become sequence, and, in sequence, they become one with us.

We will have difficulty talking directly about the song, for many reasons. Its ironies are too implicated with other things: Polish culture, Claude Lanzmann's art, life and death stories that only Simon Srebnik knows. But we might want to consider, by way of contrast, the melody of a more self-consciously naïf chronicler of the great annihilations: the professional ironist Kurt Vonnegut.

Vonnegut belongs to a special subclass of ironists: those who proclaim themselves to be hard on the surface but too tender at the center to be touched. Swift and Kierkegaard are not in that class, but Raymond Carver and Joan Didion are, humming to themselves in gentle shock. Vonnegut, indeed, is so tender that he has created a special persona to bear the shock of his story: "Kurt Vonnegut," the implied character who slyly hints that he really does exist, somewhere behind his Billy Pilgrim mask. *Ridi, Pagliaccio*, this animated mask sings tenderly to itself there, in front of its audience of high school children, and through the song's words it sings to them: Try in your limited little way, I dare you, to understand my suffering. I will make my sentences ostentatiously short and simple, but of course I'll know all the time that you think I think you don't understand. So I will say then, "I'm making this as simple as I can," and you'll take that as a knowing, friendly, *understanding* parody of what your teachers say and how tragic that makes you feel, and you and I will laugh together; but (and this is my little private joke) all the time I will be laughing at you. I will be laughing because I'll know I've shown you my scar tissue and dared you to penetrate it, and you will have failed, and you won't even know you've tried.

Those are the Vonnegut words: words implied by their author to have originated in a history so tragic that it can be signified only in irony. In fact, irony for Vonnegut is almost, but not quite, an end in itself: a way station just one stop from the unspeakable. Vonnegut appears to be a sort of Laodicean foundationalist, convinced (a) that the tragedy of history must be an ultimate referent but also (b) that this referent is so universally terrible that it can be spoken of only at a remove, concealed. We strive to speak of it approximately, but all our words are mediations between us and the light, and everything we say is necessarily a falsehood. Let us speak frankly in that falsehood, Vonnegut's words tell us. Let us understand that the joky title page of *Slaughterhouse-Five* is meant, in all its comical failure, to be understood as the prologue to a tragedy

By
Kurt Vonnegut, Jr.
A Fourth-Generation German-American
Now Living in Easy Circumstances
On Cape Cod
[And Smoking Too Much]

Who, as an American Infantry Scout
Hors de Combat,
As a Prisoner of War,
Witnessed the Fire-Bombing
Of Dresden, Germany,
"The Florence of the Elbe,"
A Long Time Ago,
And Survived to Tell the Tale.

The joke is a mode of awe.

Claude Lanzmann, annalist, believes too that what happened to his people between 1941 and 1945 was a definitive event in language. But there is this difference between his foundationalism and Vonnegut's: Lanzmann, knowing he must fail, nevertheless tries to see the source of his meaning face to face. For him, irony is only an optical instrument, a way of perceiving what is there to be perceived. When Lanzmann's Simon Srebnik sings a sentimental song to his killers, therefore, we respond to the strict dramatic irony of an innocent protagonist in the situation of *little does he know*. But when Kurt Vonnegut's persona confides his smoking problem to several million readers with a knowing leer (Grow old along with me, the best is yet to be, right folks? Har har!), the irony fails to register. Because their foundational referent is only the author's self, Vonnegut's words fail to extend beyond virtual meaning. They are grammatical, but they cannot be comprehended with reference to any feeling outside their author's sensorium. They have walled themselves into a little irony club where they speak only to one another: words speaking to words, virtuality to unfulfilled virtuality. Behind the walls of that club, inside his carapace of irony, Vonnegut will never be able to hear what William Carlos Williams heard coming from outside himself and recorded with due joy in a book called *The Great American Novel*:

> I'm new, said she, I don't think you'll find my card here. You're new; how interesting. . . . I'm new, says the great dynamo. I am progress. I make a word. Listen! UMMMMMMMMMMMM—
>
> Ummmmmmmmmm—Turned into the wrong street at three A.M. lost in the fog, listening, searching—Waaaa! said the baby. I'm new. A boy! A what? Boy. Shit, said the father of two other sons.

Listen here. This is no place to talk that way. What a word to use. I'm new, said the sudden word. (*Imaginations* 162)

Williams's word sings a single note. It is the beginning of what Williams, near the end of his life, standing on the bridge between Juarez and El Paso, between languages, learned to call "the music":

And I could not help thinking
of the wonders of the brain that
hears that music and of our
skill sometimes to record it.
("The Desert Music," *Pictures from Brueghel* 120)

Vonnegut's words, by contrast, make only the dry rustling sound of pages turning. Nevertheless, they make that sound in sequence, and sequence sometimes carries a tune of its own. We can hear it, sometimes: the sound of history, making itself known in unexpected domains of representation.

Here, for instance:

The protagonist of *Slaughterhouse-Five* lives outside the law of human syntax. He is a man constrained by many things, but not by past, present, or future. Where we are about to start reading, he has turned on the TV while "slightly unstuck in time" (73) and watched an old movie about American bombers during World War II.

The formation flew backwards over a German city that was in flames. The bombers opened their bomb bay doors, exerted a miraculous magnetism which shrunk the fires, gathered them into cylindrical steel containers, and lifted the containers neatly into the bellies of the planes. . . .

When the bombers got back to their base, the steel cylinders were taken from the racks and shipped back to the United States of America, where factories were operating night and day, dismantling the cylinders, separating the dangerous contents into minerals. Touchingly, it was mainly women who did this work. The minerals were then shipped to specialists in remote areas. It was their business to put them into the ground, to hide them cleverly, so they would never hurt anybody ever again. (74–75)

Now this passage has a generic advantage over us from the start. It comes to us, after all, as part of a historical novel: that is, as part of a text whose key words—say, "German," or "War" followed by "II"—we think of as somehow intrinsically real. As we read, we tend to think that we have been a part of this story ourselves, all along, from long before the time when the story was written. The historical novel creates a Platonic readership for itself. By the time we got to the words "so they would never hurt anybody again," therefore, many of us had probably discovered that we seemed already to know them. For us, this passage was something reread. And of course that reaction of ours is the sign that a historical transaction has just taken place between us and *Slaughterhouse-Five*.

That transaction has left us aware of *Slaughterhouse-Five*'s place in the literary history of language. If we think of the book taxonomically, we can now understand that beneath the cheap manipulativeness of Vonnegut's rhetoric pulses the rhythm of the fairytale, catching us up into itself as it has always done. But fairytales have their own historical moments, as Robert Darnton has shown. At some moments in the history of culture their plots are perceived as classically inevitable and their morals as universally true; at other moments the tales are perceived simply as stories like any other; at still other moments their only interest seems anthropological or psychopathological. Vonnegut's achievement in the genre is to translate one of those cultural moments into the historical terms of another: to make us feel one of the clichés of twentieth-century art as if it were mythic.

He does this by taking the cinematic image, one of the most pervasive, most inevitable sources of metaphor in twentieth-century literature, and employing it on us at a second remove: not in the usual way, as an immediate analogy of the passage of time, but indirectly, as an indicator of the consciousness of the passage of time. Reading, we are passed from the symbol to its phenomenological representation. If we have to give the technique a name, we might call it the scenography of time, and if we have to find an antecedent for it in literary history, we might recall Gray's "Ode on a Distant Prospect of Eton College." In Gray's poem, as in hundreds of films since then, we are standing before, but not quite in, the landscape of childhood, of faith and hope boundless and unfulfillable, seen from the beginning of a perspective receding into darkness and the future.

> Alas, regardless of their doom,
> The little victims play!

That scenography is what we have responded to in *Slaughterhouse-Five*.

And in other works of art too, of course. That is its historical importance. After the steam engine and the mass-produced clock had become a part of everyone's sense of the world, the image of time as motion became one of the fundamental ways in which people saw themselves. "Backward, turn backward, O time, in your flight," sang Kurt Vonnegut's grandparents in the nineteenth century, when that image was poignantly new. "Make me," they pleaded, "a child again, just for tonight." But time didn't turn backward. In the wake of Romanticism it brought us Aharon Appelfeld's railroad train, and before that the *Titanic*, and before that De Quincey's English mail coach. We have been apprehensive for many years about the cinema of time. That is one of the things we can learn by reading ourselves historically.

We can learn, too, that in our relation to the arts, we of this century have been particularly vulnerable to metaphors of sequence, such as Vonnegut's image of the bombers. Showing us how time might have been but wasn't, these picture words are one of our era's distinctive genres of irony. Sequence, motion, time, memory: in a literary history devoted to identifying what is distinctive about the modern era, such things ought to occupy a chapter. Reading it may help us understand what has made the other canonical headings—author, text, and audience—historical in the first place. And then, at last, we may begin to understand why we have found ourselves writing the histories and remembering the old words. We will have caught time and memory in the act, rereading.

Simon Srebnik's song, sung one last time where the death-furnaces roared many years ago, is a rereading: a retracing of the furrows plowed deep across human history by the passing time of which Simon was a part. The authors we have read in this book have also been rereaders. They have known that rereading is the part of reading into which time enters: the collaborative activity in which we and the language around us order our perceptions into a single sequence, establishing a structure in time that we can call history. History, as opposed to virtual history, is a language structure which incorporates life outside language into a sequence read as time. Virtual history, an exclusively verbal construction, has nothing to do with life or death; it is a Grecian urn of speech, waiting to be spoken by the human, forever young. History lacks this glory. It is of death as well as of life. It is an archive of mortality, as forgettable as life itself. But while we are alive to read it, history will be present for us in the text. By ordering its revelations of meaning in sequence, word followed by discovering word, history enables us to read archivally: with a sense that our vocabulary of words is a little place into which new meanings enter, moment by moment, from the manifold of the world's wordless significance. Rereading, word by word, we discover that the semantic principle of sequence in ourselves is a part of the world at large, the verbal world and the nonverbal. The zone of pure meaning is a home only for the angels of deconstruction. Humanity lives with silence and death, in the order of time. That circumstance can yield us comedy as well as tragedy. In fact, it can yield us almost any genre except literary theory.

The poets have known this all along, of course. When Milton said of himself, in the *Apology for Smectymnuus*, that "he, who would not be frustrate of his hope to write well hereafter in laudable things, ought himself to be a true poem," he was employing the language of morality to express a semantic truth. "Hereafter" is a time term, after all, and we will not be able to understand its significance until we have learned that history makes language out of us, word by word. But once we have understood, we will be able to reread in a happier way. We will understand then that our words are part of a sequence of language which has been implicated with time from the beginning. The words of the dead are a part of Simon Srebnik's song, and of us when we listen to it. Word by word, their meaning survives. We who hear the words have changed, of course. Language and culture have no claim on eternity. But as we are now, creatures bearing the knowledge of life and death in the sequence of our words, we achieve the small magic of remembering. We do that as we speak, word by word.

Works Cited

Abrams, M. H. *A Glossary of Literary Terms*. 5th ed. New York: Holt, 1988.

Agee, James. *Let Us Now Praise Famous Men*. 1941. New York: Ballantine, 1966.

Appelfeld, Aharon. *The Age of Wonders*. Trans. Dalya Bilu. 1981. New York: Washington Square–Simon, 1983.

——. *Badenheim 1939*. Trans. Dalya Bilu. 1980. New York: Washington Square–Simon, 1981.

Ashbery, John. *A Wave*. New York: Viking, 1984.

Auden, W. H. Introduction. *The American Scene*. By Henry James. New York: Scribner's, 1946. v–xxiii.

Austin, J. L. *How to Do Things with Words*. Ed. J. O. Urmson and Marina Sbisà. 3rd ed. Cambridge: Harvard University Press, 1975.

Benjamin, Walter. "A Berlin Chronicle." *Reflections: Essays, Aphorisms, Autobiographical Writings*. Trans. Edmund Jephcott. New York: Harcourt, 1979. 3–60.

——. "The Work of Art in the Age of Mechanical Reproduction." *Illuminations*. Trans. Harry Zohn. New York: Harcourt, 1968. 217–51.

Bergson, Henri. "Laughter." *Comedy*. Ed. Wylie Sypher, Garden City, N.Y: Anchor-Doubleday, 1956. 61–190.

Berthoff, Warner. *The Ferment of Realism: American Literature, 1884–1919*. 1965. Cambridge: Cambridge University Press, 1981.

Blackmur, R. P. "Emily Dickinson: Notes on Prejudice and Fact." *Southern Review* Autumn 1937. Rpt. in Blake and Wells 200–223.

Blake, Caesar R., and Carlton F. Wells, eds. *The Recognition of Emily Dickinson: Selected Criticism since 1890.* Ann Arbor: University of Michigan Press, 1964.

Bloom, Harold. "The Central Man: Emerson, Whitman, Wallace Stevens." *Massachusetts Review* Winter 1966. Qtd. in Frank Lentricchia, *After the New Criticism.* Chicago: University of Chicago Press, 1980. 320.

——. *A Map of Misreading.* New York: Oxford University Press, 1975.

Brooks, Van Wyck. *Three Essays on America.* 1934. New York: Dutton, 1970.

Casillo, Robert. *The Genealogy of Demons: Anti-Semitism, Fascism, and the Myths of Ezra Pound.* Evanston, Ill.: Northwestern University Press, 1988.

Caute, David. *The Great Fear: The Anti-Communist Purge under Truman and Eisenhower.* New York: Simon, 1978.

Chace, William M. *The Political Identities of Ezra Pound and T. S. Eliot.* Stanford, Calif.: Stanford University Press, 1973.

Chandrasekhar, S. "On Stars, Their Evolution and Their Stability." *Science* 226 (1984): 497–505.

Cody, John. *After Great Pain: The Inner Life of Emily Dickinson.* Cambridge, Mass.: Harvard University Press, 1971.

Cohen, Arthur A. "Myths and Riddles: Some Observations about Literature and Theology." *Prooftexts* 7 (1987): 110–21.

Crèvecoeur, St.-Jean de. *Letters from an American Farmer.* London: Thomas Davies, 1782.

Darnton, Robert. "Peasants Tell Tales: The Meaning of Mother Goose." *The Great Cat Massacre and Other Episodes in French Cultural History.* New York: Basic, 1984. 8–72.

Davis, Douglas. "Murphy: Life as an Invention." *Newsweek* 15 Apr. 1974: 76–78.

Deleuze, Gilles. "The Schizophrenic and Language: Surface and Depth in Lewis Carroll and Antonin Artaud." Harari 277–95.

Dickinson, Emily. *The Letters of Emily Dickinson.* Ed. Thomas H. Johnson. 3 vols. Cambridge, Mass.: Harvard University Press, 1958.

——. *The Manuscript Books of Emily Dickinson.* Ed. R. W. Franklin. 2 vols. Cambridge, Mass.: Harvard University Press, 1981.

——. *The Master Letters of Emily Dickinson.* Ed. R. W. Franklin. Amherst, Mass.: Amherst College Press, 1986.

——. *The Poems of Emily Dickinson.* Ed. Thomas H. Johnson. 3 vols. Cambridge, Mass.: Harvard University Press, 1955.

Dos Passos, John. *U.S.A.* 3 vols. (*The 42nd Parallel; 1919; The Big Money*). 1938. New York: Signet–NAL, 1969.

Duchac, Joseph. *The Poems of Emily Dickinson: An Annotated Guide to Commentary Published in English, 1890–1977*. Boston: Hall, 1979.

Eagleton, Terry. *Literary Theory: An Introduction*. Minneapolis: University of Minnesota Press, 1983.

Eisenstein, Sergei. "The Cinematographic Principle and the Ideogram." 1929. In *Film Form: Essays in Film Theory*. Trans. Jay Leyda. 1949. Cleveland: Meridian-World, 1957. 28–44.

———. "Dickens, Griffith, and the Film Today." 1944. *Film Form* 195–255.

Eliot, T. S. *After Strange Gods: A Primer of Modern Heresy*. New York: Harcourt, 1934.

——. *The Complete Poems and Plays*. New York: Harcourt, 1952.

——. *The Letters of T. S. Eliot*. Ed. Valerie Eliot. Vol. 1. New York: Harcourt, 1988.

——. *Selected Essays*. New ed. New York: Harcourt, 1950.

——. *Selected Prose of T. S. Eliot*. Ed. Frank Kermode. New York: Harcourt, 1975.

——. *The Waste Land: A Facsimile and Transcript of the Original Drafts, Including the Annotations of Ezra Pound*. Ed. Valerie Eliot. New York: Harcourt, 1971.

Ellmann, Richard, and Robert O'Clair, eds. *The Norton Anthology of Modern Poetry*. 2nd ed. New York: Norton, 1988.

Engel, David. *In the Shadow of Auschwitz: The Polish Government-in-Exile and the Jews, 1939–1942*. Chapel Hill: University of North Carolina Press, 1987.

Evans, Hiram W. "The Klan's Fight for Americanism." *North American Review* Mar.–May 1926. Rpt. in *The Culture of the Twenties*. Ed. Loren Baritz. New York: Macmillan, 1985. 85–108.

Ferguson, George. *Signs and Symbols in Christian Art*. New York: Oxford University Press, 1954.

Fish, Stanley. *Is There a Text in This Class? The Authority of Interpretive Communities*. Cambridge: Harvard University Press, 1980.

Fitzgerald, F. Scott. *The Crack-Up*. Norfolk, Conn.: New Directions, 1945.

——. *The Great Gatsby*. New York: Scribner's, 1925.

——. "My Generation." *Esquire* Oct. 1968: 119, 121.

——. *Tender Is the Night*. New York: Scribner's, 1934.

Forster, Leonard, ed. *The Penguin Book of German Verse*. Baltimore: Penguin, 1959.

Foucault, Michel. "What Is an Author?" Harari 141–60.

Freud, Sigmund. *The Origin and Development of Psychoanalysis*. 1910. Chicago: Regnery, 1965.

Frost, Robert. *The Poetry of Robert Frost*. Ed. Edward Connery Lathem. New York: Holt, 1969.

——. *Selected Letters of Robert Frost*. Ed. Lawrance Thompson. New York: Holt, 1964.

Gardner, Brian, ed. *Up the Line to Death: The War Poets 1914–1918*. New York: Potter, 1967.

Gossett, Thomas F. *Race: The History of an Idea in America*. 1963. New York: Schocken, 1968.

Green, Mark. "Amiable Dunce or Chronic Liar? And Why the Press Lets Him Get Away with It." *Mother Jones* June/July 1987: 9+.

Gross, John. *The Rise and Fall of the Man of Letters: A Study of the Idiosyncratic and the Humane in Modern Literature*. New York: Macmillan, 1969.

Grossman, Vasily. *L'enfer de Treblinka*. 1945. Grenoble: Arthaud, 1966.

——. *Forever Flowing*. Trans. Thomas P. Whitney. New York: Perennial-Harper, 1986.

——. *Life and Fate*. Trans. Robert Chandler. New York: Perennial-Harper, 1987.

Habermas, Jürgen. "Work and Weltanschauung: The Heidegger Controversy from a German Perspective." Trans. John McCumber. *Critical Inquiry* 15 (1989): 431–56.

Hall, James. *Dictionary of Subjects and Symbols in Art*. Rev. ed. New York: Harper, 1974.

Hall, William F. "T. J. Eckleburg, 'un dieu à l'américaine.'" *Fitzgerald-Hemingway Annual* 1969: 35–39.

Hamerton-Kelly, Robert G., ed. *Violent Origins: Walter Burkert, René Girard, and Jonathan Z. Smith on Ritual Killing and Cultural Formation*. Stanford, Calif.: Stanford University Press, 1987.

Harari, Josué V., ed. *Textual Strategies: Perspectives in Post-Structuralist Criticism*. Ithaca: Cornell University Press, 1979.

Hemingway, Ernest. *A Farewell to Arms*. New York: Scribner's, 1929.

Hesse, Hermann. *Blick ins Chaos: Drei Aufsätze*. Bern: Seldwyla, 1920.

——. "Recent German Poetry." *Criterion* 1 (1922): 89–93.

Hirsch, E. D., Jr. "The Well-Read Urn: A Thought Experiment." *History as a Tool in Critical Interpretation*. Ed. Thomas F. Rugh and Erin R. Silva. Provo, Utah: Brigham Young University Press, 1978. 47–50.

Hoffman, David. "The Metamorphosis of George Bush." Washington Post Service. *Honolulu Advertiser* 22 Jan. 1989: B1.

Holman, C. Hugh. *A Handbook to Literature*. 4th ed. Indianapolis: Bobbs, 1981. Based on the original edition by William Flint Thrall and Addison Hibbard. 1936.

Hull, David Stewart. *Film in the Third Reich*. Berkeley: University of California Press, 1969.

I'll Take My Stand: The South and the Agrarian Tradition. By Twelve Southerners. 1930. New York: Peter Smith, 1951.

James, Henry. *The American Scene*. 1907. New York: Scribner's, 1946.

Jameson, Fredric. *Fables of Aggression: Wyndham Lewis, The Modernist as Fascist*. Berkeley: University of California Press, 1979.

——. "Imaginary and Symbolic in Lacan: Marxism, Psychoanalytic Criticism, and the Problem of the Subject." *Yale French Review* 55/56 (1977): 338–95.

——. "Periodizing the 60s." *The 60s without Apology*. Ed. Sohnya Sayres, Anders Stephanson, Stanley Aronowitz, and Fredric Jameson. Minneapolis: University of Minnesota Press, 1984. 178–209.

——. *The Political Unconscious: Narrative as a Socially Symbolic Act*. Ithaca: Cornell University Press, 1981.

Jones, D. A. N. "Lamentations." Rev. of *The Children of the Souls: A Tragedy of the First World War*, by Jeanne Mackenzie. *TLS* 25 July 1986: 823.

Keller, Ulrich, ed. *The Warsaw Ghetto in Photographs: 206 Views Made in 1941*. New York: Dover, 1984.

Kenner, Hugh. *The Invisible Poet: T. S. Eliot*. 1959. New York: Citadel, 1964.

——. *The Pound Era*. Berkeley: University of California Press, 1971.

——. *Wyndham Lewis*. Norfolk, Conn.: New Directions, 1954.

Kermode, Frank. *Romantic Image*. New York: Vintage-Random, 1957.

Keyserling, Count Hermann. *The Travel Diary of a Philosopher*. Trans. J. Holroyd Reece. 2 vols. New York: Harcourt, 1925.

Kojecký, Roger. *T. S. Eliot's Social Criticism*. New York: Farrar, 1972.

Kolata, Gina. "What Does It Mean to Be Random?" *Science* 231 (1986): 1068–70.

Lanzmann, Claude. *Shoah: An Oral History of the Holocaust*. New York: Pantheon, 1985.

Lentricchia, Frank. "Patriarchy against Itself—The Young Manhood of Wallace Stevens." *Critical Inquiry* 13 (1987): 742–86.

Leon, Juan. "'Meeting Mr. Eugenides': T. S. Eliot and Eugenic Anxiety." *Yeats Eliot Review* 9 (1988): 169–77.

Lévi-Strauss, Claude. Preface. *Six Lectures on Sound and Meaning*. By Roman Jakobson. Trans. John Mepham. Cambridge, Mass.: MIT Press, 1978.

Lewis, C. S. *An Experiment in Criticism*. Cambridge: Cambridge University Press, 1961.

Lewis, Wyndham. *Self Condemned*. London: Methuen, 1954.

Longsworth, Polly. *Austin and Mabel: The Amherst Affair and Love Letters of Austin Dickinson and Mabel Loomis Todd.* New York: Farrar, 1984.

Lowell, Robert, *For Lizzie and Harriet.* New York: Farrar, 1973.

Lubbers, Klaus. *Emily Dickinson: The Critical Revolution.* Ann Arbor: University of Michigan Press, 1968.

Lucas, Mark. *The Southern Vision of Andrew Lytle.* Baton Rouge: Louisiana State University Press, 1986.

Lytle, Andrew, "A Christian University and the Word." *Sewanee* [1–4].

——. "The Hind Tit." *I'll Take My Stand* 201–245.

Mao Zedong. *Quotations from Chairman Mao Tsetung.* Peking (Beijing): Foreign Languages Press, 1972.

Markish, Simon. *Le cas Grossman.* Trans. from Russian by Dominique Négrel. Paris: Julliard, 1983.

Massis, Henri. *Defence of the West.* Trans. F. S. Flint. *New Criterion* 4 (1926): 224–43, 476–93.

Mast, Gerald. *A Short History of the Movies.* 3rd ed. Indianapolis: Bobbs, 1981.

Menand, Louis. *Discovering Modernism: T. S. Eliot and His Context.* New York: Oxford University Press, 1987.

Meyerhoff, Hans, ed. *The Philosophy of History in Our Time: An Anthology.* Garden City, N.Y.: Anchor-Doubleday, 1959.

Miller, J. Hillis. "The Critic as Host." *Deconstruction and Criticism.* New York: Seabury, 1979. 217–53.

Miller, Perry. *The Life of the Mind in America from the Revolution to the Civil War.* New York: Harcourt, 1965.

Morse, Jonathan. "Sweeney, the Sties of the Irish, and *The Waste Land.*" *Critical Essays on T. S. Eliot: The Sweeney Motif.* Ed. Kinley E. Roby. Boston: Hall, 1985. 135–46.

Munro, John M. *English Poetry in Transition, 1880–1920.* New York: Pegasus, 1920.

O'Hara, Frank. *The Selected Poems of Frank O'Hara.* Ed. Donald Allen. New York: Vintage-Random, 1974.

Olmsted, Frederick Law. *The Cotton Kingdom: A Traveller's Observations on Cotton and Slavery in the American Slave States.* 1861. New York: Modern Library, 1984.

Orwell, George. *The Collected Essays, Journalism and Letters of George Orwell.* Ed. Sonia Orwell and Ian Angus. 4 vols. New York: Harcourt, 1968.

Perloff, Marjorie. "Pound/Stevens: Whose Era?" *New Literary History* 13 (1982): 485–514.

Polk, Noel. "An Andrew Lytle Checklist." *The Form Discovered: Essays on the Achievement of Andrew Lytle*. Ed. M. E. Bradford. Jackson: University and College Press of Mississippi, 1973. 97–108.

Pollitt, Katha. "Atlantis." *New Republic* 1 Dec. 1986: 38.

Porter, David. *Dickinson: The Modern Idiom*. Cambridge, Mass.: Harvard University Press, 1981.

Pound, Ezra. *The Cantos*. New York: New Directions, 1970.

———. *Selected Letters, 1907–1941*. Ed. D. D. Paige. 1950. New York: New Directions, 1971.

Pritchard, William H. *Frost: A Literary Life*. New York: Oxford University Press, 1984.

Read, Herbert. Rev. of *Travel Diary of a Philosopher*, by Count Hermann Keyserling. *New Criterion* 4 (1926): 189–93.

Rich, Adrienne. "Vesuvius at Home: The Power of Emily Dickinson." *Parnassus* Fall/Winter 1976. Rpt. in *Critical Essays on Emily Dickinson*. Ed. Paul J. Ferlazzo. Boston: Hall, 1984. 175–95.

Ridgely, J. V. *Nineteenth-Century Southern Literature*. Lexington: University Press of Kentucky, 1980.

Riffaterre, Michael. *Semiotics of Poetry*. Bloomington: Indiana University Press, 1978.

Rilke, Rainer Maria. *Sonnets to Orpheus*. Trans. C. F. MacIntyre. Berkeley: University of California Press, 1960.

Rose, Anne C. *Transcendentalism as a Social Movement, 1830–1850*. New Haven, Conn.: Yale University Press, 1981.

Rosenfeld, Alvin H. *Imagining Hitler*. Bloomington: Indiana University Press, 1985.

Rosenthal, M. L. "The Two Frosts." *Reporter* 12 Apr. 1962. Rpt. in *Robert Frost: The Critical Reception*. Ed. Linda W. Wagner. N.p.: Burt Franklin, 1977. 254–58.

Ross, Andrew. *The Failure of Modernism: Symptoms of American Poetry*. New York: Columbia University Press, 1986.

Roth, Henry. *Call It Sleep*. 1934. New York: Avon, 1964.

——. *Shifting Landscape: A Composite, 1925–1987*. Ed. Mario Materassi. Philadelphia: Jewish Publication Society, 1987.

Ruthven, K. K. *Critical Assumptions*. Cambridge: Cambridge University Press, 1979.

Said, Edward W. "The Text, the World, the Critic." Harari 161–88.

Salzman, Jack, ed. *Years of Protest: A Collection of American Writings of the 1930's*. Indianapolis: Bobbs, 1967.

Scholes, Robert. "Deconstruction and Communication." *Critical Inquiry* 14 (1988): 278–95.

Schuyler, James. "Frank O'Hara: Poet among Painters." *Art News* May 1974: 44–45.

Sewanee: The University of the South. Photography by William Strode. Louisville, Ky.: Harmony, 1984.

Shaler, Nathaniel S. *The Neighbor: The Natural History of Human Contacts.* Boston: Houghton, 1904.

Shaw, George Bernard. *Pygmalion.* 1916. Ed. Dan H. Laurence. Illus. Feliks Topolski. New York: Viking Penguin, n.d. (1985 printing).

Sibyl. "With Sweet 'Rhyme of Thought.' Do Poetic Works of Emily Dickenson [*sic*] Sparkle. Mrs. Todd Tells of Her Life. Brillian [*sic*] Characterization of Her Poet-Friend—Interesting Hour of the Modern Novel Club—Insight into the Life of Miss Dickenson." *Pacific Commercial Advertiser* [Honolulu] 23 May 1896: 3

Simpson, David. "Literary Critics and the Return to 'History.'" *Critical Inquiry* 14 (1988): 721–47.

Singal, Daniel Joseph. *The War Within: From Victorian to Modernist Thought in the South, 1919–1945.* Chapel Hill: University of North Carolina Press, 1982.

Sjöberg, Leif. "Translating with W. H. Auden: Gunnar Ekelöf's Last Poems." *Comparative Criticism* 1 (1979). 185–97.

Sollers, Philippe. "The Novel and the Experience of Limits." 1965. *Writing and the Experience of Limits.* Trans. Philip Barnard and David Hayman. New York: Columbia University Press, 1983. 185–207.

Stein, Gertrude. *Writings and Lectures, 1909–1945.* Ed. Patricia Meyerowitz. 1967. Baltimore, Md.: Penguin, 1971.

Steiner, George. *Antigones.* New York: Oxford University Press, 1984.

Stevens, Wallace. *The Collected Poems of Wallace Stevens.* New York: Random, 1954.

Stoddard, Lothrop. *Into the Darkness: Nazi Germany Today.* New York: Duell, 1940.

——. "Racial Realities in Europe." *Saturday Evening Post* 22 Mar. 1924: 14+. (Rpt. in *Racial Realities in Europe.* New York: Scribner's, 1925.)

——. *The Rising Tide of Color against White World-Supremacy.* New York: Scribner's, 1920.

Stott, William. *Documentary Expression and Thirties America.* New York: Oxford University Press, 1973.

Sturrock, John. "Laughing at the Anti-Realists." Rev. of *Not Saussure: A Critique of Post-Saussurean Literary Theory,* by Raymond Tallis. *TLS* 13–19 May 1988: 541.

Taft, Robert. *Photography and the American Scene: A Social History, 1839–1889.* 1938. New York: Dover, 1964.

Tate, Allen. "New England Culture and Emily Dickinson." 1932. Rpt. in Blake and Wells 153–67.

———."Ode to the Confederate Dead." Ellmann and O'Clair 621–28.

———."Remarks on the Southern Religion." *I'll Take My Stand* 155–75.

Thompson, Lawrance. *Robert Frost*. 3 vols. New York: Holt, 1966–76.

Thoreau, Henry David. *Walden and "Civil Disobedience."* Ed. Walter Harding. New York: Washington Square, 1968.

——. "A Yankee in Canada." *The Portable Thoreau*. Ed. Carl Bode. New York: Penguin, 1977. 243–57.

Todd, Mabel Loomis. "A Mid-Pacific College." *Outlook* 1896. Rpt. in *Hawaiian Almanac and Annual for 1897*. Ed. Thos. G. Thrum. Honolulu: Press Publishing, 1897. 50–54.

Todorov, Tzvetan. "NB." *TLS* 17–23 June 1988: 676+.

Torrey, E. Fuller. *The Roots of Treason: Ezra Pound and the Secret of St. Elizabeths*. New York: McGraw, 1984.

Turlish, Lewis A. "*The Rising Tide of Color*: A Note on the Historicism of *The Great Gatsby*." *American Literature* 43 (1971): 442–44.

Veyne, Paul. *Comment on écrit l'histoire: Essai d'épistémologie*. Paris: Seuil, 1971.

——. *Did the Greeks Believe in Their Myths? An Essay in the Constitutive Imagination*. Trans. Paula Wissing. Chicago: University of Chicago Press, 1988.

Vishniac, Roman. *A Vanished World*. New York: Farrar, 1983.

Vonnegut, Kurt, Jr. *Slaughterhouse-Five*. 1968. New York: Dell, 1971.

Wadsworth, Charles. *Sermons*. San Francisco: A. Roman, 1869.

Wendell, Barrett. *A Literary History of America*. New York: Scribner's, 1900.

Whicher, George Frisbie. *This Was a Poet: A Critical Biography of Emily Dickinson*. 1938. Ann Arbor: University of Michigan Press, 1957.

Wiesel, Elie. Foreword. Trans. Richard Howard. Vishniac [i].

Williams, William Carlos. *The Autobiography of William Carlos Williams*. New York: Random, 1951.

——. *Imaginations*. Ed. Webster Schott. New York: New Directions, 1970.

——. *Pictures from Brueghel and Other Poems*. New York: New Directions, 1962.

Wolff, Cynthia Griffin. *Emily Dickinson*. 1986. Reading, Mass.: Addison-Wesley, 1988.

Yeats, William Butler. Introduction. *Certain Noble Plays of Japan*. By Ezra Pound and Ernest Fenollosa. 1916. Rpt. in Ezra Pound and Ernest Fenollosa, *The Classic Noh Theatre of Japan*. New York: New Directions, 1959. 151–63.

Index

Library of Congress Cataloging-in-Publication Data

Morse, Jonathan.
Word by word : the language of memory / Jonathan Morse.
p. cm.
Includes bibliographical references.
ISBN 0-8014-2383-X (alk. paper)
1. American literature—History and criticism. 2. History in literature. 3. History and literature. I. Title.
PS169.H5M67 1990
810.9'358—dc20 89-23931